The British Working Class Enthusiasm for War, 1914–

Millions of men volunteered to leave home, hearth and family to go to a foreign land to fight in 1914, the start of the biggest war in British history. It was a war fought by millions of soldier-citizens, most of whom had volunteered willingly to go. They made up the Army that first held, and then, in 1918, pushed back the German Army to win the Great War.

The British 'Tommy' has been lionized in the decades since the war, but little attention has been paid in the literature to what motivated the ordinary British man to go to France, especially in the early years when Britain relied on the voluntary system to fill the ranks. Why would a regular working-class man leave behind his job, family and friends to go to fight a war that defended not British soil, but French? Why would a British man risk his life to defend places whose names he could barely pronounce? This book gives the answers, in the words of the men who were there. Young and old, from cities and the country, single and married, they went to war willingly and then carried their experiences with them for a lifetime.

David Silbey is an assistant professor of European History at Alvernia College, Reading, PA. He obtained his PhD at Duke University in 1999.

CASS SERIES: MILITARY HISTORY AND POLICY
Series Editors: John Gooch and Brian Holden Reid

This series will publish studies on historical and contemporary aspects of land power, spanning the period from the eighteenth century to the present day, and will include national, international and comparative studies. From time to time, the series will publish edited collections of essays and 'classics'.

1. *Allenby and British Strategy in the Middle East, 1917–1919*
   Matthew Hughes
2. *Alfred von Schlieffen's Military Writings*
   Robert Foley (ed. and trans.)
3. *The British Defence of Egypt, 1935–1940: Conflict and Crisis in the Eastern Mediterranean*
   Steven Morewood
4. *The Japanese and the British Commonwealth Armies at War, 1941–1945*
   Tim Moreman
5. *Training, Tactics and Leadership in the Confederate Army of Tennessee: Seeds of Failure*
   Andrew Haughton
6. *Military Training in the British Army 1940–1944: From Dunkirk to D-Day*
   Tim Harrison Place
7. *The Boer War: Direction, Experience and Image*
   John Gooch (ed.)
8. *Caporetto 1917: Victory or Defeat?*
   Mario Morselli
9. *Postwar Counterinsurgency and the SAS 1945–1952: A Special Type of Warfare*
   Tim Jones
10. *The British General Staff: Reform and Innovation 1890–1939*
    David French and Brian Holden Reid (eds)
11. *Writing the Great War: Sir James Edmonds and the Official Histories, 1915–1948*
    Andrew Green
12. *Command and Control in Military Crisis: Devious Decisions*
    Harald Hoiback

13. *Lloyd George and the Generals*
    David Woodward
14. *Malta and British Strategic Policy, 1925–1943*
    Douglas Austin
15. *British Armour in the Normandy Campaign 1944*
    John Buckley
16. *Gallipoli: Making History*
    Jenny Macleod (ed.)
17. *British and Japanese Military Leadership in the Far Eastern War 1941–1945*
    Brian Bond and Kyoichi Tachikawa (eds)
18. *The Baghdad Pact: Anglo-American Defence Policies in the Middle East, 1950–59*
    Behcet Kemal Yesilbursa
19. *Fanaticism and Conflict in the Modern Age*
    Matthew Hughes and Gaynor Johnson (eds)
20. *The Evolution of Operational Art, 1740–1813: From Frederick the Great to Napoleon*
    Claus Telp
21. *The British Working Class and Enthusiasm for War, 1914–1916*
    David Silbey

The British Working Class and Enthusiasm for War, 1914–1916

David Silbey

FRANK CASS
London and New York

First published 2005
by Frank Cass
2 Park Square, Milton Park, Abingdon, Oxfordshire

Simultaneously published in the USA and Canada
by Routledge
711 Third Avenue, New York, NY 10017

Frank Cass is an imprint of the Taylor & Francis Group

First issued in paperback 2012

© 2005 David Silbey

Typeset in Times by Keystroke, Jacaranda Lodge, Wolverhampton

All rights reserved. No part of this book may be reprinted or reproduced or utilised in any form or by any electronic, mechanical, or other means, now known or hereafter invented, including photocopying and recording, or in any information storage or retrieval system, without permission in writing from the publishers.

British Library Cataloguing in Publication Data
A catalogue record for this book is available from the British Library

Library of Congress Cataloging in Publication Data
Silbey, David.
 The British working class and enthusiasm for war, 1914–1916.
  p. cm. – (Cass series–military history and policy)
 Includes bibliographical references (p.) and index.
 ISBN 0–415–35005–0 (hardback)
1. World War, 1914–1918–Great Britain. 2. World War, 1914–1918–Public opinion–Great Britain. 3. Working class–Great Britain–History–20th century. 4. Public opinion–Great Britain–History–20th century. 5. Great Britain–Armed Forces–Recruiting, enlistment, etc. 6. Working class–Great Britain–Attitudes–History–20th century. I. Title. II. Series
 DA577.S55 2005

940.3′41′08623–dc22   2004011356

ISBN 978-0-415-35005-1 (hb)
ISBN 978-0-415-65230-8 (pb)

Contents

	List of tables	viii
	Acknowledgements	ix
1	Introduction	1
2	The rush to colours, business as usual, and the coming of conscription: August 1914 to May 1916	15
3	Currents within the flood: who were the volunteers?	38
4	'A sense of the round world': the workers, Britain, Europe, and the empire	49
5	'The monotony of the trivial round': enlistment and the escape from domesticity	69
6	'Money was the attraction': enlistment and economic motives	82
7	'We were being patriotic. Or young and silly': enlistment and allegiance	104
8	Conclusion	125
	Notes	132
	References	170
	Index	186

Tables

2.1	Possible numbers of medically rejected volunteers in the general population	31
3.1	Enlistment percentages in the occupational categories defined by the National Register	39
6.1	Trade classifications and male employment, August 1914–July 1915	93
6.2	Trade classifications and female employment, August 1914–July 1915	93
6.3	Total employment growth, male and female, August 1914–July 1915	93
6.4	Trade classifications and enlistment rates, August 1914–July 1915	95
6.5	Industries with largest percentage decreases and increases in employment and their enlistment rates	96
6.6	Largest increases/decreases in employment by absolute numbers, August 1914–July 1915	97
6.7	Enlistment rates in trades classified 'A' and 'C', controlled for economic growth	98
6.8	Wage increases and enlistment rates, 1914–1915	99
6.9	Change in enlistment percentages given different medical acceptance rates	100
6.10	Enlistment percentages of 'A' and 'C' trades, December 1914 and April–July 1915	102

Acknowledgements

There are too many people to thank, and too much for which to thank them. These short paragraphs will have to do. This book could not have been completed without the help, support, and love of many people. It is theirs as much as mine (except the errors, of course). On a professional level, I have been blessed with more assistance than I could have ever imagined when I began. In Britain, the staff at the Public Records Office and the British Library were always helpful and willing to go the extra mile. At the Imperial War Museum, Nigel Steele went beyond the limits of his responsibilities to get me the documents I needed. Roderick Suddaby was always helpful, then and later. At the Liddle Archive, Matthew Richardson and Peter Liddle constantly pointed me down paths I would have otherwise missed. Peter Daniels made a crucial intervention. Andrew Humphrys has been the calming voice of patience and a model editor.

In the USA, Martin Miller and Tami Davis Biddle endured a somewhat haphazard process. Bill Scott offered wise words in the beginning; it is my great loss that he could not be here at the end. Richard Kohn always had good ideas. Judy Martin, Peter Wood, John Thompson, Ron Witt, Vivian Jackson, and Andrea Long played critical roles. Susan Thorne made insightful comments. I cannot imagine sharing my professional life with better colleagues than Tim Blessing, Victoria Williams, Donna Yarri, and Jerry Vigna. My students frequently teach me more than I teach them. But pride of professional place must go to Alex Roland. He was there at the beginning, the middle, and the end. He offered the support, encouragement, and the intensive commentary and editing that this piece needed; often, I suspect, at some cost to his own work. Without him, this would be a much poorer book.

On a personal level, too, I have been blessed. Mike Higgins made me laugh when I needed it most. Louise Cole, Anna Locke, and Debbie Nickerson were (somewhat) voices of reason. In the United States, Jennifer Siegel offered words of comfort and wisdom. James Wyatt and Paul Gries have always been there for me; I know they always will be. Nan Keohane, Sandra Walton, and Lisa Jordan taught me about toughness and grace, a priceless combination.

Charles McKinney and Rod Clare were my sounding board and support group wrapped into one; by experience, knowledge, and memory, they will always be my best men. And without Mari, none of this would have happened. She has lived with the book almost as long as I have. I look forward to her living with many more. But, above all, I thank my parents, who have supported me with love, and understanding, and kindness, since this began, and for long before. To them, this work is dedicated.

1 Introduction

If you are over the age of 18, can read and write successfully, pass the very strict medical examination, if your eyesight and hearing is to a very high standard, you may serve His Majesty King George the Fifth, the Commander of all the British Army, the Royal Navy, Emperor of India, Commander of all his Colonial Forces all around the world, the sun never sets on his Empire.[1]

Years later, J.W. Roworth, an unemployed labourer, would remember the words of the recruiting sergeant. He thought them a 'mouthful', but enlisted anyway.[2] He was not alone. After Britain entered the First World War on 4 August 1914, British men volunteered for military service at a rate never before seen in her history. By December, more than 1 million had enlisted. By the end of 1915, more than 2.5 million had joined. These volunteers made up half of all British servicemen in the First World War.[3] They fought in Britain's most sanguinary war. They were the soldiers who marched forward at the Somme. They were the soldiers who slogged through the mud at Passchendaele. They were the soldiers who absorbed the Germans' spring offensive of 1918, and then, through the summer, pushed them back to the border of Germany. They were the soldiers who fought and won the war for Britain.

Historians, however, have focused only on a small subset of these volunteers, those of the upper and middle classes. Such a focus has ignored the larger part of the rush to colours, for the vast majority of the volunteers were working class.[4] They came from the mines, from the factories, and from the workshops. They came from cities and the country. They came from Scotland, Wales, and England. They came from occupations where employment was plentiful, from occupations where employment was scarce, and from occupations where employment was non-existent.

Why were working-class men so willing to fight? The pre-war era had seemingly provided them with little incentive. They had a deep and abiding suspicion of the government, a suspicion returned by the ruling classes. There was little sense of cooperation between the two groups. The working class had experienced stagnant wages and rising unemployment. They had gone on strike for better working conditions with only limited success. They looked forward to a general strike in

November 1914, aimed at shutting down Britain's economy. Worse, they had seen the army used against strikers and been warned by the Prime Minister, Henry Asquith, that he would use 'all the forces of the Crown' against them in future strikes.[5]

The war itself apparently offered little reason to volunteer. Britain was never directly threatened. The counties, cities, and neighbourhoods in which the working classes lived suffered no occupation. Their friends and families were not directly in danger. The people the workers fought to defend spoke Belgian and French. The lands they protected lay across the English Channel, their place names nearly unpronounceable.[6]

In addition, the war itself demanded a near-unanimous effort from Britain. The First World War was an industrialized mass war. It required the mobilization of the entire society. Without what historian Michael Howard called the 'widest possible basis of consensus within society', Britain could not hope to prosecute the war successfully.[7] Pre-war, the British government did not believe such a consensus existed.[8]

Historians have not yet dealt with this question particularly well. First World War historiography has tended to dismiss or downplay the subject of working-class enlistment and popular motivation.[9] Those who have examined the 'rush to colours' have come from two very different perspectives. Social historians have started from the perspective of the working class, while military historians have viewed the problem from a military perspective. But both have treated the 'rush to colours' as a single occurrence, consisting of a mob of men driven to volunteer by either overwhelming passion or social control, a 'herd' whose 'instinct' it was to enlist.[10] Enlistees were 'lemming-like', and not individuals.[11] By treating the volunteers as a herd, historians have been able to apply a single motivation to them, often an emotional, even irrational one. The kindlier posited a 'rising tide of patriotism'.[12] The less gentle said that the men joined because of a 'euphoria ... a demoniac outburst of enthusiasm'.[13] In effect, by making the motivation singular and unreasoning, historians have been able to explain it simply and without much investigation. A single reason was a simple reason.

This perspective has allowed historians to ignore inconvenient aspects of the 'rush to colours'. Military historians have been largely uninterested in investigating the class aspects of enlistment, preferring instead to focus on the politicians, generals, and government and military policy.[14] Social historians have been reluctant to look at the majority elements of the working class, which supported the war. Instead, they have focused on the small minority of anti-war protesters.

There is thus, as yet, no answer to the question of working-class enthusiasm. The basis of the war effort, the 'consensus', that enabled the European nations to fight a total war, has been left essentially unexamined. Such a lack leaves a gaping hole in the history of the First World War. We cannot explain how national populations came to fight so wholeheartedly for their nations and states. This book aims to begin that investigation, and fill the historical gap. It will investigate what motivations the workers had for joining up, how they spoke of those motivations, and how they acted on them.

Understanding their motivations is important for both military and social history. Military history can never come to grips with the rise and evolution of total war in the nineteenth and twentieth centuries unless it understands popular support for warring states. The soldiers and factory workers are as important to understanding modern war as are the strategy, tactics, technology, and leadership. Social history cannot claim to understand the working class until it understands the enlistment, one of the greatest mass movements of modern British history, as large as the General Strike of 1926.[15]

Inevitably, the foundation of such an analysis must be the words of the working-class volunteers. Observers misinterpret or misrepresent. Historians misjudge. Thus, any study of working-class motives must begin with what the workers themselves said. Though not as numerous as middle- and upper-class sources, working-class diaries, memoirs, letters, and other documents have been collected and preserved at a number of British archives. Certainly, if used uncritically, the words of the volunteers themselves may mislead. But handled with sufficient sensitivity, they provide the fundamental entry point into the thoughts and feelings of a working class at war.

Of course, such an analysis is difficult, founded as it is on a concept – class – that is itself hotly contested. As Gareth Stedman Jones has pointed out, class remains 'a congested point of intersection between many competing, overlapping or simply differing forms of discourse – political, economic, religious, and cultural'.[16] But if there has been wide disagreement about the form and expression of class, there has nonetheless long been an unspoken consensus, derived from the foundational works on class by Marx and Thompson, that classes – especially working classes – define themselves in opposition to other classes.[17] Such an assumption can be dangerous. Any historiographical system that views a society on the basis of its 'history of internal fragmentation' obscures areas of similarities within that society. By using 'class, gender, and race', analyses may miss the existence or establishment of shared beliefs and interests.[18] Many historians have shown a pungent sense of disappointment that British workers were not more bound by their class ties. 'False consciousness' among the workers distracted them from their true responsibility, which was to lead 'the world in creating a socialist society'.[19] For many historians, workers have thus not lived up to the expectations and requirements of their class position.

Much of the current literature has thus turned away from class as the supreme defining category, and has, instead, looked to language as the defining and mediating power. Gareth Stedman Jones and Patrick Joyce have suggested that there was no independent 'class' or experience of class, merely a linguistically self-created conception of class.[20]

Perhaps the best solution is simply – for the moment – to see what classes the British themselves described. The British were and are determinedly class-aware. Of what exactly did they think they were aware? Opinions differed depending on who spoke. For some, the fundamental distinction was between manual and non-manual labour. Charles Booth, who studied the working class of London for several decades around the turn of the twentieth century, believed this. That distinction informed Booth's groundbreaking study, *Life and Labour of the People in London*.[21] Booth's working classes worked in a wide range of skilled and unskilled jobs. They might earn substantial amounts of money or less or very little, they might be employed regularly or intermittently or not at all, but they were all manual labourers, and thus – to Booth – all members of the working class.[22] The British Census, taken every ten years, took a similar approach. The 1911 Census broke down the British population into eight categories, numbered I–VIII. Classes I and II consisted of middle- and upper-class professions. The classes below – the working classes – were manual labourers, and thus working class.[23] These were distinctions of which the British themselves, of whatever level, tended to be strongly aware. I should point out that this was not merely a self-imposed conceptual distinction. The line of division between manual and non-manual labourers was only rarely crossed. Moving from a working-class profession to a middle-class job was a rare occurrence. Over 90 per cent of working-class men remained in the same economic cohort as their fathers. They might move within the working class, but they only rarely moved out of it.[24]

People on the borderline of that distinction were well aware of the gap. Members of the 'upper' working class – those who earned a relatively generous salary and had reasonable job security – were nonetheless strongly aware of their position. For the most part, they did not believe that they belonged with people from the middle class, and they behaved in ways that reflected this. James Sloan remembered 'a long-distance train driver on the old Great Northern Railway' who lived next door to them. Sloan's father managed a hat store and even though the train driver's 'annual earnings were probably double my father's yet, to him, my father was always Mr. Sloan'.[25]

More even than the language, there was an entire physical structure within British society built around the distinctions noted by Booth and by the Census. Frederick Hunt, as a young working-class man in Kirton Lindsey, north Lincolnshire, remembered that even in church, the 'leading Methodists' were careful to distinguish themselves physically from everyone else by sitting in 'two high-sided box pews which hid all but [their] hats and bald heads'.[26] Even the time when people were out on the streets identified them by class. As Allen Clarke pointed out in 1899, the different classes awoke at different times: the workers rose at around five a.m., the clerks at around seven a.m., and the managers two hours later. The obvious effect of this was to segregate the streets according to class. Workers went to work in the company of other workers, clerks in the company of other clerks, and managers with managers.[27]

Of course, there are several problems with this view of class. First, as feminist historians have pointed out, such a classification eliminated the majority of women.[28] Housework was not paid labour, and housewives were thus separated from the working class, excluded by definition. Second, this definition of class is vague at the boundary between the lower and middle class. There is no controversy over the position of an unemployed, unskilled labourer on the docks. He (or she) was working class. But what of manual labourers who earned a substantial wage? Their income often surpassed that of the lower levels of non-manual labourers, like clerks. Many of the lower middle class earned less than many manual labourers, they frequently lived in poor neighbourhoods, and their friends and relatives frequently made their living from manual work. They nonetheless insisted 'vehemently' on their separation and their 'status in society'.[29] Such stringency suggests that lower-middle-class men may have enlisted to prove their standing, a motivation rather different from that of the workers. It is thus necessary to scrutinize the sources closely to avoid the inclusion of such lower-middle-class men.

How did this class self-awareness spill into the war? Did the categories that the British organized themselves into before the war shape how they reacted after 4 August 1914? Did the rigid divides between working and middle and upper class remain dominant and whole? Or did class consciousness stop at the water's edge? In a national emergency, such as was seemingly presented in 1914, were the loyalties of the working class shaped more by economic or by national bonds, and why?

The sources

The sources I have used are working-class documents. Though not as plentiful as elite records, the remembrances of working-class volunteers do exist. The great majority have been gathered at a few places in Britain. The Imperial War Museum (hereafter IWM) in London houses an enormous number of original working-class documents among its collection. The Liddle Archive (hereafter LA) at the Brotherton Library at Leeds University also holds thousands of working-class reminiscences, mostly gathered and preserved through the energy of Peter Liddle. There are also some records at the government's Public Records Office (hereafter PRO) and National Army Museum (hereafter NAM). From these archives, my research turned up 1,702 possible working-class sources. Of these, 889 offered some tidbit of evidence, while 409 of those were men who spoke at relative length about their motivations and beliefs.

The sources contain some diaries and letters from the 1914–1918 period, but the great majority are memoirs, autobiographies, and oral interviews, created years after the fact. This presents problems. Clearly, the sources have been shaped by various different factors and in various different ways. Sometimes, the shaping is obvious. B.J. Brookes, an office boy, wrote of his wartime experiences, but:

> left out anything which I have had personally to do or put up with if it is at all out of the ordinary . . . I have penned only such things that might, and do, continually happen to any infantryman in the British Army.[30]

G. Skelton's family left out the first twenty-three pages of his memoirs because they recounted his civilian experiences before he reached France, experiences the family felt unimportant.[31] Sometimes, the shaping is less obvious. The oral interviews from both the IWM and the LA took place largely in the 1950s, 1960s, and 1970s, years after the war. The number of years between the events and their recounting is fairly large for most of these records.[32] The temporal distance creates some doubt about their reliability. The intervening years have certainly shaped the way that the volunteers remembered their motivations. When H.C. Parker talked of the war, years later, he identified what they had been fighting against: 'the concentration camp, the rubber truncheon, the gas chamber, gangster rule, and the aggression founded on bloody murder'.[33] Parker's enemy seems much more like the Nazi regime of the Second World War than the Wilhelmine Government of the First World War.

Geographically, both archives provided sources from all around Great Britain. The non-English countries of Great Britain are all represented, if somewhat sparingly. Of the IWM sources used, 29 out of 796 come from Scotland (3.5 per cent), 14 out of 796 from Ireland (1.7 per cent), and 17 out of 796 from Wales (2.1 per cent). The figures, in the same order, for the LA are 9 out of 292 (3.1 per cent), 1 out of 292 (0.3 per cent), and 7 out of 292 (2.4 per cent). These percentages do not come up to the overall share of each country in the total population of Great Britain: Scotland, 10 per cent; Ireland 9.4 per cent; and Wales, 5 per cent.[34] As the comparison shows, Scotland, Ireland, and Wales are under-represented in the source material. With Ireland, this may relate to much lower participation by Irish men in the war (6 per cent of the total male population versus 20 per cent for the other three countries).[35] But the lack of sources from Scotland and Wales are more likely to have resulted from the collection of such sources in repositories within those countries. The imbalance may also, regrettably, result from a bias by the archivists against Scottish and Welsh records.

There are geographic imbalances within the four nations. Of the IWM sources, 85 of 796 were of men from London (10.6 per cent). The LA sources show a similar tendency: 35 out of 292 LA sources are of men from London (12 per cent). This compares with the overall figures for England in 1914: 7 million Londoners out of a population of 34 million in England (20.5 per cent).[36] By contrast, the town of Sunderland is over-represented, at least in the LA sources. The Sunderland contingent is 23 out of 292 (7.8 per cent). Sunderland's share of the total population was much smaller: in 1911, the population of Sunderland was 12,700.[37] That gives it a 0.037 per cent share of the general British population. But this imbalance is not surprising. Peter Liddle began his collection project while working at the University of Sunderland in the 1960s and 1970s, and thus many of his earlier documents are from men resident in the town.[38]

There are other potential disparities. The memoirs, letters, and diaries used were of men who mostly survived the war.[39] They chose to write about their experiences. This might have changed their views from those of the larger population of working-class volunteers, many of whom did not survive, and most of whom did not write about the war. It is not clear how, though.

The oral interviews might counterbalance that bias to an extent, but even with them, it is unclear how they were selected. Was it because the men interviewed were outgoing enough to answer a newspaper advertisement or seek out a historian such as Peter Liddle? How would this distort the record? Men who allowed themselves to be interviewed might have felt they needed to explain or justify something.

Clearly, then, these men are not a microcosm of working-class Britain and do not directly mirror the British population. How representative are they? Can they be taken as representative of the larger group or were their memoirs the reflections of idiosyncratic individuals? There is no way to tell for sure. The danger is that generalizing from what these particular workers have written may obscure rather than explain the reasons behind the 'rush to colours'.

We might counterbalance the inequities with a statistical analysis. Using the government's records of the total enlistment figures from 1914 to 1916 gives percentages that are not merely representative of the larger group, they *are* the larger group. As I work through the volunteers' expressed reasons for enlisting, I will attempt to see whether the behaviour of the larger group reflected their words. If the entire pool of working-class volunteers behaved largely in harmony with the motives examined here, it would seem the motives in the pool of men are reflective of the entire rush to colours.

The meanings of patriotism

Using a statistical analysis would also help with another problem – the concept of patriotism. There are two specific problems in dealing with patriotism. First, when working-class men wrote or spoke of their loyalty to nation, how much of what they said was a genuine feeling, and how much resulted from external social and cultural pressures? Or, to put it another way, how much can the words of the workers cited in this study be relied upon? Second, how often did the workers reach for patriotism in order to conceal a less admirable emotion? In other words, embarrassed or unable to sum up their true emotions when questioned, did working-class volunteers invoke patriotism as superficial rhetoric? These two problems strike to the heart of the book. If the workers were unreliable in reporting their motives, if the motives they espoused were not their own, then this analysis is more about social manipulation than about volunteerism.

First, patriotism may have served working-class volunteers as a justification for other, less acceptable reasons. Patriotism was an easy and readily understood motive. For some, patriotism seems to have substituted when their memory proved suspect. B.C. Aitcheson's declaration is revealing: 'I joined the 7th battalion of the Durham Light Infantry and I think that was on the last day of August or the first day of September and I think my reason for joining so early was that I was patriotic.'[40] Aitcheson, who worked as a labourer before the war, was clearly unsure. He may genuinely have joined for patriotic reasons, but he may merely have been reaching for an easy and readily understandable explanation.

Men often cited patriotism in combination with other considerations when discussing their reasons for joining. A. Whiteley, an apprentice at a car factory, spoke of joining to defend his country but also recalled his wistful desire to 'see a little bit of the continent and [then] be back again'.[41] Whiteley wanted to experience adventure. Whether the patriotism he cited existed as well or whether he added it in afterwards to balance his longing for adventure is not clear. J.C. Attwood, an office boy, 'put country first', but he only joined up 'after receiving an assurance from my employers that I could expect my job to be kept open for me'.[42] Attwood's motive was patriotic, but clearly his attention was also on his economic position. Again, as with Whiteley, it is possible that Attwood adopted a patriotic stance to cover what he believed was a less respectable motivation.

Some claimed patriotism to avoid interrogation. B.L. Lawrence, an officer, wrote of questioning a man in his company:

> The other day I asked a private soldier in my company if he understood what we are fighting for, and he replied 'Why to hammer that there Kaiser' (Only he pronounced it Kaysar). When I asked him if he knew why we should be so anxious to hammer the Kaiser he merely looked vacant and could make no reply. 'Tell me then' I said. 'Why did you enlist?' 'Because I was drunk' he answered tersely and that ended the matter![43]

The soldier, in his first response, claimed patriotism. Clearly, he had no interest in discussing it with his officer. Or perhaps he wanted to please Lawrence. In any event, he used the simple and immediately comprehensible response. Only upon further questioning did he reveal a less flattering portrait. In a sense, Lawrence's questioning resembles the process that created all the letters, memoirs, and diaries used in this book. They came out of interrogations, both actual and symbolic. These were not truly the innermost thoughts of working-class volunteers as they happened. They were, instead, shaped by those volunteers to what they wanted to tell, or what they thought the interviewer wanted to hear.

The patriotism motive was affected by more than internal considerations. It may well have been shaped by external ones. Working-class patriotism could, in fact, have been the creation of outside forces. As historian Raphael Samuel has pointed out, patriotism is something 'very often, which is thrust upon us'.[44] Samuel implicitly argued for a patriotism that had been created by people other than the working class and then used to manipulate workers into enlisting. Enlistees may have been reacting to a patriotism 'thrust upon' them, rather than their own beliefs. But who created such a patriotism?

Patriotism has often been constructed by groups fighting for possession of its meaning.[45] Because of patriotism's attractiveness, groups within society fought to define it, and thus control it. The most obvious group was the government and the ruling elites. They built a patriotism which justified and perpetuated their control. They were not alone, however. Radical groups, including working-class groups, throughout the eighteenth and nineteenth centuries created their own patriotism, counter to the government's definition. That this continued even into the First World War seems indubitable. Writing in 1915, C.H. Norman said:

> The intellectual attitude of all governing classes is to insist that patriotism should be limited to the duty to defend the country, when those governing classes choose to embark upon a war; but the true importance of patriotism

and its universal value, under the present conditions, is in upholding the rights and liberties of the people against tyranny.[46]

Note that Norman was not arguing against patriotism but attempting to reconceive it. He was not willing to allow it to be defined independent of him. The very concept of patriotism was of value and thus its definition had to reclaimed.

The problem with these conceptions is that they remove the individual from the creation of patriotism. Much of the historiography of British patriotism emphasizes the role of groups, rather than the individual, in creating patriotism. But individuals did not have to accept the patriotic formulations presented to them by the groups. They were free to negotiate their own understanding of patriotism, and, indeed, of their own place in the nation, by filtering it through their own understanding and experiences. Historians have ignored this, and assumed that individuals were unthinking consumers, accepting without question the patriotic messages presented to them. The aim of this book is, in part, to reclaim those neglected individual viewpoints and see how working-class men spoke of their patriotic beliefs.

The words, sentences, and structures used by working-class men to describe patriotic feelings differed greatly from volunteer to volunteer. Some used language that echoed elite propaganda. Many used simpler, more sincere forms of expression. Some spoke in a way that makes analysis difficult. 'I joined', Walter Hare said, 'to try and get the war over.'[47] Hare's simple words defy dissection. Did he want the war over because he was patriotic? It is not clear. But others used language that does allow analysis. H.D. Watson, a mechanic's apprentice, phrased his memories of enlisting in a noticeably acquiescent fashion: 'It was felt by me that it was my place to offer my services to HM Government, so I went & enlisted for the "Duration" on 14th August 1914.'[48] His usage of the passive voice and avoidance of the pronoun 'I' in the first part of the sentence suggests that Watson, whatever his statements, felt less than favourable towards the war. That awkwardness becomes especially clear when the second half of the sentence is looked at: 'I went and enlisted for the "Duration".' Here, Watson uses a simple and declarative structure that puts him centre stage. The second part is firm and straightforward. The first part is not. It is dangerous to draw too firm a conclusion from the disjointed phrasing, but it certainly seems to suggest that Watson felt less convinced by his enlistment motives than Hare did, that Watson's passive construction of his answer reflected a larger passivity in his own mind.

Thus the fundamental question is how reliable were the words and remembrances of the enlistees. Are they faithful to their feelings in 1914–1916, even when many wrote decades after the fact? Or are they so distorted by the passage of years that they cannot be taken as a true representation of their enlistment motivations? Can autobiographical memories – the 'least convincing of all personal records' – be relied upon for this work? Are not the volunteers introducing a 'factitious coherence' to what was a disorderly and disorganized reality?[49] Is it possible to overcome that unreliability for the purposes of this book? Can autobiographical memories be used as the basis for analysis?

There are several general arguments to suggest so. First, as Daniel James has implied, though autobiographies are unreliable as sources of objective truth, they can, if treated with caution, be read and interpreted. As long as the historian is aware that the autobiographer is a 'storyteller', shaping and moulding his or her own history, then autobiography can serve as a useful source.[50] The awareness of the storyteller's biases is as important as the story itself.

Second, while a single autobiography must surely be treated with great caution, *many* autobiographies, each making the same point, are likely to be more reliable and less biased by a particular and unique experience. They must still be treated with care, but their common themes, I would argue, can be treated as having some credibility.

Both of these ameliorate but do not entirely overcome the issue of reliability. Thus, I will turn to another approach. This book will attempt to back up the assertions found in letters, diaries, and memoirs with general statistical evidence. The British government kept fairly detailed statistics concerning enlistment. We should be able to use those statistics to find reflections of what the volunteers remembered. Statistical analysis, of course, has its own flaws. Nonetheless, the combination of the two forms should provide a much stronger argument than either alone.

There is, of course, a particular problem with those espousing patriotism. Emphasizing selfish motives like economic or domestic reasons would not seem to be in the enlistee's interest. The words of volunteers talking about the army as a possible economic step-up or adventure – non-altruistic motives – can probably be relied upon. But the same argument cannot be made for patriotism. Such claims could be self-serving.

Memoirs, interviews, and diaries making such claims thus must be treated with great care. Even when the language is simple and unsophisticated, as was one veteran's declaration that he joined the Navy because 'I wanted to fight for my country', there may be grounds for suspicion.[51] How much of that particular sentiment was genuine and how much was constructed in the post-war years? Were working-class men displaying a genuine feeling for their country or were they brainwashed by a manipulative society?

Historians have argued for both. For many, patriotic feelings were externally constructed and lacked validity; they represented an outside message, forced upon a subservient working class, 'social imperialist manipulation'.[52] In this imposition, working-class patriotism consisted of little more than 'an important willingness to accept what the state demanded of you'.[53]

Others have argued with this interpretation, believing that dismissing patriotic enlistees as 'jingoistic lemmings' was deeply simplistic. Men spoke consistently about their feelings, both before and after they enlisted, and they were not shy of criticizing themselves or their government. In this view, when men spoke of patriotism, they were speaking from the heart.[54]

Others have pointed out that to dismiss such memories is worryingly like imposing an external viewpoint upon them. It fits working-class feelings to a preconceived theory. Calling such feelings 'false patriotism' has allowed historians to avoid grasping the 'nettle of British nationalism'.[55] Historians have not had to deal with the possibility of a genuinely popular nation. They have not had to reconcile the contradictions introduced by such nationalism into the Marxist conception of class hostilities. Any 'conformity and conventionality' can be paternalistically dismissed as externally imposed.[56]

By making this assumption, historians have also ignored the degree to which espousing patriotism after the First World War was *not* a popular opinion. When veterans invoked patriotism after the war, they were flouting the cynicism and disillusionment that had swept over Britain. The First World War was an ambiguous war: the war of the Lost Generation, of the seemingly needless casualties of the Somme, of 'donkey' generals who needlessly threw away their soldiers' lives. Central to this 'myth of the war' was a misguided patriotism, as Samuel Hynes recently pointed out.[57] Memories of the Great War were allowed to be uncertain. The remembrances were not triumphant messages of national victory, but equivocal remembrances of an ambiguous war: 'memories, maybe bitter, but not degrading, sad, but not depressing', said one veteran.[58] One anonymous working-class man could convey long after the war a decidedly mixed sense of his responsibility. He had not enlisted, but if he had 'I should have been only one more scrap flung on the waste-heap, but I still have a feeling that I ought to be one of the dead who leaped into cleanness.' Even those who had enlisted could wonder. Jesse Shaw joined up in 1918 before his draft class was conscripted and wrote later of his mixed feelings: 'I sat spitting and polishing, thinking myself patriotic, while a small voice insisted that I'd merely been stupid.' Veterans, in a sense, had cultural permission to question the war and their own 'mistaken mentality'.[59]

Nor were working-class men shy about using such cultural permission in later years. Jack Lanigan, born in 1890 to a poor family in Salford, thought his youthful patriotism inexplicable: 'We kids even found time to be patriotic, why and what for God alone knows.'[60] R.J. Carrier, whose father was a miner, believed later that the war had been a great lie:

> The big men – the men with money, land, stocks and shares, factories and mines – were telling the little men, the men devoid of all save health, strength, and dependents, to go out and fight, to keep the foreigners' paw off the big men's spoils . . . . What bunkum, what lies, what damnable sins.[61]

Both men were looking back sceptically at themselves and at the feelings that led them to join the army and fight for Britain.

Even those who did not directly talk of their scepticism often shaped their language in ways that reflected their doubts. They might echo the propaganda they had seen. John Allsop said 'I joined up because it was said "Your King and Country need you."'[62] They used convoluted sentence structures, heavy with passive voice. They used clichés that echoed the wartime or post-war propaganda. When Norman Smith, the son of a weaver, spoke of his enlistment, he reverted to stock phrases: 'Reason for joining highest motives, to crush German militarism, a war to end war.'[63] His answers consisted of short, staccato clauses that echo larger patriotic themes precisely: 'highest motives', 'crush German militarism', and, most importantly, 'a war to end war'. All were catch-phrases, used during the war and after to justify the British effort. Smith's explanation seems to have less to do with him than with what he imbibed in 1914 and the years following. John Ames's language seems even more indicative: 'I joined the Royal Welch Fusiliers with about twenty others, because we felt it was our duty to fall into line.'[64] Ames's language is more explicitly deferential. Ames, the son of a plate-layer, must join, not truly of his own volition, but because his 'duty' was 'to fall into line'.

The words of Smith and Ames place patriotism in the foreground by appealing to 'duty' and the 'highest motives'. But their sentences are structured so as to eliminate their own presence. Smith never refers to himself while discussing his reasons for joining. Ames nullifies his own presence by using 'we' and the passive voice. In both cases, the volunteer disappears from the account or seems reduced to joining out of helpless acquiescence. 'I got patriotic,' Arthur Beeton said, as if talking of catching a cold.[65] These men seem to have felt less than truly enthusiastic about volunteering and re-imposed patriotism on themselves at a later date.

The danger is in including men like these with those who genuinely felt an allegiance to something outside themselves: those pressured with those volunteering. Yet this may be too harsh an explanation. The use of such language may indeed demonstrate merely adherence to propaganda fed by government and press and reinforced over the years by myth-making. It may equally reflect the use of readily available phrases by men unused to writing or being interviewed and struggling to put into words their deepest motivations. R.L. Venables, a working-class youth in Mexborough, did exactly that when recounting how he asked his parents about enlistment. His mother 'replied in words approximately the same as a song which became popular soon afterwards: "We don't want to lose you but we think you ought to go".'[66] Venables' recollections relied on stock phrases, but he was conscious of that reliance.

Such self-awareness and scepticism strongly suggest that working-class men were reasonably self-aware rather than blindly manipulated. They were willing to criticize their own patriotic feelings after the fact. If they nonetheless spoke of their patriotism, then perhaps they were expressing not blind obedience but genuine nationalism. Certainly, such pronouncements should not be accepted uncritically, but to dismiss the feelings of volunteers altogether is to move from a position of reasoned scepticism to one of blanket condemnation.

The above should not be taken as an argument for an all-knowing working class. Men joined for foolish reasons, without thinking things through and without understanding what faced them. As Claude Dawson, whose father repaired boots, said: 'We were being patriotic. Or young and silly.'[67] But so too were many middle- and upper-class men. Much government policy was made in a fog, as the Liberal Party struggled to fight a war that contradicted many of its core beliefs. The War Office laboured to figure out the new form of warfare. The generals in France sought to come to grips with combat beyond their experience. None of this should be surprising, given the unprecedented nature of the war. Few in 1914 could truly claim to understand events. As Kitchener said when trench warfare came to dominate: 'I don't know what is to be done; this isn't war.'[68]

That said, however, the examination so far suggests strongly that the words of the workers can be used, if with care, to examine patriotism, as well as other motives. But how? Can H.G. Taylor's definition, 'for God, King, and Country', be used? Was this what David Pitkeathly, the son of a cobbler, was thinking of when he talked of 'the usual patriotic reasons' behind his enlistment?[69] Here again, we run into difficulty. Are the 'usual patriotic reasons' of which Pitkeathly is speaking Taylor's 'God, King, and Country'? He does not say. Patriotism is such a familiar concept that volunteers rarely felt that they had to explain their meaning. They assumed that everyone shared the same idea of patriotism. They assumed that patriotism was a single, universal concept, the same in the inner city of Manchester as in the highlands of Scotland, in the Glasgow slum Gorbals as in the rural areas of Kent.

But here we arrive at another notion. Such a realization as above opens up the concept of patriotism for examination, as well as explanation. If we avoid the label of 'patriotism' and place it in its larger context, we may find some insight into the difficulties discussed above. Thus, for the purposes of this book, 'patriotism' will be replaced by 'allegiance'. Men enlisted because they felt a sense of allegiance to something or someone outside themselves. The motive remains a selfless one, but is both narrowed and broadened beyond merely national fealty. The range of allegiances that workers felt and that motivated them to enlist took a number of different shapes. Men alluded to a wide range of bodies, areas, or people to justify their voluntarism. They believed that, by enlisting, they acted to defend what was most important to them, whether family, friends, their neighbourhood, their class, or their country. Allegiance to country was one of those, but not the only one.

Thus, the chapters that follow use both anecdotal and statistical evidence. Chapters 2–3 recount what historians understand so far about the events of the rush to colours. Their material is not wholly new, though they contain both original evidence and original insights. They are necessary, however, to set up what follows. Chapter 2 starts before the war and examines relations between the elites and the working class, and the domestic perceptions of the growing tensions between Britain and Germany. The chapter continues into the beginning of the war, analyses government recruitment policy and the initial surge of men to the military, and the slow movement towards the passage of a conscription bill in January 1916. Chapter 3 analyses who the volunteers were, what occupations they held in civilian life, and various other characteristics. Chapters 4–7 are new. They use evidence untouched by previous historians and suggest interpretations unexpressed by the current historiography. Chapter 4 suggests a common bond between all these motives by investigating the broader worldview of the 1914 generation of workers. Chapter 5 begins the examination of working-class enlistment motives by looking at the desire to escape and search for adventure. Chapter 6 examines economic motives. Chapter 7 explores allegiance.

It is not an overstatement to see this popular support as the most critical element in the total wars of the twentieth century. Marx believed that the 'extreme judgement' of war would destabilize many states and make them vulnerable to revolution. That his prophecy did not come true in the twentieth century is largely because of popular support for wars. A nation could not effectively fight a mass, industrialized war without the support of the great majority of its populace. Without the support, a nation could not muster armies, or feed them, or build their weapons. For the most part, such support has been forthcoming.[70] The sacrifices made by the working classes of Europe on behalf of the nation state, as Bernard Waites recently pointed out, dwarf any effort made by the same working classes on behalf of socialism.[71]

At its root, it was this support that made nations so resilient in fighting total war. They have been able to endure conflicts for much longer than anyone expected. Few believed beforehand, as historian Bernard Waites pointed out, that nations could long sustain total war:

> The economies of the great powers were so entangled in an international web of commerce and finance, and their social relations so delicately poised between national integration and class conflict, that these states were assumed to be extremely vulnerable to prolonged war.[72]

Nations have, nonetheless, managed to fight lengthy and ruinously expensive wars. They have done so because they have had the consent and support of their people. It is that consent that determines how well a nation will fight a total war, and it is that consent that this book aims to explain.

2 The rush to colours, business as usual, and the coming of conscription
August 1914 to May 1916

Great Britain had little to do with the start of the First World War. The roots of the First World War grew in the second half of the nineteenth century, seeded by the re-unification of Germany, her defeat of France in 1870–1871, and the slow decline of Austria-Hungary and Russia.[1] The slow encirclement of Germany made her increasingly nervous as the century ended. When France signed an alliance with Russia in the 1890s, the German elite felt hemmed in. The internal unrest which accompanied industrialization added to the pressure on German rulers. To preserve their power, they resorted to 'manipulative strategies of national distraction'.[2] One of those strategies was war. By 1912, the Germans believed that Russia, reforming and modernizing her Army, would not be able to field an effective fighting force before 1916. Until then, she remained vulnerable. This belief shaped their preparations for war. Among these external strategies was the creation of a large Navy and the aggressive quest for a colonial empire. Britain, mostly aloof until then, finally began to mark the German menace.[3]

By the first decade of the twentieth century, then, the British, both government and people, had pushed aside France and made Germany the 'popular enemy'.[4] A growing literature, both youth and adult, warned of the dangers of German invasion. W.E. Baker, a railwayman's son, remembered his childhood books: 'we had a trilogy ... called *Britain Invaded*, *Britain at Bay* and *Britain Triumphant*. Germany, of course, was the enemy in each book.'[5] Sometimes the readers of that literature fought back: H.E. Hunt and his friends attempted to defend their homeland against spies travelling with German brass bands on tour in Britain by sitting in the front row and loudly sucking on lemon drops.[6]

The government's growing suspicions of Germany manifested in a series of larger scale military and political countermeasures. The British government started moving towards alliance with France through the 1904 Entente Cordiale. Militarily, the British government brought the greater part of her fleet back to home waters and invested heavily in pushing the limits of naval technology, best exemplified by the building of the battleship *Dreadnought* in 1906.[7] The British also paid more attention to the needs of their Army. Doubly unnerved by its poor performance in the Boer War (1899–1902), the government moved to reform both the composition and the organization of the Army.[8]

Reginald Haldane, who took over as Minister of War in 1906, drove the Army reform. His goal was to produce 'an expeditionary force immediately available for use overseas in war, with a territorial organization behind, capable of supporting and expanding it'. Haldane thus rebuilt the Regular Army and made it ready to go abroad and backed it up by creating the Territorial Force for home defence.[9] The reforms were successful. By 1910 the reformed Army had both a relatively effective domestic defence force and, perhaps most critically, Regular troops trained and ready to be deployed abroad. The existence of these forces increased the British government's willingness to commit to an anti-German alliance.

But tackling the military's problems forced the government to confront social problems as well. Medical inspection of men who volunteered to fight the Boer War revealed a worrying trend. Many working-class volunteers were crippled by malnourishment, poor medical care, and the stunting effect of harsh industrial labour. As a result, a high percentage of men were rejected. To the elites of Britain, convinced they were in a Darwinian struggle for survival with other races, this racial stunting, combined with the dropping birth-rate in England, set off alarms. 'Population', as historian Anna Davin put it, 'was power.'[10] The government thus began to work to improve the health of the British populace. In addition, many private social organizations for working-class youth emerged, aimed at making them fit and hardy. These included the Boy Scouts, the Church Lads Brigade, and similar associations. An outpouring of literature exhorted the lower classes to live moral, clean lives, so as to prove themselves a truly imperial race.[11]

Despite a Social Darwinist rhetoric of race war, few within the working class applauded enlistment in the military, seeing it instead as the last refuge of the economically or socially incompetent. 'A lad who enlisted', said E. Buffey, a colliery worker, 'was considered to be idle or had got some poor innocent lass wrong.'[12] Some parents saw it as a fundamental betrayal. J.S. Handley's father refused to stand for his son's enlistment in the Territorials in 1912 and took drastic action:

> My father kicked me out because he was a Socialist and he believed wars were engineered by the capitalists. No son of his would serve in any army to keep the country safe for them. Labour was, he believed, so organized that every man would 'down tools' and prevent any future war. So, I was kicked out. ...[13]

The workers in general seem to have been unimpressed by the efforts of the elites. While the elites were attempting to rebuild the working class physically, the working class was reinvigorating itself mentally. The Industrial Revolution had created, by the end of the nineteenth century, a new urban working class which attached less importance to traditional British deference and much more to militancy.[14] As the economies of Germany and the United States grew to rival Britain's, rising unemployment, rising prices, and stagnant wages fed worker frustration. Industrial militancy grew after the turn of the century and especially after 1910.[15] In the four years before the start of the First World War, Britain suffered a wave of strikes and stoppages. To George Askwith, the government's chief negotiator during this period, it looked 'as though we are in the presence of one of those periodic upheavals in the labour world such as occurred in 1833–4, and from time to time since that date'.[16] Combined with the growing struggle over Home Rule in Ireland, and the chaotic and often violent struggle over women's suffrage, by the beginning of 1914 Britain seemed on the edge of 'a civil war, a sex war, and a class war'.[17]

Britain slips towards war

When Serbian assassins killed the heir to the Austrian throne, Archduke Franz Ferdinand, in late June 1914, most felt that Britain could and would remain uninvolved in the situation. Even after an intransigent Austrian ultimatum to Serbia in late July widened the crisis, British involvement seemed unlikely. Prime Minister Asquith said that, even if Europe went to war, 'there seems to be no reason why we should be anything more than spectators'.[18] Such continental strife was nothing new. Tensions on the continent, and in the Balkans, had been high for a long time. 'We had lived so long in an atmosphere of war and nothing had happened,' said George Barnes, a member of the British Cabinet, 'that I think most of us had come to the conclusion that nothing would happen.'[19]

Instead, during the summer of 1914, Britons turned inward. 'We were ... engrossed up to our eyes in domestic affairs,' George Barnes recalled.[20] The crises threatening Britain remained depressingly familiar: a continuation of severe industrial unrest; the suffragette campaign of civil disobedience, hunger strikes, and arson; and the struggle over Irish Home Rule. Each, on its own, was dangerous. In combination they seemed to signal, to Leo Amery among others, that British society stood on the edge of an 'appalling catastrophe'.[21]

The suffrage movement itself divided between those who believed in the efficacy of peaceful lobbying of the government and those who believed in violent, direct action, such as the burning of ministerial homes.[22] It is the latter who have received the most attention. And, if the suffragette movement did not particularly threaten a widespread insurrection, the burning of ministers' homes, attacks upon their persons, and the forcible feeding of female hunger strikers made many – especially government officials – feel that the 'women were waging war'.[23]

Adding to the atmosphere of crisis was a continuing series of strikes. In 1913, a record 40 million working days were lost to strikes. Worse seemed to threaten in 1914. The first two major strikes of the year, mounted by the Yorkshire coal miners and London transport workers, cost more than 5 million working days between them.[24] By June 1914, the three leading unions, the Miners' Federation of Great Britain, the National Transport Workers' Federation, and the National Union of Railwaymen, had formed a 'Triple Alliance' to fight industrial disputes as a single entity. Many expected a paralysing general strike and a subsequent imposition of martial law in November 1914.[25] But worst was the Home Rule crisis, which seemed to threaten civil war. The Liberal Cabinet, its majority dependent on Irish MPs after 1910, sought to transfer the governing power of Ireland to the Irish. They met with deep-seated opposition, both political and military.[26] Irish Protestants, led by Sir Edward Carson, smuggled weaponry into Ireland. They threatened violence to prevent division of the two islands. Carson organized the Ulster Volunteer Force to defend the Union. By the summer of 1914 the force was ready to fight the British. As one participant put it:

> 1914 found me, like many another Belfast lad, all keyed up to fight. We in Ulster were ready and eager for fighting – drilling day and night. Outposts were scattered over the length and breadth of Ulster and pickets were posted at every place of importance, particularly of course where we had our guns hidden. Yes, the lads of Ulster in 1914 were ready to fight.[27]

Such violence would have found political and military support in England. Lord Roberts, one of England's most revered generals, had already backed the Unionist cause by setting up shooting clubs in Belfast, where a generation of Protestants received weapons-training.[28] The Unionist Party in England, led by Andrew Bonar Law with his concept of 'managed extremism', resisted the idea of Home Rule and may even have deliberately encouraged unrest as an electoral ploy.[29] Further, and more ominously, the British Army exhibited worrying signs of unreliability in this crisis. A mutiny at Curragh in March 1914 exposed factions within the army unwilling to enforce a Home Rule bill. Support for this defiance existed within the War Office.[30] In late July, the crisis reached such a pitch that King George stepped outside his constitutional role and called for a conference of the pivotal figures. Presiding at Buckingham Palace in late July 1914, the King warned those in attendance that they must find a solution, for 'the cry of civil war is on the lips of the most responsible and sober-minded of my people'.[31]

It was not until the end of July that foreign concerns wrenched British attention back to the continent. In mid-July, Russia intervened in the controversy between Austria-Hungary and Serbia, intent on safeguarding the interests of her Slavic brethren. The crisis escalated, the Russians mobilized, and the Germans, tied to rigid military timetables, declared war and invaded Belgium, *en route* to France.[32]

Britain thus had to decide whether to help France. The British Cabinet, unaware, for the most part, of the commitment to the French, split into opposing camps over the possibility of war. Asquith, the Prime Minister, Edward Grey, the Foreign Minister, and Winston Churchill, the First Lord of the Admiralty, led the pro-war camp. On 1 August 1914, the anti-war camp consisted of the rest of the Cabinet and most of the Liberal Party in Parliament. No one, however, had stepped forward to lead. Lloyd George, the Chancellor of the Exchequer, upon whom many radical Liberals pinned their hopes, remained silent.[33] Grey and Asquith manipulated the situation deftly, using emotional appeals to British honour, outright distortions of British commitments, and threats of resignation to convert the Cabinet. In the end, the majority of the Cabinet acquiesced. There was no formal vote for war within the Cabinet, but the ministers allowed British Army and Navy deployment to go forward without interference.

Asquith and Grey next sought to win over Parliament, which had split along party lines. The Parliamentary Labour Party ascribed the crisis to imperialist governments, and deemed it unworthy of the workers' support.[34] They firmly opposed any British involvement. The Conservatives, on the other hand, favoured intervention. Though still suspicious of France, the Conservatives believed that Germany presented a critical threat. The Liberals were divided. Many felt that going to war was a fundamental betrayal of their party's ideology, while others believed the Germans a mortal peril to the British Empire. Nearly all of the waverers shifted to a pro-war position on 3 August after an emotional speech by Grey outlining British commitments. The government had its mandate to declare war.[35]

The British people followed a similar path: mixed feelings followed by near total support. Initially, there seemed to be a widespread popular peace movement. Protests occurred across the country, culminating in a large-scale demonstration in Trafalgar Square on 2 August 1914. John Maclean, a member of the Scottish Socialist Party, preached from the podium:

> Let the propertied class go out, old and young alike, and defend their blessed property. When they have been disposed of, we of the working class will have something to defend and we shall do it.[36]

Such appeals to class solidarity did not, however, convince everyone. One observer was at the same meeting:

> Banners and placards denouncing war were everywhere in evidence but a speaker was suddenly pushed off the plinth into the packed mass below. As he fell somebody lifted an umbrella and whacked him over the head. A venturesome man climbed the lamp post on the island in the centre of the road and tied a Union Jack to the top. A great cheer went up but another youth swarmed up and pulled it down again.[37]

The mixed emotions of the crowd are clear.

As the crisis unfolded, the populace moved closer to Asquith's and Grey's position. Grey's speech in Parliament brought much of the population to the pro-war side, as the philosopher, Bertrand Russell, remembered:

> I spent the evening [of Sir E. Grey's speech] walking round the streets, especially in the neighbourhood of Trafalgar Square, noticing cheering crowds, and making myself sensitive to the emotions of passers-by. During this and the following days I discovered to my amazement that average men and women were delighted at the prospect of war.[38]

The German invasion of Belgium swung popular support firmly behind the government. H.D. Watson, who worked in an engineering firm, remembered:

> In August 1914 other people in my area (North London) reacted strongly against Germany, since Belgium had been invaded by German troops contrary

to a solemn agreement by Germany that she would respect Belgium's sovereignty and national boundaries.[39]

By the time Britain declared war, most of the population had converted to a pro-war position. On 4 August 1914, Grey demanded that Germany withdraw from Belgium. The ultimatum expired at eleven, British time. Prior to that hour, crowds flooded Piccadilly Circus and Parliament and Trafalgar Squares. When eleven came and went without word from the Germans, cheering broke out and a general celebration ensued that lasted late into the night.[40] Similar crowds gathered outside Buckingham Palace. Michael Macdonagh, a middle-class observer, recounted:

> [The King] had to appear on the balcony three separate times during the evening, because of the chanting of the crowd, slowly and with emphasis, betokening that they would have no refusal, 'We-want-our-King.'[41]

Those who rued the coming of the war, whether working, middle, or upper class, were few and far between. For the most part, even those who held socialist ideals found no disjunction between those beliefs and support of the war. James Sloan's father, though a member of the lower middle class, working as the manager of a hat store in London, was a socialist. But he saw no contradiction between his ideas and the war:

> My father's visions of a world state run by the people, for the people did not, anachronistically, prevent him from being vigorously patriotic in 1914 when Germany launched its attack upon Belgium. He turned a completely deaf ear to the contention of some of his friends that this was wholly a war between capitalists for world domination.[42]

Bertrand Russell discovered that 'the anticipation of carnage was delightful to something like ninety per cent of the population'.[43]

The rapidity of events and lack of a strong leader worked against the anti-war protesters. Much of the British peace movement saw in the declaration of war an irreversible defeat against which they could not fight. The Peace Society, the oldest of the pacifist organizations in Britain, refused to condemn the declaration of war, nor did it attempt to reverse it.[44] Even those peace organizations that did struggle on, most notably the Union for Democratic Control and the Independent Labour Party (hereafter ILP) did so, for the most part, half-heartedly.[45] How strongly the ILP argued against the war can be measured by the Home Office response to one of its leaflets: 'I do not see much harm in the pamphlet – some parts are excellent. I do not think it will do much damage to recruiting.'[46] Many anti-war organizations made complete turnabouts after the start of the war. The Labour paper, the *Daily Herald*, argued loudly against the war in the opening days of August, calling for a general strike by Britain's workers to prevent her entry.

By 17 August, however, the paper was arguing that even if Labour had controlled the government, the workers 'would probably have decided that they must go into this war'.[47]

Driving this was the wave of working-class support for the war first seen on the night of 4 August 1914. Anti-war working-class leaders sometimes found their positions undercut by the pro-war torrent of their constituents. The most notable victim of this was Ramsay MacDonald, staunchly anti-war before 4 August. Soon after the war started he resigned as head of the Parliamentary Labour Party when it became clear that the membership would not support his pacifist stand.[48] Other Labour leaders managed to preserve their position only by repudiating their initial opposition to the war. On 1 August, Arthur Henderson sided with MacDonald, calling for 'vast demonstrations' against the war in 'every industrial centre' to 'compel those of the governing class' not to go to war. Within the month, however, Henderson reversed his position. He joined an all-party recruiting body, the Parliamentary Recruiting Committee (PRC), to ensure that 'the grave issues of the War [are] fully comprehended by the people, and thereby to give a powerful impetus to recruiting'.[49] The leaders of the major trade unions found themselves forced down a similar path. A conference on 5 August of the major national unions, originally called to organize 'a united proletarian' opposition to the war, decided instead to accept the *fait accompli* and set up the War Emergency Workers' National Committee, aimed at helping workers deal with the economic consequences of the war.[50]

Within three weeks, the leaders had further decided to avoid any concerted strike action for the foreseeable future. Employees and management committed themselves to avoiding industrial disputes. As a result, the number of strikes for 1914 was 972 as opposed to 1,459 in 1913, most in the first six months of the year. Though the number of working days lost to strikes in 1914 (9,878,000) equalled that of 1913 (9,804,000), most of these came in peace-time months. From September to December 1914, only 161,437 working days were lost to strikes, 1.6 per cent of the yearly total. In the first full year of war, 1915, strikes dropped to 672. Working days lost to strikes dropped to 2,953,000 in 1915, a higher rate than that of late 1914, but still dramatically below the pre-war totals.[51] Just as working-class men signalled their support for the war by enlisting, so did they show their approval by drastically reducing industrial action.

Fighting the war

It remained, then, to fight the war. The Cabinet believed that the war would not unduly affect British society or the economy. Britain could continue with 'business as usual' while the British Expeditionary Force (BEF) fought a brief war, one that would most likely be over by Christmas.[52] The new Secretary of State for War – the man responsible for organizing the fight – felt differently. Herbert Horatio Kitchener, given the job on 5 August, was a national hero and a reluctant appointee. On holiday in England when the crisis broke, he attempted to leave before the war started and return to his beloved Egypt. But duty prevailed.

When Asquith telegraphed on 5 August to offer him the War Office, Kitchener disembarked from the liner and returned to London.

Kitchener followed the Army's plan by dispatching the BEF to France. But his vision of Britain's role immediately proved different from that of the Cabinet and his fellow generals. Kitchener, alone, believed that the war would last for at least three years. He foresaw the mass armies of France and Germany deadlocked against each other in a stalemate that would only be resolved by the intervention of a vastly enlarged British Army. Expounding this vision to the Cabinet caused consternation, but such was Kitchener's authority and prestige that no one disputed his perceptions. The War Office thus immediately set about trying to organize the thousands of volunteers pouring into recruiting offices into a force that could fulfil Kitchener's vision.[53]

And pour they certainly did. From the start of the war, enlistment rates rose to levels never experienced by the British Army. Men lined up for hours to enlist.[54] The man in charge of London's main recruiting office attested eight men on 1 August. On 4 August he required 20 policeman to escort him through the crowd of waiting volunteers merely to open the doors.[55] In the first six months of 1914, before the war, 18,687 men enlisted, not enough to replace the 24,459 men lost through discharge, desertion, death, and other causes. When the Regular Army went to war in August 1914, it was 10,241 men under its legislated allowance, a gap that the War Office expected to widen by spring 1915.[56] That shortage reversed itself almost immediately. By 8 August, 8,193 men had joined nationwide; by 15 August, 43,764 more; by 22 August, a further 49,982.[57] In just under three weeks, the Army more than quintupled the input of the previous six months. The numbers continued to rise, and very quickly the enlistment structure of the Regular Army groaned under their weight.

At this point, Kitchener, whose career had been spent almost entirely in the colonies, failed to take advantage of the military structure set up by Haldane. Haldane, from the beginning, had designed the Territorial Army (TA) to be expanded in case of war, though on a much smaller scale. The TA thus had the non-commissioned officers (NCOs) and the spare capacity to train and house large numbers of recruits. Kitchener, however, bypassed the TA organization and relied on the Regular Army infrastructure to deal with the new recruits. The Regular Army did not have enough space in its camps to house them. It did not have enough NCOs left after the deployment of the BEF to organize and train the enlistees. The 'valuable machinery' of the Territorial recruiting system could have borne much of the strain of the wave of volunteers, but Kitchener did not take advantage of it.[58]

As a result, the enlistment machinery broke under the strain. At first, by drafting local doctors and working long hours, recruiters barely kept the masses of volunteers at their doors moving. But there was often nowhere to put them after they had signed up. Frank Turner, a labourer, slept at his enlistment centre for three days after joining on 8 August 1914 before his assigned training depot found a space for him.[59] And there was often no one to train them. The supply of experienced NCOs needed to control and train the mobs of new recruits ran out within days of the war beginning. Some soldiers marched from camp to camp without actually having either an NCO or an officer to command them. The army grew so desperate to lure retired and discharged NCOs back to duty that it waived the minimum physical standards for them within the first three weeks. This attempt to 'muddle through' worked temporarily, but the increase in enlistment continued.[60]

Meanwhile, events in France were quickly proving Kitchener's assessment correct. Following its pre-war plans, the BEF took up its position on the left of the French line by the middle of August. The French Army, meanwhile, attacked across its common border with Germany. This played to the German plan, which put the majority of German forces on the right of its line. The main attack poured through Belgium and the Ardennes and into northwest France, faced only by a weak French left wing, and the four divisions of the British Expeditionary Force.

The British had expected time to prepare themselves in a quiet theatre. Instead, they found themselves in the critical sector. The Regulars reacted with aplomb, inflicting heavy casualties on the attacking Germans, but the retreat was inevitable and prolonged. As the Germans closed on Paris, many of the city's inhabitants braced themselves for a repetition of 1871, when Prussian forces had marched triumphantly through the city. But a combination of desperate rearguard action by the French and British and the sheer exhaustion of the German infantry brought the advance grinding to a halt and then, for a moment, put it into reverse. But both sides were exhausted and bloody, and by the middle of September the three armies had stumbled to a halt in northern France.

The Times article and domestic reaction to the Mons retreat

In the first weeks of the war, Britain received little bad news from the front. The British press reported only what the government wished, pursuant to a pre-war agreement with the War Office and the Admiralty.[61] The result of this voluntary blackout was that, as Charles Carrington, a schoolboy and later an officer, remembered, 'there was no official information and no reliable news'.[62] What did emerge from France were reports of a string of Entente victories.

But, by late August, disturbing information about events in France and Belgium started to appear. On 25 August, the government issued *The Belgian Official Report*, which summarized German actions in Belgium and recounted a wave of atrocities against civilians. The major explosion, however, came from the press bomb of 30 August. Arthur Moore, of *The Times* (London), who was with the British forces, wrote a gloomy and accurate account of the BEF in retreat. He told of men marching 20 hours out of 24, of heavy casualties, and of a string of defeats:

> Our losses are very great. I have seen the broken bits of many regiments. . . . To sum up, the first great German effort has succeeded. We have to face the fact that the B.E.F., which bore the great weight of the blow, has suffered terrible losses and requires immediate and immense reinforcement.

The article ended with the plaintive cry that the BEF 'needs men, men, and yet more men'.[63]

The article shocked those at home:

> That Sunday, the 30th, the situation looked very black and we all had a bad attack of the gloom. . . . In London a special edition of *The Times* was published giving a report, authorized by the Press Bureau, that the whole British Army had been surrounded and cut up, a statement which was afterwards proved to have been nearer the truth than any of us knew at the time.[64]

Some blamed the messenger. Many criticized *The Times* for publishing the article. In self-defence, the paper revealed that not only had the article been passed by the appropriate government office, but that the Press Censor had added the final line demanding more soldiers.[65] Some embraced fantasy. Reports about the 'Angel of Mons', a heavenly figure who had helped British troops survive the battle, fought for attention with the rumour that a million-man Russian army had sailed from Murmansk and 'been brought down from Edinburgh to Portsmouth and thence to France' to assist the embattled Entente forces. The British witnesses knew them to be Russian soldiers from the snow on their boots.[66]

But the main effect of *The Times*' article was to increase recruitment. Enlistment figures shot up as soon as it appeared. In the final week of August, 66,310 men enlisted. After the article, in the first week of September, that number almost tripled to 174,901 men. Daily recruiting went from an average of 8,776 in the week before the article to 25,668 in the week after. Kitchener observed that: 'more recruits joined in one day than had previously joined in a year'.[67] The surge continued in the second week of September, when 136,160 men enlisted. In London, the daily average of men signing up in the week prior to the article was 1,606; the day after it appeared (31 August), 4,001 men enlisted. The average of the following week was 3,192 men. The same figures for Liverpool were 220 and 725 respectively. In rural Hertford, the numbers were 43 and 204.[68]

Recruiting figures jumped first in London, where *The Times* was published, then spread outward to the rest of the country. Thus, during August, London supplied around 15 per cent of the country's total recruits. On 31 August, the day after the article, London supplied 19 per cent of the national total. The next day, as the papers around the country reprinted the article, the London share of enlistees dropped to 13 per cent (3,479 out of 27,914). On 2 September, London's share went to 12.9 per cent and then averaged 11 per cent for the following week.[69]

The enormous response broke an already over-strained enlistment system. The recruiting centres, by speeding men through like cattle, could keep up with the load, if barely. F. Battersby, who worked in a warehouse, remembered joining up during this period:

> After many hours of waiting I entered the Town Hall and there at long tables were a number of clerks, some in uniform, some not; questions were asked and answered and as forms were filled in, a big sergeant wheeled us out to

meet the doctor, he tapped your chest, tapped your back, held your balls, made you cough, say 99, open your mouth and bawled to the clerk 'A1'. In another part, a barber with clippers took off your hair then an officer and a sergeant swore you in, gave you a shilling, another sergeant marched you to the dentist, the dentist extracted and, with no hair, a mouth full of blood, a sergeant bawled out your name and he said 'Report here, at 7 o'clock September 7th and we will send you to your regiment.'[70]

'Congestion' developed at the depots.[71] They could not handle the influx of recruits. Designed for peace-time numbers of, at most, around 5,000 men per month, the depots had to handle, at one point in September, 25,000 per day. As early as 4 September, the War Office declared that the number of men 'pouring in' had 'outstripped' the capacity of the depots and training centres. 'Buried alive' was a more succinct summary.[72]

The army could not house, clothe, or feed its new enlistees effectively. Some volunteers were asked, if possible, to provide their own clothing.[73] For those who could not, the War Office desperately fitted men out in whatever uniforms were available. A surplus of blue serge was used to make temporary uniforms, an outfit that came to be dubbed 'Kitchener's Blue'. The same shade of blue, unfortunately, was used for prison uniforms, leading to a number of unfortunate incidents as recruit units marched through the countryside during training.[74] The combination of khaki, blue serge, and civilian clothing made the initial units of Kitchener's Army 'a rag and bobtail lot', as the King discovered when, in late September, he reviewed the 'motley' Third Division.[75] Not until November did recruits start to receive uniforms and greatcoats. Other shortages lasted well into 1915.[76]

Nor were the problems limited to clothing. The supply of weapons also proved inadequate. Britain had not stockpiled weapons before the war. As a result, the new enlistees were given whatever weapons were available. Some units were equipped with Japanese rifles, in storage in England as a result of the Anglo-Japanese alliance. Some units had only one rifle, used to demonstrate drill movements to the men. Some units had no weapons whatsoever, the men using sticks as 'dummy rifles'.[77]

Living space was equally constrained. The barracks quickly filled up, and men slept outside or, in W. Barley's case, played football most of the night to keep warm.[78] When F. Palmer Cook, a middle-class architect's apprentice, joined up during this period, he found the whole system 'entirely broken down. . . . There was no food or sleeping accommodation, not even tents to house such a mixed bag of humanity.'[79] G.J. Smith turned out for breakfast on 5 September 1914 and found 2,000 men lined up single file to receive their bowl of tea and single slice of bread with jam.[80] D.A. Hodge, a printer's apprentice, remembered the feeding arrangements:

> To say conditions [in training camp] were primitive is the under-statement of the year. There was not a knife, fork, or spoon among us, and as to sanitation

the less said the better. We blessed the name of Keillor for his marmalade jars were our sole feeding equipment. At mealtimes we were lined up in two ranks between which great dixies of stew were placed at intervals. Then when the SM blew his whistle we all dived our hands into the scalding pots and then scooped up some gravy with the jamjars.[81]

Conditions for the newly enlisted soldiers grew so awful that some of the recruits considered taking action, such as marching in protest on the War Office. When one officer told his morning muster that those with complaints should step forward, R.N.P. Wilson remembered that three platoons moved forward 'solidly as one man'.[82] The Army eventually gave up on trying to fit enlistees into the depots. On 4 September 1914, with new soldiers sleeping in railway carriages at local stations, the Army began taking men's names and sending them home, to wait for a time when the infrastructure could absorb them.[83]

The War Office finally acted to stem the flow. On 11 September, Kitchener raised the physical standard for recruits. Most importantly, minimum height for recruits was raised to 5ft 6ins from 5ft 3ins.[84] As during the Boer War, many working-class men fell below that minimum and the intake quickly shrank to more manageable numbers. Enlistments dropped from 136,160 in the week ending 12 September (before the minimum was raised) to 44,679 in the week ending 19 September (the first week with the new minimum), then 27,589 the following week. Returns for all of October numbered 72,715. By combining the more stringent height requirement with the avid recruiting of retired NCOs and the use of loaned police sergeants to assist with drilling, the War Office managed to bring some order to the chaos.[85]

From the war-fighting perspective, however, the raised standards brought an unfortunate side-effect. It told volunteers that they were not needed. Combined with news from France of German reversals, the still-common belief that the war would be over by Christmas, and the touting of 'business as usual' by the government, many volunteers concluded that they were not needed, now or ever.[86] The Parliamentary Recruiting Committee discussed this problem on 21 October 1914 and issued a pamphlet towards the end of October which said:

> Who said 'Enough'? You have not yet enlisted, perhaps because somebody told you 'They've got enough already.' That is entirely a mistake. . . . A Second Half-Million are still Needed. [capitalization by PRC][87]

It was too late. The damage was done. Recruiting figures rose towards the end of 1914, but they never returned to their previous levels, not even when the height requirement was reduced back to 5ft 3ins, nor when the government started taking those between 5ft and 5ft 3ins and putting them into Bantam battalions.[88]

Voluntary enlistment and a local/national recruitment system

Although enlistment never again reached the heights of the original surge of August/September 1914, it remained, on average, the highest in British history. Half the British soldiers who served in the war volunteered, even though conscription was in force twice as long as volunteerism, 34 to 17 months. The average monthly enlistment for the voluntary period was 145,101 as compared to 73,642 for conscription. Even excluding the boom months of August and September of 1914 and all of 1918 (when, it could be argued, the government had scraped the manpower barrel dry), volunteerism still averaged 113,659 monthly against 83,780 for conscription.[89] This ratio belies two interpretations common to the historical literature on Britain in the First World War. Many historians have adopted, without question, the belief that after 1914, Britons shunned military service in ever-increasing numbers, forcing the adoption of conscription. Other histories have reported that the recruiting system was badly organized and inefficient in its execution.[90] Neither assertion stands up to close scrutiny.

In 1914–1915, manpower requirements took two forms. First, the army needed to recruit enough to replace 'wastage', the men it lost each month to death, wounding, or other incapacity.[91] Second, the massive expansion of the British Army required a large number of men over and above the replacement for wastage. How close, then, did recruiting come to meeting these needs? The worst month for voluntary recruiting was December 1915, immediately prior to the introduction of conscription, when 35,767 men enlisted. Over the seventeen months during which the voluntary system was in operation, an average of 145,101 men per month joined up. The highest monthly wastage of the voluntary period was 33,528 soldiers lost in April 1915. Over the voluntary period, wastage averaged 23,287 men.[92] The number of volunteers never dropped below replacement level and normally averaged from three to five times the wastage rate. Clearly, enough men were entering the Army in 1914–1915 to fulfil the need for both casualty replacement and expansion.

Why then the confusion? The problem lies in failing to distinguish between the recruiting system and the enlistment system. The British never had trouble *recruiting* men; that is, getting them to join the military. They frequently had problems *enlisting* men: recording their details, getting them medically examined, and then training them. For a great deal of the voluntary period, they failed to provide adequate weapons, housing, and equipment for their enlistees. But the actual numbers of men joining remained high enough to replace casualties and to continue the expansion of the force. Kitchener admitted that in September 1915. He said on 9 September that the true shortage was not the lack of soldiers but the lack of officers to command them and Maurice Hankey, the Cabinet Secretary, echoed his analysis five days later.[93]

Unfortunately, the standard for enlistment numbers was shaped by the early months. More than half a million men joined the Regulars in those two months (August/September 1914), while around 150,000 joined the Territorials. September's haul of 367,886 for the Regulars more than doubled the number for the next highest month, April 1915.[94] That wave of enlistment set the standard. When the British inevitably compared the two, they undervalued the later rates.

This misconception warrants emphasis because the belief that recruitment failed masks both the enthusiasm of the populace and the effectiveness of the recruiting system. Quite by accident, the British managed to replace their pre-war system with a local/national combination that played to the strengths of each. Local power structures ran local recruiting campaigns and handled the men who volunteered, while the War Office administered national policy and focused on the later stages of training. 'Local arrangements', Kitchener said in May 1915, could be left to local elites, 'while the general policy was being formulated by the War Office.'[95] The system provided near-universal coverage but also saved on funding and the need for War Office supervision.

Local individuals and groups had stepped in from the beginning to help the War Office. On 7 August 1914, the War Office appealed to locals to assist in recruiting. Within a month, this appeal for aid had been extended to requesting help in sheltering and feeding new soldiers.[96] Local power brokers, such as the City Council of Manchester, set up recruiting centres in 'offices and warehouses' to deal with the masses of men. In a letter to Kitchener, Lord Esher bragged of enlisting and equipping 30,000 men 'without red tape . . . without a hitch'.[97] Contributing to the efforts, were, most notably, the grassroots party organizations of Labour, the Liberals, and the Unionists; the trade union hierarchies; some of the women's suffragette organizations; the government employment (Labour Registries) and unemployment insurance offices; and even the Church or its representatives.[98]

Perhaps the leading local organizer of these campaigns was the uncrowned 'King of Lancashire', the 17th Earl of Derby, the 'most efficient recruiting sergeant in England', as Lloyd George anointed him.[99] In late August, he asked the War Office for permission to raise and equip three battalions in Liverpool. The War Office granted permission, and Derby set about recruiting on 31 August. By 7 September, he had the requisite 3,000 men and closed recruiting down. He followed in later months with other, equally successful, recruiting efforts, which came to be known as 'Lord Derby's Whirlwind Recruiting Campaigns'. His influence grew to national level, so much so that by May 1915, some men began talking of enlisting not in 'Kitchener's Army', but in 'Lord Derby's Army'.[100]

The battalions raised as a result of these local efforts gained their own specific designation. They entered the Regular Army hierarchy, but unlike normal battalions, they focused recruiting exclusively within their geographic zones of affiliation. This, and the tendency of family and friends to join the same unit, led such battalions to be known as the 'Pals' Battalions.

Not only did the 'Pals' battalions recruit in specific areas, but most remained in those areas while they trained. Thus they encamped near their recruiting catchments and were often able to return home for the evening or weekend. Some even lived at home while they trained with the 'Pals'. This created a carry-on effect in recruiting. The presence and fevered activity of so many local men, training and marching, encouraged others to join. So successful were the 'Pals' battalions that the War Office adopted the same model for those who joined through the Regular Army structure.[101]

The combination of local/national bodies gave the recruiting system, however improvised, a reach into British society far beyond that of the pre-war system. Nearly every locality had some form of recruiting agent. Nearly every locality was reasonably close to an enlistment centre. By May 1915, Kitchener could say that 'in every parish there is a recruiting agent of some description'.[102]

Meanwhile, the War Office mounted a nationwide campaign of propaganda, aimed at making the war a national issue. What had been a sporadic effort – an 'occasional poster', complained the *Daily Mail* in November 1914 – became more organized in 1915.[103] Working-class men encountered the War Office efforts frequently, in different venues. C.J. Rice, an assistant at Woolwich Arsenal, remembered being recruited in music halls. The performances would 'almost certainly end with patriotic songs and the assembly of the flags of the Allies'.[104] The War Office even tried the newfangled 'kinematography' exhibitions for some of its recruiting efforts, which included 'patriotic films'.[105]

This national campaign was aided by local involvement. The local groups tapped their specific knowledge of the people and the area to tailor the recruiting appeals. The Royal Sussex Regiment asked locals if they would 'uphold the honour of the County of Sussex', or 'must recruits be obtained outside the County?'[106] The Lancashire Territorial Force Regiments (East and West) organized exhibitions and open-air meetings in and around Manchester to draw men in, using mostly local enlistees as their recruiters.[107]

The idea of conscription

Despite this recruitment success, by the middle of 1915 many government officials believed that conscription was vital to victory. The feeling grew stronger as the year passed. Why? The answer lay not with the number of men enlisting, but with the type. The war demanded not only soldiers, but also equipment and supplies. The industries to make the equipment needed skilled workers. Further, the British Cabinet believed that exports had to be sustained in order to pay for the war, requiring even more skilled workers. The demand on Britain's industries was thus to build up production capacity in order to equip a mass army while at the same time retaining Britain's pre-war export volume.[108] The answer to this requirement was simple. Men working in these industries had to be prevented from enlisting. However much they wanted to fight, the government could not allow them to leave their jobs. The work they did at home was simply too crucial. In January 1915, Arthur Balfour, the former Unionist leader, argued in a memorandum that many skilled workers 'must not be allowed to fight at all'.[109] Unfortunately, under the voluntary system, the government could not determine exactly who enlisted. The people volunteering were the skilled workers that Britain needed at home. The result, as a War Office memorandum pointed out, was a 'very serious drain' of skilled workers.[110]

Shortages occurred within a few months. By the beginning of 1915, so many coal miners had enlisted that there was a shortage of labour even in areas that normally had a surplus. In a memorandum on the 'Crippling of Industries due to Enlistment', the government said that the 'scarcity [of miners] had become acute even in the north'.[111] By June, *The Times* was warning of a 10 per cent reduction in coal output because of labour shortages.[112]

The government tried to ban workers in certain occupations from enlisting: mining, the merchant marine, and shipbuilding. The ban had little effect. Workers in the forbidden occupations lied about their jobs or quit in order to enlist, and recruiting sergeants proved quite willing to assist in the deception. The sergeant who enlisted W. Watkins, a coal miner, saw through Watkins's lie about his occupation, but signed him up nonetheless.[113] The recruiting sergeant of William Pressey, who joined up in December 1914, went even further:

> The colour sergeant who took us in also got something, and this, fortunately, was why he never left me as I got nearer to the table. I grabbed his arm and told him that I was a turner and fitter in the engineering trade – just what they were after at that time. I told him that I had no intention of going into a factory. A soldier – or I'd walk out before getting to the desk. He said 'That's all right, son. Tell him you're a shop assistant.' I did so when it came to my turn, and on my Army Record there it was – Shop assistant.[114]

With their own people undercutting the ban, is it any surprise that the War Office was not able to keep certain occupations from joining up?

Further, a perception of unfairness hampered the voluntary system. The weight of responsibility rested on those who stepped forward. Those who remained behind could take advantage of their absence. The government and the public came to believe that there was a certain hard core of shirkers: men who avoided military service and used the opportunities left by those who had gone to enrich themselves. In one letter, a working-class woman wrote to her brother to be wary: 'those who push others forward hangs [sic] back themselves'.[115]

Kitchener believed that these shirkers were primarily working class.[116] His belief was widespread. Shirkers were spoken of in working-class terms. Witness the analogy used in the *Weekly Dispatch*: '[The shirker] is the same as the blackleg in strike time. He reaps the benefits won through the hardships of his fellow men.'[117] The *Daily Chronicle* published a Harold Begbie poem that accused those not serving of being seduced by other distractions:

> Is it football still and the picture show,
> The pub and the betting odds,
> When your brothers stand to the tyrant's blow
> And Britain's call is God's?[118]

All the distractions mentioned by Begbie are particularly working class or lower middle class. There is no cricket, no hunting, no theatre.

Under particular attack was professional football. The sport, especially popular among working-class men, came to be called 'the Football Cancer'.[119] It received criticism not directed at cricket, the elite sport. *The Times* spoke of it as an unseemly addiction: 'We may not approve of the particular sport that fascinates them. . . . [But] they have the football habit and we cannot break them of it.' The failure of recruiting rallies held at games was taken to be proof of the danger of the sport.[120]

The recruiting authorities also assumed that the 'shirkers' were largely single men. They were 'unmarried loafers', hanging back while married men did their duty.[121] The *Daily Mail*, in May 1915, went so far as to reject recruiting advertising because of this issue:

> We announced yesterday that we will not accept any more of Lord K's advertisements asking for the enlistment of men up to 40 years of age. Men of that age . . . [are] most[ly] married . . . [and] should not be asked to go to the front while the young slackers and shirkers are left untouched.[122]

The government tested its beliefs in August 1915. The National Registration Act compelled every man and woman to fill out a form stating their name, age, employment, and place of residence. The Register seemed to confirm the presence of shirkers. Registered were 4,385,600 men of military age (18–41), not counting those who had already enlisted. The essential war industries employed 2,720,200 of those men, 60 per cent. The 'Gross Total available for military service' was, in the government's eyes, 1,665,400. They subtracted 251,500 (15 per cent) from this gross total to allow for the physically unfit and thus reached a net total of 1,413,900 men available for military service. This was the pool of shirkers. This justified conscription.[123]

But are the figures valid? Even a cursory examination suggests that the figure of 1.4 million men available to serve was a gross overestimate. The National Registry apparently overlooked four statistical problems. First, the government did not acknowledge that the men medically rejected when they tried to enlist had re-entered the general population. The 2.1 million enlistees to that point came out of a large pool of applicants, many of whom had been rejected and sent home.[124] They appeared in the Register. Table 2.1 shows the different results based on different rates of acceptance.

Table 2.1 Possible numbers of medically rejected volunteers in the general population

Rejection rate (%)	Total pool (accepted (2.1m)/ 100% minus the rejection rate)	Total rejected
5	2.21m	110,000
10	2.33m	230,000
15	2.47m	370,000
20	2.625m	525,000
25	2.9m	800,000
30	3m	900,000

Those rejected were counted among the 1.4 million men who were available for military service. Though some of the rejected may have worked in the war industries and have been eliminated from the net total, many probably did not and thus were counted among the 1.4 million. Assuming an initial rejection rate of 25 per cent at enlistment (lower than the pre-war rate), 800,000 unfit men would have been put back into the general population. If 60 per cent of those worked in exempted war industries, then 310,000 of the rejected remained in the 'available' pool. The amount was already more than that deducted by the War Office. Removing them reduces the pool of fit men to 1.09 million.

Second, the Register ignored another source of unfit men in the general population. An internal War Office memo in September 1915 reported that 'wastage at home', those men who broke down physically after enlisting and had to be discharged, was 245,457. The problem, the report went on to state, stemmed 'from the quite early days of the war, when regular medical inspection was impossible, and a large number of unfit men were therefore enlisted'.[125] This number counted only those actually enlisted who were then discharged, not those who had failed the medical. Again putting 60 per cent of that number into critical war industries leaves around 98,000 men 'unfit' but still being counted as militarily available. Removing them reduces the pool of fit men to 998,000.

Third, the Register did not account for the unfit men among those who never tried to enlist. The 15 per cent figure used by the War Office was a gross underestimate.[126] At the pre-war rejection rate of 30 per cent, 377,000 men would have been found unfit. Removing them reduces the pool to 615,000. This was still a large number of men, but it also did not account for variables other than medical. It was not adjusted for marriage status, for example.

Fourth, the War Office did not actually exclude all the vital industries from its count. Though it gave a figure of 2.7 million men working in necessary war industries, the War Office, according to a memorandum from an official working on the National Register, did not include in that figure all the industries it considered critical to the war effort.[127] What these industries were, why the War Office failed to include them, and how many men that affected remains unclear. Nonetheless, it would clearly reduce even further the number of men available for service.

Certainly, some single men avoided service, but for widely varying reasons. Some were the sole providers for their families. Some could not leave sick relatives. Some were refused permission to enlist by their employers.[128] These are hardly cowards hanging back to take advantage of those gone to war.

Nonetheless, the government and society believed that a pool of shirkers existed. They looked around for a solution. The simplest seemed compulsion. As early as 2 December 1914, Walter Long, President of the Local Government Board, suggested the introduction of conscription to correct the problem. He continued his argument in August of 1915, summarizing the arguments for the Cabinet:

> Those in favour of compulsion would be strongly opposed to a continuance of the present system of recruiting because they maintain that the best men are

joining the Army, many of whom ought to stay at home, where they would be doing far more useful work for the Country, while many thousands who would make excellent soldiers and whose presence at home is not essential are standing aside and taking no share in the work of the nation.[129]

Long's memorandum summarized admirably the government's perception of the problem with the volunteer system. The wrong men were entering, while the right men were not. Something, the conscriptionists believed, had to be done.

Industrial factors and conscription

But the government's desire for conscription had another source. The government came to believe that the inability of British industry to supply the war effort was linked to the voluntary enlistment system. Kitchener, in the interests of 'business as usual', had relied on existing private munitions firms to produce *matériel* for the new armies. But such firms simply could not produce the needed supplies. They did not have the production capacity. By the spring of 1915, war production had only reached 50 per cent of Kitchener's goals, owing to a shortage of labour in the critical industries.[130]

Lloyd George was the first to grasp the problem. He blamed the shortage on Kitchener saying, on 6 April 1915, that the Secretary of State for War 'has made a mess of Munitions'.[131] A more general awareness came during May 1915. A British attack at Festubert (Aubers Ridge) failed with heavy losses. Sir John French, the commander of the BEF, blamed the defeat on a shortage of shells. He complained privately to Lord Northcliffe, the proprietor of *The Times*, who published the accusation. The resulting outcry threatened the position of the Cabinet and came to be known as 'the Great Shells Scandal'.[132]

Asquith had to respond. He moved to solidify the position of the government and to correct the industrial management problem. First, he invited the Conservatives to form a coalition government. This placed responsibility for the war effort on all the parties and silenced Unionist opposition in Parliament. Second, although Asquith kept Kitchener in office because of his popularity with the public and the King, the Prime Minister stripped the Secretary of State for War of his responsibility for munitions. That responsibility went to a newly created Ministry of Munitions. Lloyd George was its first minister.[133]

Lloyd George had to change tactics upon entering his new office. Beforehand, he had intended to rely on the voluntary spirit of British industry. Through the 'complete cooperation of employers and workmen', the government would manage the British war effort.[134] But a War Office memorandum offered a gloomy prognosis of the situation. It concluded that the shortage of munitions would not end until 1916 and, until then, Britain could not contribute meaningfully to the war effort.[135] To speed things up, Lloyd George thus decided on compulsory measures. He planned to take direct control of essential industries, such as munitions and mining, and indirect control of other economic areas, such as agriculture and the railroads.

Lloyd George needed to control two major problems. First, he had to ensure smooth industrial relations. Second, he had to prevent skilled workers from enlisting. Lloyd George attacked the first problem with the Munitions of War Act. Passed in June 1915, the Act compelled the settling of industrial disputes by binding arbitration rather than strikes or lockouts.[136] The arbitration scheme successfully reduced the number of strikes from the pre-war level.[137]

Before Lloyd George could tackle the problem of the shortages of skilled workers, he needed a detailed breakdown of their numbers. Walter Long summed up the problem: 'We have no record whatever of the resources of our country – I mean the human resources of our country – for the various purposes for which we now want and seek their aid.'[138] Conveniently, however, the National Registry of August 1915 would provide exactly such a list. In addition to simply counting the number of men left unenlisted, the National Register would give the government an accurate record of 'those who are actually doing work which is essential to the stability of the community'.[139]

With this data in hand, Lloyd George sought an answer. The solution, he finally decided, came down to conscription. In late October Lloyd George wrote:

> The whole of this very serious and menacing trouble is but part of the price we are paying for running a great war on what is known as the 'voluntary' system. An undisciplined nation is fighting the best disciplined country in the world, and some of our politicians think this terrible handicap is a real advantage.[140]

Conscription would provide organization for Britain. With conscription, Lloyd George could organize the industry as he saw fit and end the supply problems of the first year of the war.

The arrival of conscription, winter 1915–1916

Conscription worried the Cabinet. Ministers believed that Parliament and the country would oppose any form of compulsion.[141] They were particularly worried about the working class. Arthur Henderson wrote a warning about the working-class reaction to conscription, worth quoting at length for its explicit analysis of working-class suspicions:

> Conscription, except on grounds of clear military necessity, could only be introduced by Act of Parliament, with the approval of the people, at a General Election, and there are in this country thousands of working men who would deny altogether the competence of a Parliament elected under our present Franchise and Registration Laws to bind them on an issue of life and death. In the abstract, it sounds well to say that the State has a right to the services of all its citizens; but to working-class voters the proposition means that A can make B go for a soldier because A has a house and B is a lodger, and that C, who is childless, can dispose of the four sons of D and E because, in

addition to his house, he has property in two other constituencies.... In the second place the working man does not believe that the toll of conscription would be levied equally on him and his employer. As a volunteer, he feels that the rich man who is fighting beside him has, like himself, made great sacrifices. As a conscript, he would feel that he had been placed in the trenches by the votes of rich men who were not there themselves.... The suspicion of private advantage at the public cost, which is one of the main roots of our industrial difficulties, would be intensely aggravated when the point at issue was not profit but life.... In the third place, there is the belief that conscription is a capitalist weapon for interfering with the rights of the workmen. The trade unionists will view with grave resentment anything which may be represented as an attempt to circumvent their freedom of action, and if the miners, railway men, and other highly organized trades were exempt from conscription (as they would probably have to be) they could come forward as champions of their class without any imputation on their courage.[142]

Henderson's arguments are particularly interesting because they link service to the country to the right to vote. In a sense, Henderson was speaking conditionally – should his points about voting rights and the franchise be addressed, then working-class opposition to conscription would likely disappear. It is a mark of how much the situation had changed from the pre-war period that even here, at the last ditch issue of conscription, Henderson was not wholly opposed, but opposed on the basis of the exclusion inherent in the British system. This led to fundamental changes in 1918.

Despite Henderson's arguments, support for conscription grew. The Conservatives in the coalition government favoured conscription. Among the Liberals, the big three of Churchill, Grey, and Lloyd George either favoured conscription or remained neutral. Asquith, naturally, wavered. Almost alone among prominent officials, Kitchener opposed the idea. Though his position within the government had been weakened by the Shells Crisis, he still carried weight in the House and with the general public.[143] In October, to head off the conscriptionists, he suggested a modification to voluntary recruiting. Each county would be given a minimum number of men to send to the Army. How they filled that quota was up to them. If they did not meet their quotas men would be compulsorily called up, using names supplied by the National Register.[144]

Asquith resolved the conflict. Lord Derby would move south to run a national campaign aimed at bringing enlistment figures back up to the levels of 1914. A massive propaganda campaign, using the improvised organization built up over the past year, would make a direct appeal to eligible men. A volunteer presenting himself at a recruiting office would either be enlisted straightaway or would be registered and sent home, to be called up later.[145] Asquith believed that such a public campaign would make or break the voluntary system. Should the number of enlistees not jump as a result, any 'objection to compulsion' would be 'entirely removed'.[146]

In essence, the Derby campaign served as a public spectacle to assure the supposedly restive working class that the volunteer system was being given every chance. In an introductory letter to the nation, Lord Derby wrote that:

> if this effort does not succeed the Country knows that everything possible will have been done to make the voluntary system a success, and will have to decide by what method sufficient recruits can be obtained to maintain our Armies in the field at their required strength.[147]

The implication was clear. If not enough volunteers were forthcoming, then there could be no objection to conscription. 'Voluntaryism on its last trial', *The Times* said.[148]

The figures disappointed the anti-conscriptionists. The number of volunteers were double the pre-campaign figures, but they were not enough to satisfy the Cabinet. Derby reported that in the eight weeks prior to the campaign's start, 132,614 men joined. During the eight weeks of the campaign 249,238 men joined. Derby reported in December 1915:

> These figures are in themselves satisfactory. . . . On the other hand it will be seen that during the second period we only obtained 9,238 men over and above the 240,000 that were required for the estimated wastage of those eight weeks, basing army requirements on 30,000 a week. There was therefore practically no margin to make good the deficiencies of the previous eight weeks nor to make up any deficiencies which will undoubtedly exist in forthcoming weeks. . . . If the success or otherwise of the voluntary system was to be judged by the above figures I should regretfully have to acknowledge that I had failed to secure enough men.[149]

Further, the campaign failed to prevent the loss of men from war-making industries. Many firms were so desperate for workers that they tried to forbid any of their men from signing on with the campaign.[150] In the coal industry Derby finally had to appeal to the miners not to enlist.[151] The conclusion seemed clear to the Cabinet. A group of men, unmarried and working class, refused to join their brethren in defending the country. The 'last trial' of the voluntary system had failed. Derby saw no alternative to conscription, and neither did Asquith.[152]

The Prime Minister thus proposed to the House of Commons on 7 January 1916 a conscription bill for single men.[153] He did so with some trepidation, fearing a major split of the Liberal Party within the House of Commons and mass unrest among the public.[154] Within the Cabinet, several Liberal ministers protested vigorously. Outside, a special meeting of the Labour conference, encompassing the trade union leaders and the Labour MPs, condemned the conscription bill. In both cases, Asquith persuaded his opponents to come round. In the end, both parliamentary and public opinion proved surprisingly relaxed about the idea. In the House, only thirty-five Liberal MPs voted against the bill. Nationally, bodies such as the No-Conscription Fellowship protested loudly, but mobilized little public protest.[155] The bill passed on 28 January 1916.

The government and people had what they publicly wanted: the ability to force the shirkers to do their patriotic duty. Now, compulsion would force those loitering working-class men into the army where they belonged. Certainly, the turn to conscription cured one of the problems of voluntarism. The War Office, from 1916 onwards, controlled entry into the military. Essential workers were not conscripted and, furthermore, were not allowed to leave their jobs without permission.[156] Through this and other strategies, Britain managed to manufacture sufficient war supplies not only to equip her New Armies, but also, after 1917, to provide much of the equipment for the American Expeditionary Force.[157]

But, despite all the discussion, the pool of shirkers proved illusory. The enlistment total for the first three months of conscription from February to April 1915 was 203,230, an average of 67,743 men per month.[158] This, in twelve weeks, failed to match the eight-week total of the Derby Scheme. Already, on 25 February 1916, a month after the beginning of conscription, the *Daily Mail* complained of the lack of single men entering the Army. The paper blamed industrial tribunals for giving too many exemptions, but the situation failed to improve even after the government tightened the rules. In an April 1916 Cabinet meeting, Asquith predicted that 'by the end of October, the orange would have been sucked dry'.[159] He therefore introduced a bill for the conscription of married men. It passed in May. By late 1916, all men between the ages of 18 and 41 were liable to conscription.[160]

Despite the extension of the Act to married men, the numbers being enrolled in the Army never increased. Some within the government cited 'wonderful results' for conscription, but the number of enlistees in 1916–1918 never matched those of the voluntary period.[161] Medical exemptions accounted for much of the shortfall. According to one study, two-thirds of men medically examined for military service proved to have 'marked' or 'partial' disabilities.[162] Though 300,000 men reached age-eligibility every year, that pool apparently did not make up the shortfall.[163] In May 1917, the Army complained that its divisions in France were 82,783 below strength, 'while the outlook with regard to recruiting is even worse than that of the supply of drafts'.[164] In late 1917, Douglas Haig, the Commander of the BEF, predicted that the next spring would see the British Army short by 248,226 men.[165] Whether the voluntary system could have brought in more men during 1916–1918 is unclear. The supply of available men may simply have been exhausted by 1916. But it is clear that there was no great pool of shirkers, avoiding service and ready to be conscripted. The voluntary recruiting successfully brought an enormous and unprecedented number of men into the Army. The turn to conscription should not obscure that fact.

3 Currents within the flood
Who were the volunteers?

The volunteers were not a single group. They acted and felt differently depending on many factors: where they lived; what jobs they did; whether they were from England, Scotland, Ireland, or Wales; and a host of other factors. Before an examination of their motives is given, some exploration of these differences is in order. This section, then, will examine who joined the military, what class they were, where they were from, and what their ages were. The aim is to create a group picture that captures their differences as well as their similarities.

Occupations

The volunteers I have looked at were all working class, but they came from different jobs and different economic levels within the working class. Some worked for thriving industries, with job security and a regular wage. Some worked for struggling industries, with frequent lay-offs and insufficient wages. Some worked as casual labour, picking up what temporary jobs they could. Some did not work at all. Their occupations defined them for both this book and the government that they served. In August 1915, a year after the war had started, 2,008,892 men had enlisted in the military.[1]

The government broke down those enlistment figures into nine categories. The categories were: Building/Mining, Metal Trades, Chemical Trades, Textile Trades, Clothing Trades, Food Trades, Paper and Printing Trades, Wood Trades, and Other Trades. The largest of these categories, that of Building/Mining, had 2,285,300 men over 10 years old working in it in 1911, according to the Census. Of these, 1,255,800 were within the eligible age range for enlistment (19–40). The smallest, Chemical Trades, contained 121,500 men. Of these, 68,700 were within the eligible age range.[2]

Within these nine categories, the government broke the enlistment figures down into a further fifty-two subcategories. Within the Building/Mining category, for example, the subcategories consisted of Building, Coal and Shale Mining, Metals Mining, and Quarrying. The Other Trades category served as a catch-all, holding such diverse subcategories such as Brick and Cement; Leather Goods; and Gasworks, Waterworks, and Electricity Generation.

The number of enlistments from each category, unsurprisingly, correlated strongly with the number of workers in it. Thus, the highest absolute number of enlistments came from the category with the largest number of workers. By August 1915, the Building/Mining category had sent 464,500 men into service, about 36.1 per cent of its age-eligible men. The smallest number of enlistees came from the Chemical Trades, which had sent 28,600 men to the war. This constituted 41 per cent of the age-eligible men.[3] Table 3.1 gives a more analytic view of the situation.

None of the categories stand out particularly. All the enlistment rates are between 33.7 per cent and 41 per cent, clustered around the average of 36.2 per cent. The figures do suggest that enlistment enthusiasm was fairly uniform across the working class, a conclusion that will be addressed further in Chapter 6.

Geography

But the economic breakdown is not the only important factor separating working-class volunteers. Geography played a role as well, most critically the rural/urban divide. Voluntary enlistments were much higher in urban areas than in rural, a reversal of the pre-war pattern.[4] Those of the 'farming classes' were quite 'backward' according to one War Office evaluation. There is some difficulty in analysing the numbers of recruits from urban and rural areas. The British recorded where the recruits enlisted, not from where they came. Thus rural men who joined up in a town were credited to that town, not to the countryside.[5]

But this distortion can be overcome, at least partially, by analysing enlistment figures on a county, rather than city, basis. Counties without large urban centres made fairly representative rural samples; while counties with large metropolises reflected urban enlistment fairly well. The average enlistment rate for the whole country from August 1914 to May 1915 was 30.05 per cent of the eligible male population. Urban counties averaged above that number, rural counties below. The

Table 3.1 Enlistment percentages in the occupational categories defined by the National Register

Category	Men of eligible age	Men serving	Percentage
Building/Mines	1,255,800	464,500	36.9
Metal Trades	1,019,000	343,900	33.7
Chemical Trades	68,700	28,600	41.0
Textile Trades	301,000	102,200	33.9
Clothing Trades	215,200	76,800	35.7
Food Trades	178,600	73,200	41.0
Paper and Printing Trades	132,400	50,200	37.9
Wood Trades	131,100	53,300	40.7
Other Trades	189,800	74,500	39.2
Total	3,492,000	1,267,500	36.3

Source: Figures from PRO CAB 27/2, Estimate of the Condition of the Industrial Population of the United Kingdom, August 1915.

counties of Cornwall, Yorkshire, and Cheshire had, pre-war, the highest percentages of rural workers in England and no major urban centres. Their enlistment rates averaged 24.7 per cent. In the three urban counties of Lancashire, London, and Northumberland, the enlistment rate was 38 per cent.[6]

Another way to avoid the distortion is to look at enlistment rates by profession. The same imbalance appears when the statistics are broken down by urban versus rural jobs, although the gap is less. The last pre-war Census, in 1911, found 549,660 men between the ages of 19 and 41 doing agricultural work. Out of this pool, 32 per cent had enlisted by August 1915.[7] Enlistment rates for urban workers fluctuated from trade to trade but averaged near 37 per cent. Laundry workers had the highest rate (54.6 per cent) while workers in factories making explosives had the lowest (25.8 per cent).[8]

Nor does there seem to have been any uniquely rural constraint on enlistment. Some farmers told their workers not to leave, saying that their 'job on the farm was just as important as soldiering'.[9] But industrial workers often heard much the same. Some skilled agricultural workers, such as farriers and cowmen, were restricted from enlisting. But such restrictions applied to urban workers as well and seem not to have prevented them from joining up.[10] The single rural inhibition not present in urban areas was the harvest, which slowed enlistments in August and September. Billy Dixon, a labourer in Norfolk, 'joined up as soon as we had finished harvest'.[11] Indeed, the Army released 11,000 soldiers to help bring in the harvest in the autumn of 1915.[12] However the rural/urban imbalance remained much the same over the course of the voluntary period, suggesting that the harvest effect was not a major one. Thus, it appears that the gap between rural and urban workers was significant, one that reflected less eagerness to enlist on the part of rural working-class men.

Enlistment rates also varied by political geography. Men in England, Wales, Scotland, and Ireland reacted differently to the war. The Scottish were more likely to join up than men from any other country, while the Irish were much less likely to. In the nine months to April 1915, 38 per cent of the eligible male population in Scotland joined either the Army or the Navy. The figure for Ireland for the same period was 10.1 per cent. The Welsh and English joined at a little above the average national rate, 26.8 per cent and 30.1 per cent respectively.[13] For the war as a whole, the numbers are much closer together. From 1914 to 1918, 24.02 per cent of eligible English males served, 21.52 per cent of Welshmen, 23.71 of the Scots, and 6.14 per cent of the Irish.[14]

With 25 per cent as a rough upper limit, each country supplied a varying proportion through conscription and volunteering. More men entered the forces through conscription in England and Wales while volunteering supplied more in Scotland. Ireland, where conscription was never applied, had an initial bout of enthusiasm which then tailed off after the failed Easter rebellion of 1916.

Teasing an interpretation out of these figures is tricky. The Scottish, for example, may have enlisted at higher rates than the other nations because they felt more strongly about defending Britain, or because more of their population was concentrated in cities and the higher urban enlistment rate raised Scottish figures.

Anecdotal evidence supports the latter interpretation. Major-General G.G. Egerton remembered the Scots under his command as 'recruited from the lowest slums of Glasgow, many of them awful little ruffians, just "Glasgow Keelies", but cheery game fellows'.[15] As in England, 'Pals' battalions filled quickly in Scottish cities. The 15th Highland Light Infantry filled up in sixteen hours by recruiting in the Glasgow tramway depots.[16] Yet, against that, rural rates in Scotland were higher than rural rates in England, which suggests that the Scottish working class were genuinely more enthusiastic about the war.

The case of Wales is more complex. The Welsh enlistment percentage, though lower than both the English and Scottish, nonetheless came within a few points of the other two. For some sections of the populace, this support was not surprising. English-speaking Welsh seem to have strongly supported the war.[17] But the native Welsh-speakers also seem to have been in favour. This enthusiasm of the Welsh was somewhat surprising. South Wales, and the coal valleys especially, had bad memories of English economic and political oppression prior to the war. In 1911, British troops had been sent to Wales to prevent a miners' strike from getting out of hand. As noted in Chapter 2, the South Wales Miners' Federation (SWMF) condemned the prospect of war on 2 August 1914. Nonetheless, as in the rest of the country, the Welsh rallied to the British cause upon the start of the war. An SWMF meeting on 6 August 1914 fell prey to the attack of a large crowd of pro-war miners, leading to the withdrawal of the Federation's resolution. In early August 1914, C.B. Staunton, a pre-war labour activist and no friend of the English, said 'In times of distress and trouble, I stand in with my country.'[18] Wales provided large numbers of men to the military; and Welsh miners showed no hesitation in joining the forces, a fact remarked on as early as 24 August 1914 and as late as 1917.[19]

Ireland also presented an unusual case. Pre-war, there had been a strong martial tradition in Ireland. Enlisting in the Army was one way to escape the poverty of Ireland. In the first half of the nineteenth century, there were more Irish soldiers in the British Army than there were English. Further, the percentage of Irish in the Army was higher than the percentage of the Irish in the population throughout the century. In 1881, the Irish made up 15 per cent of Britain's population but 21 per cent of her Army. The growing unrest in Ireland towards the end of the nineteenth century reduced Irish enlistment. Irish men who might have joined the British Army instead stayed at home and fought with one of the Catholic or Protestant paramilitaries. By 1911, Irish military enlistment had dropped below its population share for the first time.[20]

Irish enlistment during the war reflected this new reality. This is perhaps unsurprising in a land where schoolboys were named after Boer leaders like Kruger and Kronje, but there was an initial wave of enthusiasm.[21] During August 1914 many men from Ireland volunteered, including the entire Ulster Volunteer Force (UVF), formed by Edward Carson in 1912 to fight the Catholic paramilitaries.[22] Kitchener allowed the UVF to remain a battalion within the army, but he refused Catholic paramilitaries the same treatment. Kitchener decreed that they would have to enlist singly and be assigned to a non-Irish battalion.[23] This effectively killed the desire of most Irish Catholics to enlist. A speaker at an Irish rally on 19 August 1914 argued that the Irish should not 'defend one tyranny against another'.[24] Most Irish simply did not believe that England's battles concerned them. Enlistee Frank Laird recalled that 'in Ireland it was looked at as mainly England's concern, and there was no mass movement to the recruiting office'.[25]

But the anti-British feeling was not universal. Both the Protestant and Catholic communities raised regiments, and the population sent its soldiers off to war enthusiastically as late as May 1915.[26] Irish Catholics and Protestants expressed a variety of reasons for enlisting. Some joined up because of the economic advantage. Denis Kelly, a rural labourer, recalled that he 'had nothing at home here, there was nothing in it, no work or money or nothing'. Others joined for a chance to get out of Ireland. Tom Barry joined because he wanted 'to see new countries and to feel [like] a grown man'. Some joined because of the Home Rule bill: the sooner the war ended, the sooner Ireland would be free.[27] Historian Thomas Dooley's analysis of the enlistment of James English, an Irish Catholic labourer, suggests that many Irish enlistees felt all of the above motivations to a varying degree.[28] The economic, political, and social situation impelled some into the military. But they were few. The section of the population that provided the majority of men in Britain proved, in Ireland, more interested in remaining at home and waging a domestic war. 'Unsatisfactory' was Kitchener's final judgement on Irish recruiting.[29]

Enlistment on a class basis: working-class versus elite enlistment

Perhaps the most important breakdown for the purposes of this study is class. Telling how many of these men were working class and how many were middle and upper class is difficult. First, the government broke down enlistment figures in the Register by industries and did not include either agriculture or the professions (middle-class occupations).[30] It is possible to work out the number of men who enlisted from the agricultural sectors because another section of the National Register gives the total number of agricultural workers left in Britain in August 1915: 910,094. Using that figure and the 1911 Census figure of 1,001,442 agricultural workers in Britain gives the approximate number of enlistees from the agricultural sector as 91,348.[31] Unfortunately, for professional occupations there is not even this limited information. Unlike such industries as coal mining, the government was not interested in controlling enlistment from the professional industries, so there are no detailed numbers.

There is a second problem. Unemployed men who enlisted were counted in the Register either as a member of their occupation or as a separate category. How the differentiation was made is not clear. Those unemployed included in a particular occupation were also counted in the enlistment figures for that occupation. But there was no enlistment figure for those unemployed men separated into the 'Unoccupied persons' category. There were 227,972 'Unoccupied persons' listed in the National Register, and it is unclear how many of those had enlisted.[32]

Thus, the August 1915 working-class enlistment total of 1,358,848 reached by adding the sum of the working-class industrial (1,267,500) and agricultural enlistees (91,348) is only a rough approximation.[33] Nonetheless, it seems close enough to draw some tentative conclusions. In percentage terms, the first year's worth of volunteers was 67.4 per cent working class. The remaining 32.6 per cent was probably middle- and upper-class men, with some unaccounted-for unemployed men and agricultural workers thrown in the mix. The industrial working-class enlistees made up 20.2 per cent of the total number of industrial working-class men. The agricultural working-class enlistees made up 8 per cent of the total number of agricultural working-class men. The total number of working-class enlistees (industrial and agricultural) made up 18.1 per cent of the total number of working-class men in the United Kingdom.[34] The approximate percentage of middle- and upper-class men who joined in the first year is higher than their percentage of the population, while the working-class figure is lower. Could this imbalance be taken as evidence that working-class men were not as enthusiastic about the war as middle- and upper-class men?[35]

The problem with assuming that this was the case is that, as they stand, the numbers measure *enlistment* rather than *recruitment*. That is, they measure the number and percentage of men who not only volunteered but also successfully passed through the enrolment process. The men who showed up to volunteer and were turned away are not reflected. Thus, if working-class men were turned away at higher rates than middle- and upper-class men, then the figures do not reflect the true number who wished to volunteer.

Could this be the case? Did any part of the enrolment process eliminate many more working-class men than those of the upper and middle classes? Was there something that would make the evaluation of enthusiasm based on the raw figures, as *The Times* (London) put it, 'less than fair to certain classes of people, and more than fair to others'?[36] The answer seems to be yes. The Army's physical requirements clearly hampered the enlistment of working-class men. A higher percentage of working-class men than men from the middle and upper classes failed to pass their medical examination.

This was a continuing problem. Years of poverty, malnutrition, and back-breaking labour had left their mark on the workers. The 'quest for efficiency' in the pre-war years had done little to help them. They were stunted, unthrifty, and often beset by a range of chronic respiratory and digestive problems.[37]

As a result, during the Victorian era, the Army rejected a large proportion of its volunteers. So desperate had the Army become by the end of the nineteenth century that it allowed the enlistment of marginally unfit men who the recruiters believed could become able soldiers anyway. In 1892, such exemptions made up 32 per cent of the Regulars.[38] These difficulties continued in the Boer War, resulting in the 'quest for national efficiency' described earlier. From 1900 to 1905, 31.3 per cent of applicants were rejected for medical reasons.[39] For the ten years leading up to the war, the Army rejected between 284 and 355 out of every 1,000 recruits for medical reasons.[40] In contrast, France and Germany, where all men had to serve regardless of their economic position, suffered rejection rates of 13 and

8 per cent respectively.[41] The War Office explained Britain's rejections by noting that recruits came from the 'lowest classes of the population'.[42]

The outbreak of war hardly changed the situation. The men volunteering included many whose physical condition was woefully inadequate, most especially the large proportion coming from urban backgrounds.[43] In the first few months of the war, these men, however, were not always or easily refused entry. The overwhelming rush of August to October 1914 meant that steps in the enlistment process were skipped. Some men enlisted without ever actually being examined.[44] The examinations that were performed tended to be hurried and mechanical, 'a perfunctory examination calculated to exclude the one-legged, the hunch-backed, the man moribund of cardiac disease, and the blind,' as one Army doctor put it.[45] Thomas Edmed, a working-class enlistee, recalled that the 'doctor gave us a medical exam by pressing his head against their chest and then saying "Now, go and kill Germans."'[46] Even when a serious examination took place, volunteers often found ways around it. Some enlistees passed the eye test, for example, by memorizing the chart before they entered the testing room.[47] If the volunteers failed their first examination, they simply kept trying until they found another doctor to pass them: K. Palmer succeeded in enlisting on his twenty-eighth attempt, ironically, of all things, by joining the Royal Army Medical Corps.[48]

The breakdown of the medical examination meant that men who were 'unfit when they enlisted' nonetheless made it into the Army.[49] Some had serious medical conditions. E.A. Bond recalled that a deaf man with a crippled right leg was rated 'A1' by the medical board examining him and allowed into the Army.[50] Syd Carroll successfully enlisted in 1914, even though he was deaf. Confronted with an eye-chart, A.G. Whyte randomly said a letter and the doctor passed him, though, even with his glasses on, he could not see the chart. Some simply ignored the doctor's verdict: when H.E. Wright was rejected because of his bad heart, he simply waited until the doctor wasn't looking and then joined the 'passed' group.[51]

Despite this laxity, many working-class volunteers nonetheless failed the medical. The dental requirements and the height and chest measurements proved most challenging. The War Office initially insisted that volunteers have a certain minimum number of teeth.[52] Robert Roberts remembered a Boer War veteran returning after being rejected on dental grounds. '"Turned down!" he said disgustedly – "Bad teeth! They must want blokes to bite the damned Germans!"'[53] Soon, however, the dental rejection rate proved to be too high. The policy was changed in February 1915 and men were accepted if insufficient teeth was their only defect.[54]

Many encountered similar difficulties with the minimum height and chest measurement. The minimum for enlistees started at 5ft 3ins, went briefly to 5ft 6ins, dropped to 5ft 4ins, and then back to 5ft 3ins, all with proportionate chest measurements ranging from 34 inches. Many men failed even the 5ft 3ins minimum. But even if they came up to the height minimum, many men failed to make the chest-size minimums. The experience of J.T. Baldwin and his friends was not uncommon:

We visited London for the purpose of enlisting in the RAMC. I was there rejected on account of small physique, chest, and heart. Reg was rejected on account of eyesight, Harold was rejected as not reaching the required height. My medical examination particulars were: Height five ft 4.5 inches, chest measurement 30 inch normal, 32 inch expanded.[55]

The War Office found in 1915 that the medical rejection rate 'remained constant for some time at between 22.5 and 25 per cent'.[56] But the War Office did not analyse the rejections by class. The available evidence suggests that the rate of rejection varied dramatically between socio-economic groups. The rates for middle- and upper-class men seem to have been quite low, in the 5–10 per cent range. The Leeds Pals, the 15th (Service) Battalion of the Prince of Wales' Own (West Yorkshire Regiment), was a gentleman's battalion, open only to middle- or upper-class men. It experienced medical rejection rates of volunteers of about 8 per cent.[57] Figures for working-class men, on the other hand, seem to have increased on the pre-war figures, ranging from 30 per cent. In Sheffield, a local battalion raised by the mostly working-class city ran into great difficulties in trying to enrol men. The 'rife' malnutrition had left many too scrawny to pass the medical standards.[58] By December 1915, a Sunday paper, the *Weekly Dispatch*, claimed that the rejection rate for working-class men hovered around 50 per cent.[59]

Rather than analysing the rejection breakdowns, the War Office assumed, as a general rule, that 70 per cent of those aged 19–40 were physically fit to serve.[60] The recruitment figures in different industries produced by this assumption led the government to understate working-class enthusiasm and overstate upper- and middle-class ardour. For example, 61,600 men out of the 160,200 who worked in 'Central Government', a heavily middle-class occupation, had enlisted by October 1915. Using the government's 70 per cent fit figure gives an enlistment rate of 58 per cent. A similar calculation for working-class men who worked in shoe factories gives a figure of only 45 per cent. Using different rejection rates, however, the percentages change. If only 10 per cent of middle-class men were rejected, then only 42 per cent of those eligible in 'Central Government' volunteered. Even assuming that only 30 per cent of working-class volunteers failed their physicals, then the 45 per cent achieved by the workers from shoe factories exceeds that of 'Central Government' workers. If the working-class rejection rate was higher, then the disparity in favour of the working class would be greater.

These numbers suggest that medical rejections reduced working-class enlistments more than middle- and upper-class rates. The figures are not broad enough to generalize authoritatively about the entire country. Nonetheless, the rate of medical rejection among working-class men seems to have been about three times the rate for middle- and upper-class men. If this difference was indeed general across Britain, then it would go a long way towards explaining the disparity between the enlistment rate of the social classes.

Volunteers and the age breakdown

When S. Lewis was sent home from the Somme after six weeks of fighting, he had just turned 12.[61] The Army created by voluntary enlistment was very young. The men joining were sometimes surprisingly callow. The youthfulness of the enlistees reflected the youthfulness of British society.[62] In the 1911 Census there were 3,157,547 men aged 15–25, 2,831,655 men between 25 and 35, and 2,336,508 aged 35–45. The 15–25 age group provided the largest number of recruits (1,150,000) during the voluntary period. By contrast, the 25–35 age group, all of whose members were within the military's age requirements, provided around 850,000 recruits.[63] The disparity may reflect youthful exuberance or the fact that the older men were more likely to hold positions as skilled and thus exempt workers.

Of the 1,150,000 men aged 15–25 who joined in 1914–1915, 300,000 seem to have been under the Army's minimum age of 19.[64] The breakdown of the enlistment system extended to checking the ages of volunteers. In the mad rush to get them signed up, many boys seem to have slipped through the cracks, making getting in underage relatively easily. Recruiting sergeants were not eager to turn away underage men. Many volunteers prepared themselves, lied about their age, and were admitted by unquestioning recruiters.[65] S.T. Kemp, a farm labourer, recalled that no one 'asked for a birth certificate, you said you were such an age and they believed you. Boys of fifteen were saying they were nineteen or twenty.'[66] If they did not want to lie, S.H. Hopkins, a clerk, remembered, they would 'put "20" inside their hats so that they could say – quite correctly – that they were just under 20. They were often only 17.'[67]

Those who forgot and revealed their true age were often given another opportunity to come up with something acceptable.[68] When F. Turner, the son of a compositor, 'said I was 18, the sergeant said "have another think, lad." So, in ten minutes, I became nineteen.' Some recruiting sergeants gave up when the underage volunteer showed persistence. Walter Bennett, rejected in his first try, returned to the end of the line. When he got back to the table, the Sergeant-Major looked at him with 'instant recognition' but allowed him in anyway. Some recruiting sergeants accepted bribes to pass a youth.[69]

Nor were all the underage boys nearly 19. The Army formed a company of boys aged 16 and under who had managed to enlist and actually serve overseas before they were caught. Called the 'A4 Boys', they numbered over 200.[70] Howard Benwell, Walter Grove, and W.F. Billingham, all working-class enlistees, joined at age 16. Thomas Edmed, a milkman, successfully joined at age 15. G.W. Albin, a farrier, and Jeff Pritchard, a cart-handler, managed to join at age 14.[71] Underage and undersize, such an Army often looked like children playing at soldiers. One of the boy soldiers remembered:

> That night we dressed up and thought that we were very big, walking down the street. My trousers were about a foot too long, my great-coat was dragging on the floor and my tunic was a bit too slack, sure, but we thought we were looking great.[72]

Conclusion

Several conclusions are obvious. Working-class voluntarism rivalled, perhaps exceeded, that of the middle and upper classes. Certainly, the working-class presence in the volunteers was obvious. One middle-class observer reported:

> Their [his fellow volunteers] degree of intelligence was obviously of the lowest. They were just drink sodden, unclean and foul mouthed brutes lacking the mental capacity of even a decent dog but you must by no means run away with the idea that this applies to the whole collection. Some were of a very good class, others were poor and ill kept but yet decent fellows enough and anxious to do well again. There was the countryman simple and badly educated but muscular and healthy who will with training make a better soldier than I can ever hope too [sic].[73]

Other middle-class men viewed their fellow soldiers with more charity:

> If they weren't old soldiers, they [his section] were old prison lags, and one soon learned their particular skills in crime. I had base coin makers, pickpockets, swell mobsmen, 'get away men', and petty thieves. The back-chat in the tents and huts was fascinating for the uninitiated listener. The merits of Strangeways Prison, Manchester as compared with Winson Green, Birmingham, or even Dartmoor, with the names of the Governors, chaplains, and warders, bandied about in a familiar fashion. . . . The 'get away man' explained to me that he worked with break in thieves who brought out the swag, usually jewellery and small articles of value, and in order to prove their innocence if caught 'red-handed' passed it to him to sprint away with. He must have told the truth because he won all the flat races, over the hurdles and obstacles at the regimental sports later on.[74]

Even the medical problems of working-class men had an oddly beneficial effect. Working-class men, though by absolute numbers the largest segment of the population and the Army, were less likely to be admitted to the Army. Once in the Army they were less likely to be sent to front-line units. They thus suffered, as J.M. Winter has shown, proportionately fewer casualties than did middle- and upper-class men. The idea of the 'Lost Generation' of middle- and upper-class men has a substantial basis in fact.[75]

Nonetheless, working-class men constituted both the largest pool of military manpower and the largest section of Britain's fighting forces. Within that group, urban workers were more likely to enlist than rural ones. No particular segment of the working class dominated the enlistment sheets, but some industries sent greater percentages of their men to the front than average. Some regional differences seem significant, but none are so remarkable as to suggest a fundamental disparity between the countries of Great Britain, with the singular exception of unenthusiastic Ireland.

What motivations did these working-class men have? Why were they willing to enlist in such numbers? Their reasons were neither singular nor unconnected. Men joined for a range of different reasons, but their common link was a newly expanded worldview, an unprecedented consciousness of the world at large and their place within it. That is the subject of the next chapter.

4 'A sense of the round world'
The workers, Britain, Europe, and the empire

'We were the most powerful nation, our Navy the strongest, and the King-Emperor, the acknowledged leading monarch among the Heads of State.'[1] A former office boy, F.L.B. Burns, wrote those words of the pre-war years. They testify to his pride in Britain and his identification with its glory. Burns linked himself to the nation, just as the workers linked themselves to Britain. Burns felt that Britons had 'the experience gained and world knowledge acquired as our position in international affairs improved. We achieved a broad-mindedness obtainable only by travel and endurance in the hard school of life.'[2] This worldview, more than anything else, was the common thread running through the motives of all enlistees. The workers conceived of themselves as occupying a significant place in the British hierarchy, just as Britain held a particular position within Europe and empire. They consciously located themselves within that national, continental, and imperial hierarchy. They believed themselves part of the 'concrete community' of nation.[3] They conceived of themselves as part of a larger whole, not separate from it, and their actions were based on that belief.

But what created that view, and did the 1914 generation differ from its predecessors? Several influences created this global view. First, nearly the entire working class was literate by 1914. By 1893, 95 per cent of workers could read. Twenty years earlier, the figure had been 78 per cent.[4] Furthermore, the type of literacy differed between the two generations. The earlier generation's literacy was minimal and unequal to the task of regular reading. It had been only what historian R.K. Webb called 'a potential reading public'.[5] The generation of 1914, by contrast, enjoyed a near universal, functional literacy. It was an actual reading public. This mass literacy spurred the growth of mass, national newspapers. National papers with circulations of over 500,000 became common.

Through these papers, the workers, especially urban workers, had daily contact with the larger world of politics, culture, society, and empire. The working-class generation of 1914 grew up in a world in which information was much more widely accessible than ever before. Their horizon extended beyond neighbourhood, village, or city. This sustained contact with the outside world broadened and deepened their evaluations of their own position, both in Britain and in the world.[6]

Second, the working class encountered new and helpful bureaucracies and government bodies. The creation of unemployment insurance, the labour registries and exchanges, and various public and private health care charities brought, on a large scale and for the first time, assistance and aid to working-class communities. Social Darwinism and the Boer War spurred the interest of the upper classes in the health of working-class children.[7] Such concerns brought elites who were trying to be helpful into contact with workers. Meanwhile, the Liberal government's social reforms did much the same thing on an economic level. The economic well-being of the working class went from being a 'peripheral concern of the Poor Law guardians into a central problem of public administration'.[8] The workers, in addition to seeing a larger world, were acknowledged by such administrative efforts as being a valuable part of that world.

Such contact shaped the working-class view of the world. Historians have emphasized the internationalist class-consciousness promoted by such changes.[9] The emphasis of this conception was economic and the weight was on conflict. But such a formulation is incomplete, for workers did not conceive of themselves as merely part of an economic group, but also of a national one. Workers had a sense of Britain, and the British Empire, and of themselves as a class. They had found both a class and a national consciousness. Much of their information was biased, incomplete, or simply wrong, but it nonetheless connected them in way that was foreign to their mothers and fathers. This generation viewed themselves as elements in a larger, global entity, in which they had an investment, and upon which they had some influence. They understood that they were part of a larger working class, a larger country, and a larger Europe.

Both the government and much of the upper classes recognized this change. For perhaps the first time, the cultural agenda of the British elites included the workers. The workers began to have prominent places in newspapers, books, and invented traditions.[10] When the war began, the government turned to these national forms of communication to reach the workers. They could reach the working class through an 'advertisement in the Press, a cinematography film, distribution of booklets and other recruiting literature, an Information Bureau at the Earl's Court Exhibition, recruiting marches, and improvements in recruiting machinery'.[11] It was this knowledge that led the workers, for a variety of motives, to enlist when war broke out. The First World War was the first large-scale industrial war, but, for the working class, it was also the first large-scale war of knowledge, heroic and chauvinistic as it may have been.[12]

The roots: education

The working classes' new literacy grew out of the educational reforms of the late nineteenth and early twentieth centuries. The Educational Reform Acts of 1870 and 1902 had created a nationwide system that instilled literacy in a majority of the working class. By the turn of the century, the great majority of working-class children attended at least several years of school. They might, like A.E. Brown, a farm labourer in Sunderland, go to school without shoes, but they did go.[13] Though many left school between the ages of 12 and 15 in order to go to work and

86 per cent of them had left by age 17, they nonetheless established a fairly solid command of written English.[14]

These newly literate children usually coexisted in households with older generations who were often barely literate or illiterate.[15] Sometimes, the gap was between parent and child. When Tom Stockton's father gave him permission to go to war in 1915, it was by putting 'his mark' on a piece of paper. He could neither read nor write.[16] P. Creek's parents could not help him learn to read while he went to school because they themselves had only the basics of literacy: 'My Mother and Father could not help me to become a good scholar because they had difficulty in writing their own names.'[17] For most families, however, the transition to literacy happened across several generations. J.H. Hird's grandmother 'could not read at all. She made fun of me when, as a young boy, I stood by her chair and read to her. She did not believe that "them marks" meant what I said; I was making it up.' By contrast, his mother 'could read a little, having had some schooling'.[18]

Working-class society, as a whole, thus slowly shifted from a mostly oral society to a literate one after 1870. The fundamental structure of working-class society came to depend on people being able to read. Economic interactions and social interactions grew increasingly to be shaped by the assumptions of literacy, rather than orality.[19] For example, throughout much of Britain, newspapers replaced the traditional form of spreading information, the town crier.[20]

Fundamental economic interactions such as the job market were transformed by the spread of literacy. Growing up, R.T. Wallace, the son of a gardener in London, remembered how the domestic servants of his parents' generation used to change their employers:

> Whitsuntide, and Martinmas were the time when the farm servants, both men and women used to change their situations. The men would stand in the market place with a straw in their mouth to show that they were prepared to be hired.[21]

When, shortly before the war, Wallace went to change his position, the system had changed:

> During this period I saw an advertisement in either *The Times*, or the *Morning Post*, I forget which, I applied for, and got the position as first footman with Mr Vernon Watney, and Lady Margaret Watney at Cornbury Park, Charlbury, about 15 miles from Oxford.[22]

In the first instance, the procedure used pre-industrial methods of both setting dates and signalling. The choice of a traditional time of year (Whitsuntide and Martinmas) that everyone could be expected to know, and the method of signalling availability (the straw in the mouth) demanded nothing in the way of literacy. By contrast, the newspaper advertisement assumed a broad range of working-class literacy. By placing the advertisement, employers implicitly showed that they assumed that potential domestic servants could and would read newspaper want ads regularly.[23] Further, the advertisement spoke not only to a literate audience, but to a national one. The job was in Oxford. By advertising in *The Times* (London), a newspaper sold throughout England, the employers probably expected that they would get responses from around the country. The advent of newspapers and literacy had made such an advertisement possible. It had made a want ad a method of national economic communication that habituated both workers and elites to such interactions. Such advertisements were imitated by recruiting ads used during the war. Usually small and almost always placed in the classified sections, the government's requests for soldiers echoed those of any other economic transaction.[24]

Education also opened paths of advancement that had been unavailable to a previous generation. R.J. Carrier remembered the route his father had taken to advance within the mines:

> [My father] drifted into the coal-pits, and by hard work and a natural aptitude he became a mine official. Among the local colliers, his gift of pit work became a byword, and was looked upon by many as uncanny. More important still, in an age when bribery and corruption were rife in the mines, when many an official made his pile out of the men and the company, he remained honest.[25]

Carrier's father had become a mine official by dint of 'hard work and honesty'. His reputation spread orally; it 'became a byword'. Neither his honesty nor his work ethic required literacy or education. R.M. Luther, a generation later, used a different route:

> I was a young miner, working on the coal face of a very big steam coal pit, known as the Bargoed Powell Duffryn Colliery. It was possible to earn about £2 per week, as I was a proficient Collier with five years' service on the coal face. I had just turned 19 years of age, and was considering the idea of studying mining and becoming a colliery manager; in fact, I was attending evening classes for that purpose, together with ambulance class, surveying and other mining subjects.[26]

Luther's route to becoming a colliery manager was education. Classes would give him the knowledge to become a manager. Luther may have been just as industrious and skilled a worker as Carrier's father, but the way he saw of advancing his position involved education and literacy. On a fundamental level, literacy and education proved useful: learning returned value.

Nor was Luther alone in recognizing the value of learning. Many others aggressively went beyond the lessons they were given in school and educated themselves outside the formal boundaries of their educational institution. P. Creek, the son of a stable hand, remembered:

> I had difficulty in reading at first and many words I did not understand and I remember asking my eldest sister who was bright and had done well at school the meaning of a good number, gradually I began to read better.[27]

Later, when Creek worked at a bakery, he kept a pocket dictionary with him and during slow times would copy out words and memorize their definitions.[28]

Of course, this is not to say that the schooling was uniformly good. R.J. Carrier remembered his teacher with fondness but he had no illusions about her weaknesses:

> Poor old 'Mammy Maykin' – that was our name for the old schoolmarm. She would be getting on for sixty at that time and had taught most of the children's parents and, indeed, some of their grandparents. What education she herself had received or what she gave, I have never fathomed. Dear old lady! Like an old duck, she brooded us all under her wing, teaching us only the elementary truths of life. That was the extent of her knowledge, and probably, after all, the best of knowledge. Educationally, a child of ten today would be her superior.[29]

Part of the reason why P. Creek had to work so hard outside school was that he had learned little there. 'I could just about write my name when I left, the three R's were a mystery to me and the other children.'[30]

Children learned the basics of literacy even as school served to inculcate broad national values. Both the lessons and the reading children did on their own served to introduce them to a larger Britain. For urban children, the distant England to which schooling linked them was the rural countryside. Alun Howkins has recently demonstrated the degree to which England's image in popular culture has been a rural one.[31] Urban children were shown an English countryside that bore little similarity to their urban England, but was nonetheless labelled as their England, as their nation. Such schooling connected urban children to a larger England that contained fields and forests and mountains. It was an England that they themselves had no experience of, that they themselves had to make part of their imagined community, in Benedict Anderson's enduringly useful formulation.[32] That message, it should be noted, was most efficiently and effectively absorbed by urban children. Unlike rural students, they were unlikely to be pulled out of school regularly for the harvest. Unlike rural students, they were unlikely, after the turn of the century, to have to travel far to reach their school houses. They thus received regular visions of an England not of their experience but one to which they were connected. They had to imagine themselves as part of that England. Their school lessons also forced them to imagine empire.[33] Their environment and schooling also gave them visions of foreign lands with different people and different customs. Working-class children learned of Britain's far-flung empire and her powerful Navy. E. Buffey remembered that 'at school my most interesting subject was history with its wars and I could vividly picture the Indian Mutiny, Charge of the Light Brigade and the many battles our troops had fought and won'.[34] Such history often gave children a connection and understanding with their own families. Herbert Wootton's uncles were both Regulars who had fought in South Africa during the Boer War (1899–1902). Reading 'books on War' gave Wootton a sense of their experiences.[35] Imperial examples were even used to discipline unruly children, as James Murray, the son of a boot maker, remembered: a 'succession of missionaries on holiday from Africa, [told] us how well the black children were taking to Christianity, and behoving us to be as good as they were'.[36] As a result, the empire came into working-class lives not only in a celebratory fashion but also in a domestic way.

Another factor that differentiated the new generation from the previous one was the role of education in accelerating the spread of English as a national tongue, even in Wales, Scotland, and Ireland. Britishness had become 'multi-ethnic', with a wide number of races living under a single royal family. But what wove those races together was the English language.[37] Converting the children of non-English users to English thus gave them entry to the national culture. It was a particular kind of English, of course, one in which dialect and accent immediately revealed a person's social status, but when L. MacDonald went to school and learned to read and write English, something that his parents, Gaelic speakers, could not do, he was made aware of a larger Britain than they could ever know.[38]

Working-class children were not, however, simply empty vials to be filled. They sought to influence and control their schooling, even as children. The most extreme form of this was children's strikes, in which schoolchildren used industrial tactics to demand changes in the education system. Such strikes were quite common before the war.[39] Children disputed adult control of the classroom in smaller ways, as well. One example was schoolyard traditions that implicitly showed the teachers that they were not in complete control of school. J.H. Hird remembered

> a long-established custom, which was that some of the older boys tied the door admitting to the porch, so that the teacher on duty would not be able to come out after the bell sounded to start morning school. It was, of course, only a temporary, and symbolical, piece of mischief, intended to reduce briefly the superiority of the staff over the pupils.[40]

Working-class children used what they learned for their own ends and to draw their own conclusions. R.J. Carrier, beaten as a child for not saluting the daughter of the local squire, found that 'the French Revolution had a wonderful charm for me'.[41] It was the ability and knowledge to make that connection between the French Revolution and a personal situation that marked this working class; it was an ability and knowledge that would profoundly influence their decisions after 1914.

The roots: reading newspapers and 'halfpenny dreadfullers'

The workers took advantage of their education by using the new skills, when and how they could. 'We were all avid readers,' R.A. Cockell, the son of a marine engineer, said of himself and his siblings.[42] They read newspapers. They read books. They read whatever was accessible. To meet this demand, a broad range of new reading materials came on to the market, mainly cheap newspapers and books.

The new material first appeared around the turn of the century. Before that, there was little for the working class to read. The working-class periodicals that did exist used pictures to transmit information, which inevitably curtailed the complexity and depth of the message. Other sources of information, newspapers such as *The Times*, tailored their publications and prices to upper- and middle-class tastes. Publishers of magazines and books did so as well.[43] As a result, they were priced too high for workers to afford.

Technological changes helped feed the new demand for cheap reading material. Improved printing techniques allowed mass publication at relatively low cost. Press barons could now print a million copies of a newspaper, sell them at a halfpenny each, and still make a profit. The first to exploit the possibilities was Alfred Northcliffe, who began the *Daily Mail* in 1894. The *Mail*, aimed at a lower- middle-class and upper- working-class audience, proved a phenomenal success, gathering circulation numbers that dwarfed anything seen previously.[44] By 1912, the *Daily Mail* was selling between 850,000 and 1,033,000 on a daily basis. *The Times*, by contrast, sold 150,000 copies per day in 1914.[45]

Workers from all economic levels found in these new newspapers information that connected them to the world they had learned of in school. H.E. Hunt, whose working-class family was well enough off to afford an annual holiday, would sit, with his father and brother, 'on a seat on the promenade perusing the morning papers before returning to the boarding house for breakfast'.[46] But impoverished working-class families subscribed as well, as J.H. Hird remembered from his days delivering the paper:

> Not far away, a door would open, and the stench issuing took my breath away. There were ragged clothes piled up against the wall, and the woman herself was a bundle of the same sort. Why she wanted a newspaper I could not understand.[47]

The newspapers connected the workers to a world outside Britain. In north Wales, John Ames, the son of a plate-layer on the Mersey Railway Tunnel, recalled that 'a lot of news was obtained from the Liverpool "Weekly Post" and I can clearly remember the sinking of the Titanic'.[48] A.G. Ransley, the son of a domestic servant, remembered getting the very latest editions of the papers, the 'stop-presses', to follow the story of Captain Scott's ill-fated expedition to the South Pole.[49] It was a source of information that workers clearly valued highly. When E. Rolph enlisted in 1908, having failed to find a job, his family and especially his father disapproved strongly. Nonetheless, said Rolph, '[my father] must have had some regard for me because he sent me the local paper each week. This was always a great joy to me, for it allowed me to keep in touch with all the home news.'[50]

Through this new outpouring of affordable newspapers, a new generation of workers became acquainted with an imperial and European world. It became a regular and interesting part of their lives. The emphasis on the British experience of empire made the workers feel that these lands and peoples were not impossibly distant and out of reach, but were part of their heritage, their nation.

This new world sometimes made the concerns of their parents and grandparents seem provincial. J.H. Hird thought that his parents' generation knew 'nothing beyond their immediate social experience. They did not read newspapers or anything about what was going on in the wider world.'[51] Newspapers made that 'wider world' familiar and apparently attainable to workers. They, unlike their predecessors, understood more than their 'immediate social experience'. They knew the world.

Newspapers were not the only reading material available. As the strength of the market became clear, publishers focused their energies on adventure tales, magazines, and other works, all of which sold. The 'penny dreadfuls' of the mid-century period, priced for middle-class consumption, were replaced in the 1880s and 1890s by the 'halfpenny dreadfullers', affordable by working-class adolescents. By the end of the century, it is estimated that there were over 50,000 weekly periodicals being published in England. By 1914, over 3,000 works of fiction were being published each year, using 1.8 million tons of paper.[52]

Subsidized by advertisers, such weekly serials as *The Union Jack* carried stories of fictional heroes like Sexton Blake, whose detective work carried him through Europe and the empire.[53] Many of the heroes of these works were recognizably working class, such as Sergeant King of 'Sergeant King of the Marines Spins a Jolly Good Yarn'. Sergeant King's tale is one of military heroism across the empire, as he and his fellow Marines take on 'savage blacks on the West Coast of Africa, and semi-civilized Mohammedans on the East Coast'.[54] It was a working-class view of the experiences of empire, clearly aimed at workers.

Boys found them enthralling. 'It did not matter what it was that came my way in the shape of print, I read it,' said R.J. Carrier. 'Boys' adventure tales, school tales, love tales, penny novellettes, anything and everything.'[55] Despite the poverty of P. Creek's family, he found a way to get his hands on the stories of Sexton Blake:

> When the weather was cold, wet, and dull I used to sit in a chair on one side of the hearth and read the weekly editions of Sexton Blake. I was fortunate to get these little booklets from a friend who lived near us and whose parents were in better circumstances financially than mine, thus he had the pocket money to buy the exciting tales which Sexton Blake was all about, the stories were thrilling [and] always beset with danger for Sexton but he triumphed every week, and was the hero of every boy who read his books.[56]

But more than simply teaching workers about the outside world, reading taught the working class about their place within that world. The belief in such a hierarchy can be seen in the celebratory reaction to the Boer War. Far distant and not a direct threat to Britain (though some had relatives fighting), the war nonetheless captured public interest at home. Eventual British victories provoked an outbreak of celebration among all classes. Arthur Ward, the son of a first-class goods driver, remembered:

> News from far away South Africa was received much less quickly than today when battle news is transmitted almost as soon as it happens. . . . The success of our arms was often far from encouraging. Little wonder the relief of Kimberly and Ladysmith and Mafeking were occasions for unbridled jubilation. Processions of decorated carts and cycles toured the streets, children's amusements were organized, bunting and union jacks appeared everywhere.[57]

In Herbert Chapman's neighbourhood, the celebration took the form of a fancy-dress parade. Chapman went as a jockey and shared in the experience, thus also sharing, in some small way, in empire.[58]

There have been attempts to elide this working-class enthusiasm for the Boer War, but whether or not the workers approved of the war, they cheered the triumph of British arms.[59] They saw themselves as part of a greater whole for which the war was important. They linked themselves to Britain and empire. For some, that linkage was somewhat less than voluntary and lasted a lifetime, as a friend of Harry Forrester, a miner, discovered. Born soon after the relief of Ladysmith, this friend was christened by his enthusiastic father after the relieving general and thus gained the somewhat unmusical name of 'Redrust Buller Mould'.[60]

In addition to Britain and empire, the workers grew aware of Europe and Germany. Just as they were shown imperial visions, so too were they subject to European visions, ones which usually portrayed Germany as the enemy. C.H. Rolph, the son of a police sergeant, remembered that 'Germany at that time [1910–1914] was the popular enemy. . . . All our boys' weeklies, when they needed a bungling spy or a foreign villain, used German ones.'[61] Possibly the most popular genre within this literature was the invasion novel, in which England was threatened by the landing of an enemy army. Of the sixty-seven invasion novels counted by historian Cecil Eby for the period 1871–1914, forty-one had the Germans invading, eighteen had the French, and eight had the Russians.[62] A common plot was Britain, under attack and invasion from the Germans, emerging triumphant only after much violence. H.E. Hunt remembered:

> Quite a lot of our boyish literature dealt with a war with Germany, three paperbacks were very popular with us boys. The Boys' Friend 3d Library entitled respectfully *Britain Invaded*, *Britain at Bay* and *Britain's Revenge* these sold like hot cakes, and we boys revelled in the gory details revealed therein.[63]

Up to the turn of the century such works often included a working-class revolt against the British government following such an invasion. 'The East End had slipped its leash, and its fangs were dripping,' wrote one author.[64] The twentieth-century literature, however, no longer portrayed the workers as the enemy, but as part of the popular defence of Britain. They were given the privilege of fighting alongside the upper classes. In essence, they were invited into society's conception of the British nation. The workers became part of the British polity in the view of both the elites and the workers themselves.[65]

As a result, workers analysed the political situation in Europe with knowledge and some precision. Their analysis remained largely focused on Germany. In 1911, Joseph Leftwich broke down the political situation thus:

> Turkey has been becoming friendly with Germany and Austria recently – Italy is the third member of the Triple Alliance and fears that Turkey would soon be joining the other two and compelling the Triple Alliance to become a Quadruple Alliance.[66]

The significance of Leftwich's thought is not the analysis itself, but the fact that he received and reflected upon information about an area seemingly so remote to his concerns. His vision and knowledge extended beyond the East End of London.

Certainly the views the workers read presented them with a pro-British view of the world and offered little in the way of critical analysis.[67] The imagery, as Raphael Samuel has pointed out, adhered to the 'grand theme. . . . of national greatness' by presenting the 'stirring events' of history.[68] Such information favoured the British viewpoint and presented the empire as a force for unalloyed good. The civil servants of that empire were the custodians of the 'white man's burden', selflessly guarding the lesser races and bringing to them the benefits of British civilization.[69] Imperial glory seemed inexhaustible abroad, as the British fought numerous colonial conflicts in the later half of the nineteenth and first decade of the twentieth century. From North and South Africa, to India and China, the British Army waged a series of small, usually successful wars, which presented to the people at home a picture of imperial splendour.[70] It was the height of empire, and the world was coloured British red. S.T. Stanbridge, who later worked on the railway, grew up, as he remembered, 'during the great days of empire, and I was accustomed to looking at maps with their large areas of red indicating the extent of the empire "on which the sun never sets"'.[71]

But the working classes hardly accepted these messages uncritically, surrounded as they were by counter-examples from their own life. The vision of British glory and power existed for many in the middle of the squalor and poverty of their everyday lives. As G.W. Archer, the son of a gamekeeper, recalled:

> Empire Day was regularly celebrated by a lecture on the great British Empire, salute the Flag, etc., even if some of the pupils were too poor to be provided with boots and stockings.[72]

Even as Archer listened to a message of triumphant imperialism, he could see around him his fellow students without shoes, a linkage that he explicitly made and explicitly remembered. When Joseph Leftwich, from the East End, read the paper in 1911, he made the linkage even more clear:

> The *Daily Express* has an article to prove that strikes cause infant-starvation and mortality. The writer suggests that persons responsible for strike-agitators or [?] shall be treated as criminals or lunatics and incarcerated in an asylum or gaol. He also suggests that John Burns as the responsible minister should compel medical men to put 'strike' on death certificate, where the strike is the cause of 'rickets', 'fever', or 'malnutrition' or any other cause of death. The man who thinks this will prevent strikes must be very ignorant of working-class conditions.[73]

The newspaper could send whatever message it chose about the strikes, but Leftwich was just as free to accept it or not.

Though it is dangerous to generalize for an entire population, it seems that many workers reached their understanding of the world not from a blanket acceptance of the newspaper stories, but through a negotiation between their own learning and the viewpoint presented to them. They tested what they read against their own experiences and knowledge, and rejected received wisdom when it did not pass.[74] This was not true of all workers. Some accepted the official line. R.J. Carrier believed his father thought that the 'newspaper was his weekly oracle and . . . that Lloyd George was the modern Jesus Christ'.[75] Nor should this be taken as an argument for a deeply critical and reasoned scepticism on the part of the working class. Working-class Britons had a view of the world that was their own. They gathered their knowledge from the sources available to them and shaped it according to their own experiences. The conception that resulted may have been liberal, conservative, revolutionary, reactionary, or even implausible and illogical. But it was their worldview, and they made decisions based on it.

When the war started, many workers turned to the lines of communication they knew, the newspapers. A.E. Tritton, a labourer, sought out various sources on 4 August 1914: 'I well remember that day, newspapers which were published frequently were scanned eagerly for news of the great crisis.'[76] The message presented was usually less than impartial but it gave people such as A.G. Meacham, the son of a butler, a sense of events. It was the 'flare of beaten up war enthusiasm in the London newspapers [that] aroused' in Meacham the desire to enlist.[77] Their education gave them the background to evaluate their own position and Britain's. S.T. Stanbridge, who worked on the railway, remembered:

> There was no doubt in my mind that with the resources of our great empire and the strongest navy in the world, we would win the war. At the time I was 15 years old; my boyhood had been spent during the great days of empire, and I was accustomed to looking at maps with their large areas of red indicating the extent of the empire 'on which the sun never sets'. At school [I] was taught little about the United States of America or Russia, but the British Empire loomed large in geography lessons, and to entertain the thought of defeat with such strength was just unthinkable.[78]

Stanbridge made explicit connections between the history he knew and the events in France. He was not alone. William J. Tucker, a labourer, recalled that 'the press [was] representing it [the Marne] as an exploit akin to the famous charge of the Light Brigade at Balaclava. I wanted to be in such a charge!'[79]

Working-class soldiers at the front relied on reading for contact with home. Arthur Cave, who had worked in a clothier's shop, set up a reading library for his unit, receiving a donation of 104 books from Britain. It was popular, 'crowded out'.[80] Even in German prison camp, Wilfred Kay, a working-class POW, complained because he could not get newspapers from home. When W. Daly was imprisoned for being absent without leave in 1915, he arranged with a kindly jailer to receive daily the two essentials: cigarettes and a newspaper.[81] Clearly, just as workers craved news of the outside world before the war, so too did soldiers in the trenches seek out news of their domestic world.

Some of the previous generation's suspicions about reading clearly remained among the working class, however. A soldier who read too much might be thought of as not authentically working class. Reading, it seems, may have been perceived as something exterior to normal working-class life. It thus could be done by working-class soldiers only in moderation. P. McGregor wrote from the front to his family asking to be sent papers, but not too many:

> You might send me some dainties – a cake, fancy biscuits, toffee, sweets occasionally, and papers. We get none here. Some of the magazines are dated 1905. In fact, they are the latest we have. Don't send too much as I might be considered a toff – you know – just a little.[82]

The roots: alternate contacts

But education, literacy and reading were not the only ways that workers came into contact with the larger world. In the years after 1900, the national hierarchy increasingly intruded into working-class lives. The stunted and unhealthy working-class volunteers during the Boer War had led the British upper classes to fear that their 'anaemic slum population' could not stand up to the Germans.[83] The elites began to change their conception of the poor and unemployed. National leaders began to accept that the evil lay in the environment of the working class, not the working class itself.[84] The result of this shift was an attempt to improve the health and welfare of the working class. New government bureaucracies emerged to help save the race.

These bureaucracies had an important effect on the working-class conception of the world. On a regular basis, workers encountered representatives of the state and of the nation ostensibly acting in their interest. Perhaps the most widespread of these bureaucracies were those created by the Liberal government after 1906, especially those concerned with unemployment. The unemployment bureaucracies created a working relationship between trade union officials and government bureaucrats. It made them 'co-founders of the new consensus'.[85] But the effect was not limited to labour officials. The initial old age pension bill covered 668,000 people. Many of those pensioners lived with their extended families, making the economic benefit and social contact much broader. By 1911, 2.25 million workers had unemployment insurance.[86]

Workers thus had daily contact with a more helpful government, one that treated them with relative respect. R.S. Patson recalled his experiences of the new employment bureaux:

> Things were improving in employment after Lloyd George brought in his National Insurance Bill in 1911, and Labour Exchanges were set up. I registered at one near the Angel public house at Islington, and obtained several interviews for jobs thereby. There was no unemployment pay but we did come under the new health insurance scheme in due course.[87]

Here was a government office providing employment assistance and health insurance. Here was a concrete example of the rewards the working class gained from being British.

These same offices proved a ready-made infrastructure through which to set up and organize recruiting after 1914. Conveniently located in working-class neighbourhoods, both libraries and labour exchanges soon hosted recruiting offices; where better to gather working-class men? The labour exchanges and unemployment insurance offices proved especially useful to the War Office, because they usually had lists of men in each district, with their addresses, ages, and physical status. The War Office took advantage of that knowledge by asking for lists of men stating age and employment.[88]

The campaign to improve the British race quickly came to include working-class children. The growing number of youth movements aimed to bring working-class youth into a strictly regimented and healthy environment. When Robert Baden-Powell founded the Boy Scouts in 1908, he did it 'to counteract, if possible, the deterioration, moral and physical, which shortened our rising generation'. Youth organizations were certainly avenues for the 'reinforcement of social conformity', but this was not the whole story.[89] Youth movements also served to bring working-class youths into contact with each other as a national group. They familiarized working-class boys with a larger, martial world around them.[90]

Most working-class sons could not afford to join the Boy Scouts. Thomas Baker, his father a gardener for the banking family the Rothschilds, was a rare exception. The Rothschilds purchased his uniform for him.[91] But most found the cost of a Boy Scout or Girl Guide uniform to be an insurmountable barrier. As a result, the church-sponsored youth movements, which mostly provided the uniforms, proved more attractive. In the Church Lads Brigade (CLB), Frank Turner, the son of a labourer, received 'a full uniform, a pill box hat, leather belt and haversack'.[92]

Jack Armstrong joined the CLB because he 'fancied soldiering', and the uniform was not the only resemblance to military service.[93] Members undertook a range of overtly military activities. 'You learned all the army drills and everything,' Arthur Groves remembered. Fred Dixon recalled that he and his unit practised 'signalling, gymnastics, map-reading, night operations on the local commons, and, I mustn't forget, we used to use an old naval gun [to have] naval gun drill'.[94] Many of the youth movements, in fact, affiliated themselves with the local Territorial units, and aped their practices, including having a summer camp much like the two-week gatherings of the Territorials. The training the boys received proved helpful when the war started. R. Pearson's CLB experience meant that upon enlistment in 1914, he 'soon found [himself] in charge of a section, instructing them in the art of forming fours and other movements'.[95]

They explicitly connected what they were doing with the larger and historical world around them. F.H. Kibblewhite, the son of a railway inspector, was typical:

> Here was I in the CLB with an actual rifle, breech-loading doing the absolutely same as Slope Arms! Present Arms! Also the rifles had, I imagined, been in use in 'The Crimean War' with a Cut in the Breech. Also we had an old seven lb Field Arm used I should imagine on HMS Victory with Nelson.[96]

Kibblewhite makes a point of noticing the history of his rifle, of its connections to the past. He, in fact, extends his vision past his rifle to talk of another weapon with a history and connections. Such links gave the working class an investment in what Eric Hobsbawm has called the 'invented traditions' that defined British symbolic life.[97] Just as the elites created a public, national symbolism that self-consciously evoked the broad span of English history, so too did the working class create links to that symbolism.[98] Such creations linked them with elites in the celebration of imperial ritual. They, in essence, included themselves in the pomp and ceremony so elementally crucial to British society.

But they did not accept what H.G. Taylor called 'a very good grounding' in patriotism uncritically.[99] Working-class boys seem to have figured out their own meanings. Rather than absorbing it without demur, they negotiated the significance of what they were told. Nor were they necessarily shy about expressing their opinions. R.A. Hobby, an errand boy, swore at his scoutmaster and was thrown out of the Boy Scouts as a result.[100]

However sceptical the boys were of what they heard, membership in a youth movement did have a critical effect. It brought working-class boys into contact with other members of their own class, and, often, with members of other classes.[101] Membership involved working-class boys in a large, nationally organized group that interacted with similar organizations like the Territorials. It opened connections for them between their local groups and a larger, if martial, world. Influenced by his experience in the CLB, Jack Armstrong joined the Army in 1913 because he 'wanted to see the world'.[102]

The effects: connections

Connections between the workers and the wider world were not limited to those created or initiated by the upper classes. Workers established and broadened their own links. The formation of working-class political parties and industrial unions created links, if sometimes adversarial ones, between workers and elites. The late nineteenth century saw the growth of a working population that viewed itself in class-specific ways and, in its labour battles, explicitly contrasted itself with the capitalist class. 'The new unionism' created a working class that conceived of itself as a community with a stake in the polity as a whole.[103] The growth of the Labour Party in the pre-war years reflected the movement of those workers as a self-conscious group into the political arena.

As we note the adversarial relations between labour and the government/governing elite, we should not be blind to the interactions. Both these organizations linked the labouring classes to the government, links that the War Office and the Cabinet quickly took advantage of during the war to facilitate enlistment. The party machinery and the trade unions were both vital in helping further enlistment.[104]

On an individual level, workers actively demonstrated their growing sense of national and personal connections. They went to a wide range of meetings and activities. They discussed politics and considered themselves political beings. H.S. Bartlett, the son of a carpenter, went to the political theatre that was the House of Commons, witnessing among other things the suffrage debates:

> I used to go in and listen to the debates and talks on the proposal to give women the vote and witnessed a good many scenes of these women chaining themselves in and around Parliamentary area to railings and police hustling them on.[105]

Their sense of themselves and their connections to the world also undercut traditional working-class deference. Observation and contact led many workers to doubt the capacity and ability of the upper classes to rule Britain. Joseph Leftwich thought that the men who ruled England, produced by the Oxbridge system, were 'limited in outlook, crammed with useless knowledge, learned and tremendously ignorant and terribly, terribly bumptious and conceited because of their education'.[106] E. Rolph, a pre-war soldier, was the wicketkeeper for his regiment's cricket team and thus mixed with the officers regularly. His close contact made him sceptical:

> Although I was treated as an inferior, I enjoyed the strange atmosphere of the officer class and their peculiar ways of communicating with each other. The more I observed them, the more I questioned their ability to govern the lower classes and be able to jeopardize a man's whole future.[107]

But some did not limit themselves to observation and evaluation. They used their knowledge and beliefs to fight for their rights. Arthur Ward, after the establishment of unemployment insurance in 1911, insisted his employer adhere to the new unemployment laws, in the face of stiff resistance:

> In my case I met with considerable resistance from my employer vowing he would never pay. The first quarter period came to an end and . . . with much

> trepidation I had to point out again the situation and press for the money. Finally he relented and almost threw at me the four shillings and four pence needed coupled with a string of hard words.[108]

Ward clearly understood his rights and responsibilities in the new system, and was willing to be aggressive to get his due.

During the years 1911 to 1914, the growth of working-class awareness became so noticeable that government members began to comment on it. George Askwith, the Cabinet's chief labour negotiator, pointed out in 1911:

> The cheap press and the increase in all means of communication have made the workmen more homogeneous and more in touch with one another. They are more inclined to act in masses, and more conscious of their numbers and strength.[109]

Askwith highlights the linkages between workers, their growing sense of each other, and their group inclinations. But he again focuses – perhaps not surprisingly given his position – on the adversarial nature of this new generation. Was he right to think that the workers thought themselves strictly adversaries of the government and all its positions?

On the surface, Askwith certainly seemed correct. The labour unrest of 1911 to 1914 strongly suggested a hostile working class. And, perhaps more pertinently, the developing working-class view of the world seemed opposed to war. Joseph Leftwich remembered a speech at a working-class association he attended in 1911 at Bethnal Green:

> We fight against war . . . because the people suffer from the war. Think who does the dirty work in the war! Tommy! And what benefit does Tommy get from the war? I tell you what benefit Tommy gets from the war. Tommy gets shot in the war. That's what benefit Tommy gets from the war.[110]

This analysis makes the implication that elites start wars and benefit from them, and that it is not in the best interest of the workers to support them.

Nor, as we have seen in Chapter 2, did things seem to have changed by the summer of 1914. Up to almost the very moment of Britain's entry into the war, the workers still seemed opposed. Yet, as soon as the war started, the working classes demonstrated an immediate and active support. Was this not a paradox? How could the working class reverse itself so completely after 4 August 1914 and fight for a government of which it remained suspicious? Did the workers simply bow to the weight of social pressure and support a war in which they had no interest?

More confusingly, the evidence suggests that the working classes enlisted without relinquishing their scepticism. Working-class men formerly opposed to the government enlisted. Despite James Murray's 'socialist leanings', he 'felt sufficiently patriotic to offer my services to the Army in that first week [of the war]'.[111] T. Macmillan remembered the stories going around at the beginning of the war:

> There were yarns in the air about the sons of lords and the sons of crossing-sweepers joining up and serving the ranks together. We were told that class barriers had broken down, and that all were going forward to meet the foe as brothers-in-arms.[112]

Macmillan was clearly sceptical of the 'yarns in the air'. The passive construction of 'we were told' and 'all were going forward' reveals a sense of doubt. Despite that, Macmillan enlisted because he believed that 'all classes were agreed' on the need for an 'equality of sacrifice'.[113]

How could what seems to have been a class-based consciousness turn so easily from resistance to cooperation? How could active union members join a campaign by and for their oppressors? This is perhaps the central question behind British enlistment in the First World War. Any attempt to prosecute the war would have been useless without sustained popular support. And popular support meant working-class support. Did the 'hurly-burly' of enlistment truly drown out the 'rationalists'?[114] Were the volunteers simply 'cannon fodder', 'infected' with the 'virus of right-wing patriotism' to be used by an uncaring government?[115]

The simple answer is that the paradox is an illusion, fostered by a misunderstanding of the fundamental attitudes of the working classes. The endorsement did not, in fact, contradict the earlier industrial militancy. Too much literacy and knowledge did not make the workers rebellious, as the elites had feared in the nineteenth century.[116] Instead, their knowledge made the working classes believe that, for good or for ill, they had an investment in Britain. Their wider worldview led them to fight for better working and living conditions in peace-time; in wartime, it made them willing to consider defending the larger nation. Horace Astin, a cotton mill worker and member of J.P. Hindle's Weavers' Union, had fought the labour battles of the pre-war years. When the war came, he reacted with the same activist sentiment:

> I felt like a lot of patriotic people felt in those days, that Germany was against us and we wanted to do something about it and that we were doing the right thing.[117]

'Us' – Astin believed that Germany was against 'us'. He explicitly lumped himself in with the larger nation, with the rest of the working class and with the middle and upper classes. He included himself as part of a larger whole, a whole responsible for Britain's defence.

Astin was not alone. Workers followed the war news and related it to their own positions. It existed not merely as an adventure play to be read, but events connected intimately to their lives.[118] E.E. Rickus, afloat off the Dardanelles, analysed the action of the minesweepers in a letter home:

> I should like to tell you about thoes [sic] Brave fellowes [sic] they are continually going up the Dardanelles sweeping for the mines and they have very little protection and when you come to think of the guns and the number

66 *'A sense of the round world'*

> of them that are at the narrows you will see that their job is run with considerable Danger [sic]. They have had the thanks of the Admiralty and they certainly deserve the thanks of the whole of the working classes of Great Britain for until the mines are clear we cannot get to Constantinople and with the fall of that city means the fall of the price of bread as there is tons of grain here waiting to come home.[119]

Rickus linked, in his mind, the action of the trawlers, distant from Great Britain, and the price of bread in the marketplace. He believed that the crews of the minesweepers were making an effort on behalf of all of Britain, including the working class. He implicitly placed the British working class in a larger hierarchy that encompassed the Dardanelles, Constantinople, and Russian grain. More importantly, he gave the workers a place of responsibility in that hierarchy. It was the same sense of responsibility that led the workers before the war to go on strike or to force their bosses to comply with the unemployment laws. They acted as members of a national polity with rights and responsibilities.

The difference between working-class generations showed clearly in these enlistments. Men enlisting often found themselves unable to talk to an older generation about their actions. Rather than the pre-war 'parental wrath', as E. Buffey put it, workers found parents who simply did not understand.[120] Rather than understanding but disapproving, many working-class parents simply failed to comprehend their children's actions. When W. Jaeger, a labourer, told his mother of his enlistment, she 'said "Don't take so silly." I laughed it off, glad that I had broken the ice and caused no argument.'[121] Jaeger's mother reacted not with disapproval or by forbidding the attempt, but with denial. She seemed not so much to disapprove of it as to find it out of her realm of comprehension.

Even in September 1915, a conversation between Percy Ogley and a friend's mother revealed the way in which the two generations talked past each other:

> My pal Jerry Platts came bursting into the house, and knocked me for six off the stool. 'Come on, Percy, I am going to try to enlist, are you game?' 'Game? Good Lord haven't I been eighteen times? Hasn't my mother caught me in the Recruiting Office, hopping about with only a smile on? Yes, I am game for anything, come on.' 'Don't go,' says Mrs Butcher. 'Look at all those poor lads, who went from here. Poor devils, all shot up, gassed, blinded, shell-shocked, and ruined. What does the Ruddy government care? Look at me, five kids, youngest two, and goodness knows when my boss will come home.' 'Ah well, Mrs Butcher, we all can't stay at home, somebody must go.' 'Why? You're only babies, they'll not have you.' 'Well, good morning, Mrs Butcher, we'll go and see,' and we went.[122]

Percy did not so much disagree with Mrs Butcher here as simply act as if the reasons were beyond her comprehension. He responded with a platitude ('we all can't stay at home, somebody must go') and when that failed to convince her, simply left. He did not bother to argue with her, as if someone of her generation was not worth the effort. Some of this reaction may be the natural incompatibility of teenagers and parents. Still, it is striking to see that, in September 1915, talking of the horrors of trench warfare produced such an indifferent reaction.

Sometimes the indifference went the other way. J.H. Hird's parents were noticeably apathetic to their son's enlistment:

> The war was something remote. They had become aware that I might become involved, but that would be my affair. They knew, when I did not come back home, that I had done something about it.[123]

It was not that they supported or opposed the war, or disagreed with Hird's decision to enlist. They simply did not care: it was his 'affair'.

Unsurprisingly, when many of them reached the front and experienced fighting for the first time, they found the world little resembled their conception of it. When W.J. Shewry briefly encountered his brother Leonard, who had enlisted before the war, in France, all that passed between them were 'those three immortal and historic English words "You bloody fool"'.[124] Many of the volunteers came to agree with that assessment. The mud, decay, and danger of the trenches provided a rude shock for many. Though the British character forbade the too-explicit display of emotions, especially negative ones, some hints of dismay travelled home. In a letter to his family in 1915, J.A. Wilkinson avoided any mention of his unhappiness, but it rang through nonetheless. 'What I have done cannot be altered so I will have to go through with it. . . . It is done now and cannot be undone.'[125]

But whatever their reaction when they got to the front, the fundamental point remains that the 'rush to colours' of late August 1914 and the steady and large-scale enlistment that occurred afterward was fundamentally shaped by the new working-class view of the world. This wartime generation of workers came of age in an era which inundated them with information, most warning them of the imminent war with Germany. James Brady, who was working half-time in a cotton factory when the war started, believed that 'we'd been steeped in war, really, the generation of Edwardians. The Boer War had just finished, you see, and it was Buller and Kitchener and Wight and Baden-Powell and bands in the park on Sunday.'[126] The workers did not receive such propaganda uncritically or without scepticism. They were influenced by it, but they shaped it to fit their needs and their concerns.

This working-class paradigm formed the foundation for all of the enlistment motivations. Men could not have enlisted for allegiance reasons if they had not understood for what or whom they were fighting. They could not have made economic calculations without grasping the economic hierarchy of which they were a part. They could not have sought adventure and escape without having a vision of the world outside their home. At the root of their motives, varied and different as they were, lay a single supporting factor: their increased awareness and sophistication and their belief in a larger empire and nation. H.G. Wells, the writer, identified the change:

> The working man today reads, talks, has general ideas, and a sense of the round world; he is far nearer to the ruler of today in knowledge and intellectual range than he is to the working man of 50 years ago.[127]

As John Horne has put it: 'Nation and labour, nation and working class, were perceived . . . to be intimately connected.'[128] Workers were repressed, acted upon, and manipulated, but they also showed a fundamental understanding of their place in society and their society's place in the world. They believed in a Britain that was not necessarily the state. It was a Britain in which they had a stake. It was a Britain worth defending, whatever the sins of the government. As R.W. Farrow said: 'At a public meeting I strongly denounced the warmongers who had stumbled into this terrible situation; "but," said I, "we are actually in it; we shall have to see it through; all of us must help."'[129] The 'we' that he spoke of was both a working class and a national 'we', one that linked the workers and the warmongers into a single alliance, however awkward. Historians may or may not agree with their actions, but robbing them of responsibility for their actions is both inaccurate and demeaning. Workers realized that they had choice before them, and made their decision. It was for war.

5 'The monotony of the trivial round'
Enlistment and the escape from domesticity

For working-class men, their view of the outside world contrasted badly with the confinement of their own lives. Some working-class men saw enlistment as an opportunity for adventure, a chance to see foreign lands, and a way to experience the world. The war promised escape and adventure. It was fought in foreign lands, against a well-known enemy. It seemed likely to end quickly. Working-class men could join and be paid for the excitement of fighting. They would get away from the confinement of their familiar world and break out to a recognized but never experienced foreign world. And, often, they could go with their friends. It was adventure in familiar company. For many, such enlistment resembled a larger version of the territorial summer camps they knew well.

This quest for adventure grew from an overwhelming sense of constraint. Workers before the war lived tightly contained lives, captured in a cycle of work and home life, rarely able to escape from either. Work had become much more regimented than it was for previous generations: stricter working regulations, the need to be in the factory within certain hours, the inability to escape the machine for which they were responsible, all tied workers tightly to their servitude.[1] This routine was mirrored at home by comparably restrictive domestic and matrimonial roles for both men and women.[2] Such confinement bred frustration and a longing for release.

The physical circumstances of workers were similarly circumscribed. Though many workers moved frequently in search of jobs, they usually ended up in a replica of the place that they had left; industrial slums like the Merseyside in Liverpool and the East End in London strongly resembled each other.[3] A male worker lived his life in the narrow confines of neighbourhood and workspace, and within that, in the cramped quarters of crowded houses and factories.[4] Perhaps the only break from this was the pub, the theatre, or, for some of the better-off workers, a week by the sea in August. Women were, if anything, even more confined.

This domestic confinement was all the more galling coexisting, as it did, with the 1914 generation's broadly expanding sense of the world around them. They read and encountered newspapers, magazines, books, music hall performances and the like, that introduced them to Britain, Europe, and empire, and all they had to compare those stories to were the shabby limits of their domestic world.

When the war started, many working-class men believed that it offered an enticing alternative to their lives. They could escape abroad. For the first time, they could join the Army without fear of censure from their neighbours and families. The combination proved irresistible. Most believed the war would end by Christmas, or spring of 1915; by enlisting, they thought they had agreed to six months of travelling. Few gave much thought to the danger of wounding or death. This idea of adventure focused not so much on killing Germans or invading Germany as on a simple escape from England, from the warrens of the inner cities, from the dully repetitive factory work.

Only after a few months, after the continuing reports of massive British casualties, did men come to understand the full scope of the industrial war they were fighting. Even then, the quest for adventure did not die away completely. There were always some who believed that nothing was worse than their current situation, and that the army offered escape and freedom. They joined thousands of like-minded compatriots in the Army.

Confinement

The fundamental escape was physical. The houses and flats in which the workers lived tended to be both cramped and crowded. The demands of the industrial economy drew thousands of labourers into densely packed urban communities. Those slums were not pleasant. One reformer described an industrial slum in Southampton in 1890:

> The small, close, dirty, and evil-smelling streets, generally blocked up at one end, sometimes at both, the maze of little courts and passages leading out of them, with their wretched tumbledown houses closely packed with human beings, with no provision for decency or cleanliness, [are] dismal, wretched, squalid and hideous beyond words.[5]

In the late nineteenth century, the government had acted to limit the density of these slums, most critically in the 1890 Housing of the Working Classes Act, which set minimum standards for house size.[6]

But continuing requirements for housing caused a wave of building in the late nineteenth century that aimed to get the maximum number of people into the minimum space. Building uniformly, entrepreneurs found they could get forty-one houses to the acre. The results were long, parallel rows of houses, 15 feet wide, with a few square feet of garden space in front and an alleyway at the back.[7] All the houses looked much the same, with three bedrooms upstairs and two rooms below. Such residences frequently housed large numbers of people. In Barrow in 1911, an average of 6.7 people lived in such a three-bedroom house. Three-bedroom houses containing ten or more people were not uncommon. Tom Stockton remembered growing up in such a situation, the eldest of eight children living with his parents in a two-bedroom house.[8]

Routine bound working-class families. They might rise at five or six in the morning, have a small breakfast consisting of tea and bread, and then go their separate ways. The wife, after the husband left, began the household chores which dominated her day: laundry, cleaning, mending, shopping, tending to the children, stoking the stove, and hundreds of other domestic tasks.[9] Though not tied to set work hours, women rarely had the opportunity to stop and rest. Infrequently, if ever, did a working-class wife go further than the nearest shops. Mick Burke's mother in pre-war Liverpool hardly ever escaped the physical confinement of her neighbourhood or the hard work of her domestic routine. Only at holiday time could she arrange some sort of relief:

> The only time she had off was Whit week, when the house would be stacked with food and we all had to help ourselves. She'd say, 'It's my week this week,' and be on the booze all week, made up like the first lady of the land.[10]

The walls of a working-class woman's house defined the greater part of her world.

By contrast, the husband's world encompassed the work-place as well, but this offered little improvement. Most workers worked ten- to twelve-hour days, with only brief breaks for lunch and tea. G. Phippen's father, a farrier, worked from six a.m. to late evening, Monday to Friday. On Saturday, he only had to work until six p.m.[11] The work usually involved highly repetitive actions that offered little of interest to workers. Joseph Leftwich complained in 1911: 'I am just weary of having to do work which has no interest for me – weary of having to do the same thing over and over again, every day, from a certain hour to a certain hour, measured and weighed and found correct.'[12] The conditions were usually cramped and insanitary. Albert Williams remembered the situation at his factory in pre-war Manchester.

> There was one toilet on each floor to fill the needs of about 24 males and this small room was so much infested with the repulsive-looking insects that a thick stick was permanently kept there to deal with them.[13]

B.L. Fensom remembered the faces of the people travelling with him on the seven a.m. 'workman's train' to Southwark Bridge. 'There was no happiness in this ride, people looked tired and dejected and hardship was plainly discernible on those faces.'[14]

Upon leaving work, the men might find time to drink in a local pub or a working man's club, but many simply went home and collapsed in front of the stove. William Holt's father, who hauled coal for a local firm, had no energy left at the end of his day to do anything more than nap. 'He rarely played his fiddle now. No sooner had he sat down in his armchair after tea than he fell fast asleep.'[15]

As a result of these conditions, both husband and wife spent the larger part of their lives in the house. The wife, because that was where her responsibilities were, and the husband, because he was simply too tired after work. William Nicholson, whose father was a railway worker, remembered that 'the only time my mother went out was on Saturdays to do the shopping and my father never went out after he came home from work.'[16]

Food was routine as well. For many, the take-out of a 'penny piece of fish and ½d worth of potatoes' constituted the only luxury in an otherwise meat-poor diet, heavy with bread and potatoes.[17] Each worker consumed an estimated 6.7 pounds of bread and 1.6 pounds of potatoes per week. Meat was, as historian Ellen Ross has pointed out, a luxury. In the working-class world, to eat meat was to signal prosperity.[18] The quality of their everyday diet is reflected in working-class volunteers' reaction to Army food. Non-working-class enlistees were 'disgusted' with the 'unpeeled potatoes, gristly meat, and watery gravy'. Working-class men, by contrast, thought the military food 'splendid', as H.V. Jones wrote to his mother in 1915.[19]

Workers did fit some recreation into their lives. A working-class family might go to a music hall for entertainment, or to a football game, or simply for a walk in the park. C.R. Allcock talked about the diversions available for working-class families, both children and adults, in pre-war Bakewell:

> For [the working class], life was confined to town activities, mainly organized by the religious bodies, with regular periodic diversions provided by the bustle of cattle and produce markets, the fairs, Volunteer Reviews, and the visits of travelling concert and theatre companies and circuses.[20]

Children had things both better and worse. In many ways, they had more freedom than their parents. But they were also largely at the mercy of their parents, a mercy that was not always kind. B. Rudge's father used to say '"I'll see as you blighters have nothing of mine," and he used to swear at us, he used to call us his Arabs, he didn't know our names, he didn't want to know our names.'[21]

Physical abuse was not terribly uncommon. How widespread abuse actually was is unclear. Child abuse, as George K. Behlmer recently pointed out, was only fully criminalized in a series of laws passed between 1857 and 1880.[22] Available figures for domestic violence are unreliable, but suggest that reported cases of child abuse declined in the late nineteenth century.[23] Abuse certainly does not seem to have been a general condition. Nonetheless, clearly, some children did experience physical mistreatment. George Ashurst's father, who worked in a quarry, drank and beat his children.[24]

But the most universal pressure on a child was economic. Though they did not have the primary economic or domestic responsibilities that the adults did, most children were expected to help around the house or work to earn extra money for the family while they were in school. During their school years, most working-class children helped their mothers about the house or worked at a job part time. Female children typically stayed home and helped their mother with the domestic chores and taking care of the younger children. They became 'little mothers' at an early age.[25] Male children were most often sent to work. Frank Turner 'worked in part time jobs to help swell the family budget'. Horace Calvert took on a common job for working-class boys by delivering papers from an early age.[26]

But even with part-time jobs, working-class families could not afford to keep their children in school into their teenage years. Families frequently needed full-time income from their children as soon as possible. As a result, most working-class children usually left school at age 14 or earlier and went to work full time. Robert Sim, the youngest of eight, remembered that all his brothers and sisters went to work by age 13, either in the mines or in domestic service.[27] The child's earnings were handed over to the parents, and the child received an allowance. J.W. Horner gave his mother all the wages earned during a 48-hour week at an engineering factory. His only spending money was the daily halfpenny he received for coming in early and lighting the fires. That he spent on fish and chips and a weekly seat at the local music hall high up in the 'cattle pens'. 'Riotous living', he called it.[28]

Working-class children thus rarely made their own economic choices. Once the child reached an age at which he or she could earn money, further familial outlay on education or other training was a luxury. Any apprenticeship which required 'reasonable clothing' or 'tools of the craft' was normally out of the question, according to A.W. Hancox, the son of a bricklayer.[29] Even if the child won a scholarship for further schooling, the loss of income was normally impossible to manage. D.J. Price won such a scholarship but could not take it because his family needed the income he could provide.[30]

The children's working situation thus came to resemble that of their parents. They worked long hours, for little pay, with little leisure time, and little control. W.J. Kemp remembered the unhappiness of his job as a stable lad: 'I was soon fed up with it all YET tied to the job. . . . Life like this was not worth living.'[31] In some ways, the children's situation was worse than their parents'. Their smaller size made many jobs more dangerous for them. At age 13 or 14, most working-class children had still not reached their full growth. Put into adult, full-time jobs, they often struggled. When W. Watkins went down into the pit at age 13, he could barely keep his lantern from dragging on the ground because he was so short.[32]

Family gender relations exacerbated the sense of powerlessness felt by working-class boys. As the historian Ellen Ross has pointed out, the working-class home was one of the places where the patriarchal power was the weakest. Working-class women, to a large extent, controlled the expenditures and decisions made.[33] This constraint affected working-class husbands, but it bound young working-class men, out of school and still living at home, even more. With little money, both mother and father imposing rules upon them, and little chance of future relief, working-class boys most probably felt an urgent desire to escape. The war seemed to offer them that chance.

Visions of escape

This description is meant to show not the futility of the working-class experience, but the limitations upon it. Workers lived constrained lives, with release through travel, emigration, or upward economic mobility available to only a few. Some observers at the time, like Norman Angell, believed that this 'constant pressure of the social problem' distracted the working-class from larger visions.[34] In fact, the result was the opposite: a constant longing for escape. Workers thought and dreamed of ways to break out of their lives and to have an adventure. This was not entirely a new feeling. P. Boydell, whose father worked as a painter, remembered how his grandfather emigrated to the United States:

> Grandpa took time off in order to make the journey to Liverpool with a few friends to see one of them board a ship as an emigrant bound for America. . . . None of them had ever seen the sea and what they saw on arrival at Liverpool put the fear of God into at least one of them and he was the prospective emigrant. The ocean was too ominously big, the ship too dangerously small and nothing could be done to get him aboard. The passage was booked, the fare had been paid and the ship would have sailed with an empty bunk had not Grandfather then and there made up his mind to take his place. Whether this quick decision was made because he could not bear to see so much money and opportunity wasted or that he saw this as a heaven sent excuse for reckless adventure and a temporary release from his responsibilities as a husband and father we shall never know. Anyhow he left on that ship sending messages back to his wife and family.[35]

That Boydell's grandfather would so casually and recklessly leap at the chance to go to the United States reveals, I would argue, a deep-seated lust for escape. But it also reveals the lack of knowledge of that earlier generation. Boydell's grandfather had never seen the ocean. Once given that awareness of and opportunity to escape, he seized it. He left his life behind without, it seems, much of a second thought. In 1914, by contrast, the ocean came to the workers. They had seen the sea. When the war came, they felt that 'the passage was booked, and the fare had been paid'. They could not let the ship sail with an empty bunk.

For at the same time as the restraints on working-class life became stricter, a new generation had started to grasp the size and complexity of the world around them. Their schooling and their environment offered them images of a larger Britain and of distant lands. These images linked them to a larger national and global hierarchy. Their schooling connected them to an increasingly familiar Britain and an increasingly familiar empire. Such a mind-set made the younger generation unsatisfied with their lives. They wanted something more and it had to be something that fitted into the history that they had imbibed. A. Sharpe, a miner in Northumberland, 'did not know' specifically what he wanted, but it had to be 'something better' than the mines. It had to be a 'thumping good time'.[36]

Before the war, there were some opportunities for escape available. Even a fixation upon a gateway to escape could serve as a substitute. Thus, Frederick Hunt and his childhood friends focused on the railway station in their home town of Kirton. For them, it seemed an avenue of departure, a gateway out of their lives:

> We children regarded the station as a door to adventure and excitement which only the well-to-do and a few other privileged townspeople could enter –

doctors and lawyers, a few businessmen, and of course those intrepid young people who 'went for a soldier'.[37]

The railway station became for Hunt, as it did for many workers, a source of 'transfiguration', a way to remake their lives.[38]

Some found a limited release through fantasy. Many working-class children play-acted imperial and nationalist rituals at home. Dressing up as soldiers and other imperial adventurers brought the empire into the children's everyday world. A.G. Meacham recalled his Boy Scout camping trips and how he and his comrades had 'played at attacking other camps sometimes . . . delighting in mock battle with blank ammo, war cries and slogans'.[39]

Travel also offered escape. For many, emigration offered a chance to escape the confinement of their lives.[40] But, for most, travel was on a much smaller scale. Many working-class families managed an annual week at the sea .[41] For many jobs, however, there was no annual holiday. The only breaks from work were the bank holidays. Most important of these was the August bank holiday, the last holiday of the summer. Some workers, like D.A. Hodge, schemed ambitiously to break away from their life for that single day:

> 1914 found me in my fourth year of an apprenticeship as a printer, cycling seven miles to work and back on water-bound roads and in all weathers. There were, of course, no 'holidays with pay' in those days, and in fact a day off work was severely frowned upon. In consequence, bank holidays had a special significance and became occasions to be planned far ahead. The August one in particular was something special, as the last before Christmas and real summer to boot. Any travel beyond cycling distance was perforce by railway as the internal combustion engine was still in its infancy and a motor car the preserve of the upper classes. The railway companies issued leaflets concerning their excursions and I had been especially attracted to one advertising a day trip to Boulogne. The cost would be £1, which was quite a lot of money for one earning no more than ten shillings a week. But I talked it over with a friend, and we planned to make our first journey to the 'Continent'.[42]

Hodge's almost reverential view of the bank holiday, and the detailed (and expensive) preparations for an excursion to the continent, revealed the effort and imagination that he put into a momentary break from his apprenticeship. His account clearly showed the desperate need to break out and the lengths to which workers were willing to go to escape. They sought to break out of their lives, even if only a little, and for a little while.

Finally, young working men could flee their confinement by enlisting in the Army. It offered them escape from their home life. H.A. Biggle, the son of a hairdresser, left his family and joined the Army because he 'was fed up with home life'.[43] It offered them adventure. A.W. Hancox, a labourer, enlisted to 'find a channel through the uncharted seas, to the land of fulfilment, via the Armed Services'.[44] Enlistment offered them a way to begin a journey, to break out of the domestic straitjacket binding them tightly. But such enlistment was little favoured by the working-class community and men who enlisted had to overcome the disapproval of their family and neighbours.

One 'big attraction' that seemed to offer the advantages of the military while not suffering from such domestic disapproval as the Regulars was the Territorials.[45] The Territorials were attractive to working-class men for a number of reasons. They offered, as H. Moulds, a working-class man, said, 'activity to occupy my spare time'.[46] Perhaps most attractive of these activities were the two-week summer camps. Every year, members of the Territorials would go out into the country for two weeks and train.

Such a fortnight was powerfully attractive to many workers. S.P. Shepherd, a miner, felt that way:

> You worked full time and seven days a week. . . . [Joining the Territorials] meant that every year . . . you did a fortnight's camp . . . a fortnight's holiday with pay, food, and everything.[47]

Note, perhaps most importantly, that it was a *paid* camp, critical for working-class men. 'They were poverty-stricken days,' said A.E. Smith, an office boy, 'so that the prospect of a fortnight by the sea [i.e. the annual camp] for which one was paid a few shillings was enticing.'[48] The prospect of the two-week holiday even overwhelmed fears of getting involved in combat. Mr Hannah, whose father worked in the shipyards, recognized the possibility of being involved in a war when he joined in 1913. He nonetheless felt that the prospect of the two weeks' holiday was too enticing to pass up: 'I was taking a chance but we could have a fortnight's holiday.'[49] In a sense, the Territorials almost served as an adult version of the boys' clubs that so many working-class men had grown up with. It offered similar activities, and a break from their everyday lives.

But for the most part, escape routes remained expensive, limited, or simply unavailable. Men could break free of their domestic bonds only with great effort or large amounts of money. They lived a life of confinement, even as they continued to read of distant lands and distant adventures. They were trapped. The barriers to escape were simply too high.

The outbreak of war

The outbreak of war in August 1914 seemed to offer the workers an easy way out. It was an important event not restricted to the newspapers or the history books, and 'it were an adventure' in which they could join. C.H. Rolph remembered that he and his friends 'must have been typical of millions in our excited and rather bewildered surprise that war was not, after all, confined to the history books'. The conflict seemed to many working-class men to be an opportunity both to get a 'bit of relief' from the monotonous daily routine and travel to the world they had previously encountered only second-hand. During the initial 'rush to colours' in August to September 1914, many men took enlistment as an opportunity to escape the desperate circumscription of their lives, whether temporarily or permanently. 'Blow this!' thought Charlie 'Ginger' Byrne, an apprentice blacksmith. 'I'm off!'[50] They were no longer mute and passive spectators in the pomp of imperial pageantry but active and valuable participants.

For those who thought the war would be over by Christmas, it seemed to offer a brief respite. It was a short furlough, of the order of a bank holiday or week by the seashore. 'A glorious holiday', T.J. Simpson called it. The comparison to the Territorials' summer camp is inescapable. Working-class men could join up, wear a uniform, fight the Germans, and be home for the holidays. It was seductive. M. Martin, a miner, 'thought we were going to get three months' holiday and it would all be over'. The war was a break, a chance to interrupt their normal daily lives. A. Whiteley, an apprentice in a car factory, thought of it as a paid holiday: 'I will go and join up. It will probably be a six days' wonder. I will see a little bit of the continent and I will be back again.' But they had to hurry, so as not to miss it, they had to, as J.H. Hird remembered, 'get in before the end of the excitement'.[51]

Some workers, however, saw the war less as a holiday and more as a permanent escape from their current circumstances. They could enlist and change their lives in a lasting way. T.A. Bickerton, a carpenter's apprentice, hated his apprenticeship and the war gave him an 'opportunity to get away' from it. Robert Bird, a messenger boy who was going to night school, decided that he could escape from school by enlisting: 'When war broke out, Kitchener was in charge, so I joined Kitchener's army. I joined for adventure. I'd had enough of school.'[52]

But a common feeling ran through both sets of men. They compared their daily lives with what they conceived of as soldiering and found their daily lives sorely lacking. Enlistees mentioned most often unhappiness with their jobs. J. Jackson joined because he 'didn't like blacksmithing'. 'To be quite candid,' J. Murray, a miner, remembered, 'I wasn't particularly fond of working in the mines.' For Ossie Burgess, a single event crystallized his and his work mates' feelings. When a tunnel collapsed in their seam, Burgess said, 'I'm not having this. I'm going to enlist.' A number of his friends went with him.[53]

The pre-war experience of joining the Territorials formed their conception of soldiering. The two-week summer camps had led them to believe in an idyllic vision of military endeavour. J. Hartsilver, an office boy, contrasted such a perceived open-air nature of Army life with the stifling confines of an office. His language reflected such beliefs:

> Here was my golden opportunity for a healthy open-air life. The idea of war was a huge joke to me, as it must have been to other youngsters. I promptly asked permission to go off and join the army. . . . Better be a soldier in any capacity than a wretched office boy.[54]

That the reality of the war had not come home to Hartsilver is apparent. He thought it was 'a huge joke'. His anticipation of a 'healthy open-air life' suggests strongly the pre-war motives for joining the Territorials more than it does a patriotic rush to colours. Hartsilver wanted to go not because he was unemployed or because he felt the need to defend Britain, but because he was bored as a 'wretched office boy'.

The enlistees placed their adventures in the context of their knowledge of the larger world. They fitted them into the history that they had learned. William Tucker, the son of a labourer, linked his enlistment in August 1914 to British history:

> Analysing my feelings as I remember them, I would say that it was not 'King and Country' that held any special appeal for me. Nor was it the propagandized cause of Belgium that induced me to enlist. Rather it was the urge to seek adventure: the desire for thrills and new experiences. . . . the press representing it as an exploit akin to the famous charge of the Light Brigade at Balaclava. I wanted to be in such a charge![55]

Tucker's remarks suggest both the conscious historical awareness of the working class and the dubious accuracy of some of that knowledge.[56]

Some workers worried that joining to escape was not as acceptable a motive as patriotism. They believed that their society would condemn them for enlisting for a non-selfless reason. They thus cloaked their true motives in patriotism. B.L. Fensom, a salesman in a clothier's, though not feeling much in the way of patriotism, allowed his firm to believe that he did:

> The declaration of war offered an escape for me and the possibility of a new outlook on life and I decided to join the forces and take an active part in the fighting. . . . [My firm] accepted my gesture as an act of patriotism, but for me, it was to act for freedom and a new outlook on life.[57]

But for some, the desire for adventure genuinely coexisted with other motives, including patriotism. The war gave them an opportunity to be selfish and selfless. They could have an adventure, but also serve their country. The patriotism justified their other reasons. They were doing good for both themselves and Britain. James Macdonald remembered how he weighed his reasons:

> I was sitting in a chair deep in thought, my mind in a quandary whether I should keep on working, I was a hand putter at Bearpark Colliery near Durham, it was very hard work shoving eight cwt tubs of coal up very steep gradients, and under extremely wet conditions, or whether I should take Kitchener's advice, he was constantly pointing his finger at you, and saying, Your King and Country needs you. In the end, and after much thought, he won.[58]

Macdonald presented it as a problem with two opposing sides. Either stay in work or take Kitchener's 'advice' and enlist. But his description of work suggests that he had no love for the job. He abdicated the responsibility by saying that Kitchener 'won'. Clearly, though, Macdonald lost little in the outcome.

This first wave of enlistees signing up to escape seems to have been different from those who came later. The first wave had little concrete knowledge of the war. Instead, they relied on their pre-war experiences and beliefs. They wanted to escape the deadly dreariness of their domestic lives. What they were going to seems to have been, in their minds, a larger Territorial camp in a foreign country. H.F.M. Clark, who laboured for the London County Council, summarized the general feelings of the first wave of enlistees who joined in August–October 1914, 'seizing the opportunity to break the hitherto unspoken monotony of the "trivial round"':

> 'Join the Army and See the World', the slogan of recruiting posters during recent years certainly had its attractions for the volunteers in the early days of the First World War: travelling abroad was then the privilege of a comparatively few folk. In the main, only those with special responsibilities at home wanted to avoid foreign service. . . . The majority were anxious to 'see the world' and meet the enemy anywhere. True, the latter were then unable to appreciate all this decision would involve.[59]

They, like the rest of the British, had little idea of what they were going to. They knew only too well what they were leaving, but they had only shadowy visions of their destinations. Those visions, nonetheless, drew them.

The end of the rush and 1915

That first rush reflected pre-war conceptions of conflict. What the men knew or thought they knew when the war started shaped their decisions. 'Join the Army and See the World', H.F.M. Clark remembered. The volunteers in August and September were indulging an imperial fantasy, riding to the rescue of the embattled BEF and nation. After the end of the August–September rush to the colours, things changed. When Christmas passed, belief in a short war died away. As casualties grew, many stopped believing that the military was a happy alternative to their former lives. Now, they could see the reality of war.

Enlistment to escape nonetheless continued. Some of it was merely an earlier desire delayed by external factors. Jim Crow waited until December 1914 to enlist because harvest came in August–October and '[I was] doing more benefit for the country at large by staying on the farms.' When the harvest finished, he joined up.[60] H. Bartlett, a counter boy at a food shop, had tried when the war first started because it was 'an opportunity to get away from a distasteful job'. He was rejected as medically unfit and gave up until early 1915, when he talked to a soldier friend on leave: 'Walking out with him and yarning with him "fired" me anew. I'd get in "by hook or by crook".'[61]

But some of the enlistments were new. The desire for escape, even as knowledge about the war percolated through British society, still impelled men to enlist. Here, again, the difficulties with regard to sources make a quantified analysis problematic. Of those who enlisted for reasons of adventure and can be pinned down as to the exact date they joined, 58 per cent enlisted in 1914, while 42 per cent joined in 1915.[62] This suggests that adventure motivations became less powerful as the war continued, but nonetheless affected men throughout the voluntary period.

Certainly, the anecdotal evidence suggests as much. J.G. Barron joined in November 1914, desperate to escape the mines:

> Not from any sense of patriotism but as a means of getting out of the pit.... I didn't like it. It was too much hard work, it was rough.... It wasn't fit for humans. It was like rats and mice burrowing. It was terribly hard work.[63]

Even in January 1915, James Lowry and his friends down the pit in Houghton joined up for a holiday: they 'got out of the pit and ... thought [we] were going for [our] holiday'.[64] Though it was clear, by then, that the war would not be short or pleasant, neither Barron nor Lowry seemed to factor that into their calculations. The opportunity for escape seemed to blind them to their destination. Escaping the mines to go to the Western Front hardly qualified as going to something 'fit for humans'. They went, nonetheless.

This wilful blindness continued through the rest of 1915, as men continued to enlist for reasons of adventure. The continuing stream may have been made up by a more youthful group of men than the initial wave. Young men just reaching the age of enlistment or close enough to pass were particularly fixated on the idea. J.A. Malcolm, who had just reached the age of 18, joined in March 1915. He remembered that he 'suffered from the exuberance of care-free youth and looked upon war as a delightful adventure and nothing would serve my desire than to get into the fighting line as quickly as possible'. W. Slater thought that his 'main motive' for joining in March 1915

> was a desire to see the world in a way that had hitherto been quite impossible. As a boy a few years earlier, I used to think ... that it would be a wonderful experience to see London even, let alone any foreign country....[65]

Horace Calvert, still only 15 years old in 1915, nonetheless enlisted in September. The 'exuberance of care-free youth' can also be seen in his reasoning:

> I wanted to be in the services, to take part in the war. I looked upon it as a big adventure. I'd read all those adventure stories in the wide world magazines in the local library. It made me feel, what a nice life, adventure! ... I thought it might be more exciting. It was a dull life, just work.[66]

Perhaps a large proportion of the 'escape' enlistments came with this sort of adolescent mind-set. Again, a note must be made of the unreliability of any statistical analysis. The sources, especially the oral history sources, are distinctly biased towards younger men. Using such sources to identify the age of those enlisting for reasons of adventure risks reaching a wildly inaccurate answer. But, perhaps, a limited sense of the relative number of teenagers present among the adventure volunteers can be found by eliminating the more obviously prejudiced sources. Throwing out all the oral history interviews (which took place in the 1960s, 1970s, and 1980s) eliminated the largest source of bias in this pool of enlistees. The percentage of teenagers in what remained was 60 per cent.[67] This suggests that teenagers did form a large subset of those enlisting for adventure. The particularly powerless position of adolescent males in working-class households and a teenage sense of invulnerability may have led many to overvalue the adventure they would find in the mud of Flanders.

It should be noted that service in France did not necessarily disappoint them. Horrifying as the Western Front could be, some found what they wanted in the military. B.A. Keogh wrote back from France in December 1915:

> It is nearly four months since I crossed the waters and I, like others, have seen a few things which I never dreamt of seeing when I was plodding along in my unchanging Leeds haunts. The most exciting time I've ever had on the front was not long in coming for it awaited me as soon as my draft reached the firing line.[68]

Even in those sanguinary times, the military promised and sometimes delivered adventure and escape from the realities and confinement of working-class life, an escape that workers seized. That the adventure for many ended with an anonymous gravestone in France or Gallipoli or the Middle East is without a doubt. But if workers failed to understand the length or magnitude of the task they undertook, so did the politicians or generals who ran it. The workers who enrolled in the spirit of adventure sought not primarily to kill Germans but simply to experience the larger world they had read about for many years. They thought less of death and destruction than of escape. Less of killing and being killed than a simple chance to taste the world of which they had heard so much. It was innocence, of a sort.

6 'Money was the attraction'
Enlistment and economic motives

Working-class men also had very practical reasons to enlist. The state of the British economy meant that for many enlistment was preferable to their existing circumstances. Such economic motivations ranged from the simple to the complex. Volunteers saw the military as an avenue of economic advancement, a way to improve their skills, gain new ones, or find a job. The wages offered by the Army rivalled those of many working-class industries. When the free food, housing, and clothing were added to this wage, the economic incentive became even stronger. On top of the personal benefits, an enlistee's family received a separation allowance. A man could join, earn money, take the burden of housing and feeding himself away from the family budget, and deed a weekly allowance to his parents, wife, or children. In an uncertain economic environment, marked by stagnant wages and unemployment and under-employment, this seemed a reasonable bargain for many men.

The pre-war industrial situation increased the economic pressure on Britain's working class. Beginning in the second half of the nineteenth century, Britain steadily lost economic ground to other industrial powers, most notably Germany and the United States. Britain began the half-century as the strongest economic power in the world. But while her economy grew in absolute terms, other economies grew much faster, thus shrinking Britain's relative lead. In 1900, the United States surpassed Britain in manufacturing output. In 1913, Germany also passed the British. Imperial assets, as one contemporary noted, were supposed to act as a counterbalance and provide a 'bulwark against . . . cosmopolitan competition'.[1] But the colonies proved a mixed blessing. Though the empire contained riches, the subsidies required to organize and defend the imperial hinterland meant the profit to be made was minimal, if not non-existent.[2]

The empire put two more stresses on the British economy. First, the sea-borne communication lines between metropolitan Britain and the colonies demanded that Britain remain the pre-eminent naval power to ensure her empire's survival. When Germany started to build up her Navy with the aim of rivalling the British, His Majesty's Government had to respond.[3] The ruinously expensive naval race that resulted diverted capital away from investment to naval ship-building. Second, the empire diverted capital. External investment opportunities, in both Europe and empire, pulled money out of Britain. As a result, the pool of money for financing the industrial infrastructure shrank.[4]

The group suffering the most from this economic stress (with the possible exception of the colonized peoples) was the British working class. Workers at the very bottom of the economic scale bore the heaviest burden, but even those industries that had previously provided secure and reasonably well-paid positions suffered. Shipbuilding, textiles, and steel manufacturing felt keen competition from cheaper producers in America and Germany. The coal industry, although still globally dominant, slipped from its position of near monopoly in the 1880s to mere preponderance in 1900.[5] The rise of wages, explosive during the last twenty years of the nineteenth century, slowed down and unemployment increased.[6]

Working-class incomes and safety nets

By 1914, workers felt economically insecure. The slow movement of wages, underemployment, unemployment, and the lack of completely comprehensive safety nets meant that many believed themselves only a misstep or two away from the poor house. The obsession was to find a job with a 'keeping wage', that paid enough to feed, house, and clothe one's family.[7] This could be very difficult, and if a family's income was not enough, certain items had to be gone without. For many working-class children, that meant going without shoes.[8] For many, though, it meant going without enough food. Frank Turner's father found enough work to 'just . . . keep out of the workhouse', but Turner often went hungry for days at a time.[9] At the time, because of lack of money, around 30 per cent of working-class families lived a state of constant malnourishment.[10]

Single men, unlike families, had a range of choices. They were not tied to their families and were thus more geographically and professionally flexible. One option was emigration. The two leading choices in the period 1880–1914 were Australia and North America.[11] Another option was enlistment. Before the war, men who sought to escape unemployment filled the ranks of the British Army. J.M. Lane was one. The son of a shipyard riveter in Sunderland and one of three children, he could find work only rarely before 1914. He finally joined the military: 'I was off [from work] and I was sick of doing nothing and I went and joined the Army.'[12]

But joining the Army pre-war was viewed with suspicion by working-class communities. The exception to this suspicion was the Territorials. Men could join the Territorials without making a lengthy or time-consuming commitment and without leaving their family and friends. Most importantly, becoming a Territorial had economic benefits, though not as large as the Army's. For A.E. Smith, the 'few shillings' earned as a Territorial kept him out of a 'poverty-stricken' state.[13] Even those earning a wage found the added money attractive. 'Two weeks' camp, Two shirts, and a pair of boots free with pay, more than we were receiving at work,' wrote one working-class man.[14]

Working-class men with families were in a fundamentally different situation from single men. Their freedom of movement was more restricted, and the economic burden they carried was higher. Children caused both the biggest drain on and the biggest addition to a family's budget. The worst time for most working-class families was just before the eldest child finished school.[15] At that point, the children were too young to work or could only work part-time because of school. Their feeding and clothing demanded the lion's share of the budget, but they contributed little or nothing to their upkeep. The 'long years' was how E. Buffey's father described this period.[16]

This picture of insecurity and poverty did not apply to the entire working class. Some industries survived and even thrived, and the result was an upper stratum of well-paid and reasonably secure earners. W. Slater's father had a full-time job as a compositor that lasted throughout Slater's childhood and paid a reasonable wage. As a result the Slater family was relatively well off. Slater never suffered the shortages that other working-class children did. His family could even afford the luxury of a week by the sea, or an 'Edison phonograph costing two guineas'.[17]

But even such a privileged situation did not prevent feelings of insecurity. Slater's family was dependent on a single bread-winner. Its status was unstable and could change drastically for the worse with little warning. If anything happened to his father, they would have been quickly impoverished. Slater's mother 'was haunted during a great part of her married life' by the prospect of a 'long spell of unemployment or illness'.[18] Either could have reduced them to the status of other families who had difficulty in merely feeding themselves.

These feelings of insecurity were not helped by government and charitable safety nets. Only a few institutions helped the un- or under-employed. The Poor Law offered some help, but its tendency to split up families made it a solution to be avoided at almost all costs.[19] Short of the poor house, local authorities did attempt to help alleviate poverty. Mick Burke grew up in Ancoats, a slum in Liverpool. The help there was doled out by the police and the schools. Each day, his teacher would ask whose father was unemployed. Those children who raised their hands would be given breakfast and dinner free. The teacher would also inspect the children's footwear. Children without shoes would be given 'free lace-up clogs' by the police. Made of wood, they marked the poorer children out by the 'clatter' they made.[20] Some religious institutions also offered support, as Frank Turner remembered: 'the various Churches in the district did their best to help with such as Dinner Tickets and aid to Children and Down and Outs'.[21]

But the greatest source of relief in the immediate pre-war era was the unemployment programme introduced by the Liberal government in 1909.[22] The programme had two main effects. First was unemployment insurance. No longer, as Arthur Ward remembered, did the old mantra 'no work, no pay' hold true. The insurance was a 'great change' that ended for many working-class families their feelings of economic insecurity.[23] Second was the network of bureaucracies set up by Lloyd George to assist in job-finding. Labour Exchanges opened in working-class neighbourhoods and provided unemployed men with help in searching for jobs. R.S. Patson was one of those unemployed men. In 1911, he registered at one and received 'several interviews for jobs thereby'.[24]

Unemployment insurance, however, reached only a limited number of people. Though the Liberals broadened the coverage in March–April 1914, many remained outside its purview.[25] Either they did not work in a protected occupation or they did not work consistently or long enough to gain coverage. William Cowley's father, a bricklayer, could not receive unemployment insurance payments because he rarely had a single employer for a substantial period of time.[26] As a result, although the government schemes helped, the workers' economic position remained fundamentally insecure up to 1914, with few options for advancement or safety nets against disaster. Most working-class families remained a prolonged illness or two away from poverty, and the little done by either private citizens or the government reduced that risk only marginally.

The beginning of the war

The war did not bring an end to the difficult economic times. The initial months of the war were actually a time of economic decline. 'Slack times', one observer called them.[27] Many industries lost the markets for their goods, either because of the blockade of Germany or because the European nations at war could no longer afford foreign purchases. As a result, during the first months of the war, unemployment increased. And, although wages went up, the cost of living increased faster, a disparity that would not correct itself until 1919.[28]

Several industries were notably affected during the early days of the war. The coal industry initially weakened. The shipping and storage industry, dependent on the movement of goods into the European market, suffered. The textile industry in the north, robbed of some of its main markets, declined. Closing of northern mills pushed Lancashire into a sharp economic downturn.[29]

This downturn seems to have pushed men into the army. There are no general statistics on the number of unemployed who enlisted in the first months of the war. Nonetheless, a lot of anecdotal evidence suggests that men joined because they needed the cash. As Isaac Rosenberg said: 'There is certainly a strong temptation to join when you are making no money.' F. Battersby, who worked in the storage industry, turned to the Army. He said that he 'wandered around the town looking for work and on the 3rd of September feeling very fed-up . . . I got into the [recruiting] queue'. When Bill Albin, the son of a domestic servant and a construction worker, looked around at his fellow enlistees, he concluded that they had enlisted because 'they were all out of work'.[30]

Underemployment also played a role in enlistment. The number of men on short time (less than a full week's work) increased to 26 per cent of the active labour force.[31] Men who could not get full-time work found joining up an attractive option. The instability of the civilian economy contrasted negatively with the surety of the army wage. J. Newsted, a miner in Hetten le Hole, enlisted because '[t]he pits were only working two days a week and we couldn't get kept'. G.E. Ramshaw worked in a colliery. The lack of business there meant that he could only get three shifts a week. The underemployment decided him on enlistment, and justified his long-held interest in the military: 'I always liked to be working and I couldn't get enough work and I always had the desire to be in the Army. It was in my blood somewhere.'[32]

Some of the unemployment had nothing to do with the economic downturn. Unemployed men of an eligible age found it difficult to find a job because companies refused to hire them. When Arthur Bonney's firm shut its doors at the beginning of the war, no one would hire him. 'Nobody else would take you on, because you were 19, of military age.' As a result he joined up, just 'for a job, really'.[33]

Some of the strikes during the early period of the war seem to have helped recruiting. Men out of work, without wages, saw the Army as an opportunity to earn money. When George Pollard, an apprentice at an engineering firm, and his work-mates went on strike in September 1914, they felt the loss of wages keenly. Some joined up to replace the salary:

> There was a strike on then and this was why so many joined up. I can't say it was mine. I just wanted to go into the Army. As an apprentice my wage was 10/6d a week. Because we were on strike we got nothing. When you joined up you got 21/- a week.[34]

Pollard's co-workers joined to replace their lost wages and even his denial rings slightly hollow, in view of his detailed knowledge of the relative salaries of the apprenticeship and the Army.

Army wages could be attractive. Pollard cited a wage of 21 shillings a week, which must have been for a specialist position, perhaps a mechanic. A private (second class) earned 8 shillings 9 pence in 1914. The Army considered that the food it served was worth a further 5 shillings a week, bringing the soldier's pay to 13 shillings 9 pence per week. As the soldier rose in the ranks, his pay went up: a corporal earned about 12 shillings a week and a sergeant earned 16 shillings a week.[35]

This wage was low, but it compared favourably to certain working-class professions. The weekly pay of agricultural workers when the war started, for example, ranged from a low of 13 shillings in Oxford to a high of 23 shillings in Northumberland. Other workers earned more. Men in the building trade earned from 29 shillings a week (bricklayers' labourers) to 43 shillings a week (bricklayers). Coal miners averaged around 33 shillings a week. Some professions earned substantially more. Cabinet-makers brought home 46 shillings a week and police constables earned 72 shillings a week.[36]

But though the Army wage was lower than that of many working-class professions, a married soldier could multiply his weekly pay. A soldier could send home part of his wages, and the Army added an allowance to support the family. Married men received a further 7 shillings a week separation allowance. Those with two children received a further 18 shillings a week.[37] Bringing those together, a soldier with a wife and two children could receive the equivalent of 31 shillings 9 pence per week for himself and his family, a not inconsiderable sum.

Even if that wage did not quite match payment for full-time employment, the steadiness of the job often appealed to men whose civilian occupations were less than reliable.[38] P. Carroll figured in 1914 that, combined with the separation allowance of 15 shillings a week, enlistment meant that he could support himself and his family more easily than in his domestic job of carrying firewood, a notoriously weather-dependent occupation.[39]

The economic calculations proved particularly potent for younger men. Younger men earned less, averaging 11 shillings 10 pence per week in 1914.[40] As a result, the military wage alone often surpassed their salaries. R.E. Foulkes was earning 11 shillings a week as a plumber's apprentice and so the Army salary seemed to be 'great wealth' to him. A.G. Ransley, an office-boy, though he was 'no war hero', found out from a colleague that he 'could earn more in the Army'. That decided him and he joined in late 1914.[41]

Younger men could also use the separation allowance to their benefit, by providing for their parents and siblings. The allowance meant not only money for the new recruit's family, but a higher allowance for him as well. Suddenly, they had become bread-winners, responsible for a respectable contribution to the family welfare. Many of those men had been pulled out of school at the minimum age to work and support their families. They were expected to make money immediately. Many found that difficult before the war. Unemployment and underemployment limited their earnings. Their continuing status within the family as a mouth to feed exacerbated that failure. 'My mother was poorly in a country home and my father had six other mouths to feed,' Jeff Pritchard remembered. The situation led him to join in 1914 at the age of 14.[42] J.W. Roworth's mother had a fairly typical reaction. His enlistment dismayed her but only until she found out about the weekly allowance. That, Roworth remembered, 'made her very happy'.[43] In some cases, it allowed the son to supplant the father. Winnie Parker's father, who worked on the Ship Canal in Lancashire, came home during the first week of the war and said that 'there'd be no more work for who-knows-how long'. Her teenage brother spoke up with a solution: 'he told Mam not to worry, as he'd join the army and give her his pay'.[44]

The men who volunteered were thus continuing the economic calculations that they had been forced to make all their lives. How could they arrange the situation such that they and their family would get the most benefit? Joining up promised them a regular wage, a potential allowance for their families, and one less mouth to feed. It meant that they confirmed their status as bread-winners. And with the end of the pre-war attitude to enlisting, working-class men could now make that economic choice without courting disgrace.

Complex economic calculations

Enlisting for a wage was a simple monetary calculation. Many men made more complex economic reckonings when they signed up. Some men looked at the soldiers on leave, often men they knew, and saw how their position had improved. Civilian men saw enlistees who were better dressed, healthier, and, in some cases, physically larger, and decided that such benefits made enlisting worthwhile. On a more tangible economic level, the Army also offered work in a range of specialisms. Many men looked to these openings to use or improve their own skills. Some saw them as a way to learn a new profession. Some saw them as a way to gain experience that would prove useful in civilian life.

The Army played up the specialized positions in its advertising. Frank Turner, a clerk, remembered seeing 'adverts in Daily Papers applying for men with special trades [the Army] wanted and they offered special rates of pay [for] trades like Blacksmith, Fitters and Turner, Saddlers, Bakers and Butchers, and Motor Drivers'.[45]

The availability of such slots affected men differently. Some men planned to enlist anyway, but the chance to join as a specialist confirmed their choice. A.J. Kingston looked to use his blacksmithing skills: 'Being a smith I tried for farrier jobs as horses was the transport of the day.' Some who otherwise might have remained civilians saw the openings and changed their mind. F.J. Orton ignored the initial recruitment call in August 1914. He had finished his apprenticeship and had found a job as a journeyman fitter in a lace factory. He was reluctant to leave his new job. Later, however, he found a position that suited his skills in the Army. Given the chance to continue in his chosen trade, he enlisted as an 'Armament Artificer Staff Sergeant' in the Army Ordnance Corps.[46]

Some men, employed or not, believed that the Army offered them training for a chosen profession. Particularly sought after was the position of officer's servant (batman), which many believed would prepare them to be domestic servants in civilian life. L.S. Price felt he could 'advance my station in civvie life' by becoming a batman:

> Like a good many at that time, I was employed in service – a footman to be precise – and as you may guess, not overpaid. It occurred to me that if I could obtain a post as officer's batman, it would further my credentials and [might] lead to all sorts of possibilities.[47]

In a profession like domestic service that did not have apprenticeships, the Army served as formal training for these men.

For some men, the military offered training not readily available in the civilian world. This proved especially true of jobs that required technological skills. In the civilian arena, the schooling required for these jobs was either not up to date or was prohibitively expensive. Charles Burne worked as an apprentice in a car garage prior to the war. But that job did not offer as much cutting-edge technology as did the ones available in the Royal Air Service (RAS). For someone who was 'mad on anything mechanical', the only choice was enlistment. So he joined the RAS as a mechanic.[48]

Others joined simply to keep their civilian positions. When an upper-class man enlisted, he generally left behind several assistants or servants. Sometimes, one of those servants refused to accept the separation. Guy Buckeridge encountered a man who was 'in ordinary life, a man servant. . . . His civilian chief had re-joined as an Engineer Officer and he had joined in order, if possible, to accompany him, as his Army servant.'[49]

Working-class men made economic calculations that did not necessarily include consideration of jobs or wages. Sometimes men felt that the physical benefit of joining up was enough to bring them to enlist. Soldiers returning on leave often exemplified the effects of such benefits. Seeing those soldiers convinced numerous others to go as well. For many men Army life proved the first time they ate or bathed with regularity. The food, alone, made a big difference to many. Robert Roberts, a youth in the slums of Salford, believed that the Army food was, for many, the best that they had ever had.[50] The training men received extended to more than the arts of warfare. G. Bird wrote home in 1914 that 'we have learned a lot about cleanness, to clean your teeth well, and to keep all the dirt off your heads, for it just causes bad germs and they cause diseases.'[51]

The enlistees, often stunted by years of hard, indoor labour and malnourishment, found that cleanliness, nutritious food, and physical training had an unexpected reward. After weeks of training and eating, H. Clegg and his comrades 'grew out of all recognition'. Men grew taller and gained weight. F.W. Webster had been roughly the same height at age 15 as he had at age 10. After he enlisted in the Army in 1915, he grew at a 'phenomenal' rate.[52] Such growth retroactively validated their decision to enlist. Whatever doubts they had about joining disappeared in the flush of good health.

When those men returned home on leave, remade by their training, they had a substantial impact on those they had left behind. Other men looked at them enviously and the soldiers' vitality often overrode reasoned objections to enlistment. Robert Roberts remembered the reaction:

> In the first few months of hostilities many local recruits returning on their first furlough astonished us all. Pounds – sometimes stones – heavier, taller, confident, clean and straight, they were hardly recognizable as the men who went away. Others, seeing the transformation, hurried off to the barracks.[53]

It may not be too strong to see this as a symbolic counter to the later reaction to dead and mangled men returning from the front. The memory of the physical health of the soldiers on leave may even have added more poignancy to the sight of many of them years later, maimed and crippled.

Speculation aside, however, it is clear that men made complex economic calculations about their prospects once the war started. Whether it was because they felt it would help their civilian career, give them skills training impossible to find in domestic life, or simply remake them physically, men joined to gain economic benefits. They saw the military as a place where, materially, they could get what they wanted.

Economic motivations, the government, and anti-war groups

Both the government and anti-war groups were aware of such economic calculations. Both tried to use such reckonings. How they attempted to do so reveals much about the way in which the British perceived the war.

The government tended to talk about economics as a subset of other issues. The implication of much government propaganda was that men were joining for patriotic reasons but, nonetheless, were wisely considering the monetary aspects. Anti-war groups, on the other hand, tended to address such ideas in a more class context, ignoring patriotism in favour of appeals to class solidarity.

90 *'Money was the attraction'*

Army propaganda from the start addressed the financial issues of joining the military. An August 1914 recruiting pamphlet emphasized:

> You are not asked to serve for the money you can make out of it, but to help your Country. At the same time it is worth mentioning what the conditions of service are.... The private soldier in the Infantry on joining gets six shillings/eight and a half pence a week clear of all expenses. In other branches of the service, the pay is higher. It is also naturally higher for those who become non-commissioned officers or do special duties. For terms consult the nearest Recruiting Officer, whose address you can ascertain at any Post Office or Labour Exchange.[54]

Two features mark this discourse. First, the lead line of the quotation neatly sidestepped the issue of patriotism. By making it clear that it did not believe that men should join for purely economic reasons, the government assumed an unspecified, presumably patriotic motive for enlistment. The 'it is worth mentioning' of the second sentence reinforces that implicit point. The pamphlet thus implicitly freed men from feeling defensive about any financial reckonings they might make. Second, the last line revealed the bureaucratic link between Recruiting Offices and Labour Exchanges, further evidence of the military's awareness of the economic motives of enlistees. Where better to convince a man that his best interest lay in enlisting than in an office designed to find jobs for those unemployed? William Beveridge, head of the Board of Trade and the man who oversaw the Labour Exchanges, specifically ordered his divisional managers to 'draw attention of unemployed men to the posters, and in every way assist the recruiting officers as much as possible'.[55]

Nor was the government alone in making economic arguments about the war. Those who opposed the war used similar reasoning. On 21 August 1914, the Independent Labour Party (ILP) passed out a pamphlet at a Welsh colliery, arguing against the war in explicitly economic terms:

> Hardly less dreadful is the position of the women and children at home who are dependent on those who are under arms, and the countless workers and their families who are plunged into unemployment and destitution by the war. Almost no conceivable effort – even if the food supply of the country holds out – will prevent the occurrence of fearful privation amongst them.[56]

This was a more general, collective argument than the one made by the government. The ILP used language that appealed to the workers as a group, and emphasized the need for group solidarity to stand against the war. But the appeal was to economic interests, nonetheless. Some of these collective appeals also recalled the pre-war situation. At an anti-war meeting in London on 4 September 1914, organized by the ILP, the lead speaker, Ernest Pack, argued that:

> I do say this – a man has no right to volunteer [to join the Army] – if by volunteering he leaves his wife, his child, or his mother at the mercy of the

charity of his country.... Is this the way the richest country in the world ought to behave?... You see at every street corner 'Your King and Country Need You'. I suppose they do, but it's rather a new discovery, isn't it? Charlie Wilson didn't say that during the strike, did he?... Plenty of death and a hell of a lot of 'glory' but precious little grub for your wives and kids at home.[57]

This direct language aimed at the day-to-day economic struggle of workers who might enlist. But the language and example harked back to the union unrest of 1911–1914. Pack attempted to repair the severed connection between the pre-war and wartime and remind his audience of the fundamentally adversarial relationship between labour and government.

The war progresses, the economy grows

As the war continued, the situation changed. After the first few months of the war, the domestic economy expanded, led by the north. After December 1914, demand and pay for skilled workers increased in both the military and the civilian world as Britain geared herself up to build and equip a mass army. Wages increased by 10 to 15 per cent in 1915. In the industries controlled by the Ministry of Munitions (and thus clearly critical to the war effort) wages went up by a minimum of 25 per cent and a maximum of 70 per cent. Unemployment fell to 1.1 per cent in 1915 and to 0.4 per cent in 1916, the 'irreducible minimum'.[58]

'There never were such times for the working class', H.J. Cripps, a domestic servant, thought in 1915.[59] The poverty driving much of the earlier enlistment began to disappear. Unemployed men found jobs. Underemployed men got more shifts. Working-class families began making enough money to feed themselves. Robert Roberts recalled visible signs of this turnaround: 'abject poverty began to disappear from the neighbourhood. Children looked better fed.... The number of pupils taking free dinners at our school fell to one fifth of the pre-1914 figures.'[60]

Despite this upturn, economic motivations still led men to enlist. In March 1915, J.W. Horner felt dissatisfied with his pay at an engineering firm. Seven shillings for a 48-hour week was not enough for him. The military wage seemed to him to be a great improvement, and so he enlisted.[61] Nor did the news from the front discourage men from joining for economic reasons. W.E. Baker was the son of a railwayman and had a job in late 1915. On his way to work, he 'often bought a paper to read how our troops were faring'. Despite the stories he read and despite his employment, he was, 'as usual, short of pocket money, [so] I called at the local recruiting office, and signed-on'.[62]

In late 1915, the threat of conscription began to weigh in the balance. Men could no longer expect either to remain in work or to choose a particular branch of the military. For those making the enlistment decision based on patriotism or a desire for adventure, this change probably meant little, although the shame of being conscripted as opposed to volunteering did affect those with patriotic motivations. But, for those with economic motives, the change loomed large. Choosing a particular specialism could mean a better wage and exemption from combat. If a

92 *'Money was the attraction'*

man was conscripted, such a choice would not be offered. Joe Woollin, a miner from Yorkshire, revealed the blunt economic calculations that went into many workers' decisions to enlist and their ready willingness to use the system to their advantage. Patriotic or not, workers, as Joe put it, had their 'eye on the main chance':

> To understand why he [Woollin wrote in the third person] enlisted from what could well have been a reserved occupation [coal mining] it is necessary to know something of his background. When war broke out in 1914 Joe was in his early twenties, married with a young daughter. He was a coal miner and his upbringing had not been easy.... Joe will readily admit that he always had his eye on the main chance, and soon found out that in the army the pay in the transport corps was well above that of the humble footslogger. He decided that when he joined up it would be as an ex-driver rather than as an ex-miner.... Joe was aware that, being young and physically fit, there would be no question of his future in the event of such conscription.... He decided that he would not wait to be conscripted, almost certainly into the infantry. He enlisted into a transport corps, diplomatically omitting to mention his occupation as a miner. By so doing he ensured that his army pay, plus his wife's allowance together totalled more than his earnings had been as a coal-miner.[63]

Clearly, Woollin, and no doubt other working-class men, included conscription in their economic calculations. With conscription on the horizon, those who wanted to choose a specific occupation had to hurry before they were drafted into the infantry.

Economic motivations: general?

Clearly, there is strong anecdotal evidence for economic motivations affecting enlistment. But were the sentiments expressed by these men representative? Did economic considerations influence many, most, all? Unlike other dimensions of working-class motivation, the anecdotal evidence on this issue can be easily tested against hard statistical data. The British government broke down enlistment by job, allowing a detailed dissection of the percentages of men joining up from individual industries. If economic motivations truly played a large part in enlistment, then workers in trades with rising wages and low unemployment would likely volunteer at lower rates than those in less successful businesses. Enlistment percentages would be lower in thriving industries than in failing ones.

The government's trade breakdowns roughly paralleled economic growth in the various industries. The government ranked occupations according to their importance to the war effort: those classified 'A' were industries in which more than 50 per cent of the workers worked on government contracts; those classified 'B' did 25–50 per cent government work; and those classified 'C' did less than 25 per cent. Thus, for example, shipbuilding was an 'A' industry; sugar-refining was a 'B' industry, and lace-making was a 'C' industry.[64]

As can be seen in Table 6.1, those trades without much government work (the 'C' trades) grew at a slower rate (1.7 per cent) than those with some government work (the 'B' trades, 4.3 per cent) and both expanded much more slowly than those industries with a great deal of government work (the 'A' trades, 15.5 per cent).

This employment trend becomes even more pronounced if female workers are included. Women workers made up a specially large percentage of the 'C' trades. The absolute number of women employed in the 'C' trades shrank after July 1914, reducing its employment growth substantially (see Tables 6.2 and 6.3).

Table 6.1 Trade classifications and male employment, August 1914–July 1915

Trade classifications	Number of men employed (1911 Census)	Employment growth (men)	Employment growth (per cent)
'A' trades	1,821,500	283,500	15.5
'B' trades	2,198,000	95,600	4.3
'C' trades	2,353,600	40,500	1.7
Total	6,373,100	419,600	6.6

Source: Figures from PRO CAB 27/2, Report from the CID on War Policy, 30 October 1915, Appendix XIII.

Table 6.2 Trade classifications and female employment, August 1914–July 1915

Trade classifications	Number employed (1911 Census)	Percentage of total workforce	Employment contraction or expansion (since July 1914)	Employment growth (%)
'A' trades	214,500	10.54	+39,200	18.2
'B' trades	475,800	17.79	+47,200	9.9
'C' trades	1,696,600	41.89	–16,700	–0.9
Total (female)	2,386,900	27.25	+69,700	2.9

Source: Figures from PRO CAB 27/2, Report from the CID on War Policy, 30 October 1915, Appendix XIII.

Table 6.3 Total employment growth, male and female, August 1914–July 1915

Trade classifications	Number of men and women employed (1911 Census)	Employment expansion (since July 1914)	Employment growth (%)
'A' trades	2,036,000	322,700	15.8
'B' trades	2,673,800	142,800	5.3
'C' trades	4,050,200	23,800	0.5
Total	8,760,000	489,300	5.6

Source: Figures from PRO CAB 27/2, Report from the CID on War Policy, 30 October 1915, Appendix XIII.

94 *'Money was the attraction'*

The economic expansion that started in late 1914 clearly concentrated in the 'A' trades (see Table 6.1). As a result, they offered working-class men steady jobs and reasonable wages. How did this affect enlistment? If economic motivations did play a role in enlistment, then the rates from the 'A' trades should have been less than the 'B' and 'C' trades. Table 6.4 shows the enlistment rates for the various trade classifications, both overall and of those within the eligible age range and fit.

The figures reveal heavier enlistment from less successful industries. Enlistment rates are lower in the 'A' and 'B' trades than in the 'C' trades when taken as a percentage of the total employed. Enlistment as a percentage of eligible men reveals the same pattern. Enlistment in the 'C' industries is again higher than both the 'A' and 'B' sectors by approximately three percentage points. These figures suggest that economic motives did indeed affect enlistment on a nationwide basis. Industries which, because of their government work, thrived during wartime sent fewer of their eligible men than industries that did not.

But this creates two problems. First, the different enlistment rates from the various trade classifications might not reflect economic motivations. Men in a 'C' trade such as, for example, the preserved meats industry, might have felt that they were doing little to help the British war effort. They thus might have left their jobs and enlisted out of patriotic motives, rather than economic ones. Conversely, those in an 'A' trade, such as explosives, might have felt that they were aiding Britain and thus stayed put in their jobs. Second, the 'A' and 'C' classifications are only a loose guide to economic success or decline. Not all 'A' trades expanded enormously. Not all 'C' trades collapsed. Within each set of classifications, some industries prospered or decayed more than others.

It is possible to correct for these problems. By examining the industries that grew or shrank at the most extreme rates, without regard to their trade classification, it should be possible to see whether the economic state of a particular industry affected enlistment. The results can be seen in Table 6.5.

They reinforce the earlier conclusion. Shrinking industries sent 20 per cent of their total workforce to the military, while the growing industries sent only 14 per cent. When only eligible and fit men are considered, the gap widened further, with shrinking industries having sent 58 per cent of their eligible men, while the growing industries sent 29 per cent. The highest enlistment for growing industries was 37 per cent (leather goods) while the lowest for shrinking industries was 46 per cent (tinplating). Nor does trade classification seem to have had much of an effect. The 'A' trade among the shrinking industries (tinplating) – although it had the lowest rate of the shrinking industries – still sent 46 per cent of its eligible men into the armed forces, a higher rate than any of the growing industries. The 'C' trade among the growing industries (preserved meats) sent 35 per cent of its eligible men, well below any of the shrinking industries.

The extreme cases, however, tended to be those with a small number of workers. Together, the ten industries in Table 6.5 made up only about 10 per cent of British industrial workers. They were thus perhaps not truly representative. The ten industries with the largest absolute number of jobs gained or lost (which were also, for the most part, those with the greatest number of workers) are given in Table 6.6.

98 *'Money was the attraction'*

The results are roughly the same. In industries which included 60 per cent of Britain's male industrial population, declining industries saw enlistment rates of 57 per cent of eligible men, while growing industries saw enlistment rates of about 43 per cent. Thus, whether classified 'A', 'B', or 'C', growing industries sent fewer of their eligible men into the army. But Table 6.5, though it suggests their power, does not conclusively prove the existence of economic motivations. All of the shrinking trades in Table 6.5 are classified 'B' or 'C'. All of the growing trades are classified 'A' or 'B'. Men still might have been leaving because they felt that their jobs did little to support the war effort.

To find out if this patriotic effect existed, an analysis of the enlistment rates from various industries should compare 'A' and 'C' industries that grew at similar rates. If the 'C' group in such a comparison nonetheless sent many more men to the Army, then it would suggest that patriotic rather than economic reasons were a better explanation for enlistment. Table 6.7 shows the enlistment rates for three 'C'-classified industries and three 'A'-classified industries.[65]

The average growth rate for the three 'C' industries was 6.86 per cent. For the 'A' industries, it was 8.57 per cent. The enlistment rates are roughly the same. In fact, the 'C' trades enlisted at a slightly lower rate than did the 'A' trades. Though this is not conclusive, it does suggest that economic motivation played a role in enlistment. It was not the only motive, otherwise men in growing industries would not have enlisted at all. But it suggests that economics had an influence.

There is another way to check for economic motivations. Rapid wage increases might tend to prevent enlistment, as workers realized that it would be to their economic benefit to stay in their civilian jobs. If economics played no role, then rising wages should not have had an effect. Did they?

Wages, on average, rose 5–10 per cent in the first year of the war.[66] Table 6.8 compares the enlistment rates for industries where wages grew at a higher rate than this average with those for industries that grew at a lower rate.

Table 6.7 Enlistment rates in trades classified 'A' and 'C', controlled for economic growth

Trades	Growth in employment, from August 1914–July 1915 (per cent)	Enlisted (as percentage of eligible), by July 1915
Textile dyeing (C)	8.1	49.5
Publication of newspapers (C)	5.4	39.5
Stationery (C)	5.5	58.5
Cutlery (A)	7.1	40
Manufacturing (A)	10.2	53.3
Wood boxes (A)	8.4	63.4
Total (C)	6.86	49.17
Total (A)	8.57	52.23

Source: Figures for Table 6.7 are from PRO CAB 27/2, Report from the CID on War Policy, 30 October 1915, Appendix XIII.

Table 6.6 Largest increases/decreases in employment by absolute numbers, August 1914–July 1915

Trades (class)	Number of workers employed	Number of workers of suitable age and physical standard	Growth/shrinkage in employment[a]	Enlisted	Enlisted (as percentage of total workforce)[b]	Enlisted (as percentage of those fit and of age)[c]
Building (C)	1,022,700	369,200	−46,000	196,400	20.11	58.28
Brick, cement (B)	77,800	29,200	−11,100	14,600	21.89	68.13
Quarries (B)	98,700	35,800	−10,300	14,100	15.95	49.32
Jewellery (C)	44,300	15,500	−5,600	7,700	19.9	66.49
Printing (C)	165,600	68,600	−4,000	34,900	21.6	53.04
Engineering (A)	588,400	233,900	76,500	114,700	17.25	39.9
Shipbuilding (A)	163,800	64,100	49,600	27,000	12.65	27.32
Iron/steel (A)	311,400	124,400	44,200	56,700	15.94	36.5
Coal mining (B)	1,121,400	458,000	40,400	247,800	21.33	50.96
Boots and shoes (B)	198,700	64,800	23,300	31,600	14.23	38.96
Total (shrinking industries)	1,409,100	518,300	−77,000	267,700	20.1	57.64
Total (growing industries)	2,383,700	945,200	234,000	477,800	18.25	43.08

Notes
a This figure is addition to the replacements for those enlisted.
b Formula is: Number Enlisted divided by (1911 Workforce added to Growth or Shrinkage since August 1914)
c Formula is: Number enlisted divided by (Number of age and fitness added to 70 per cent of growth or shrinkage since August 1914)

Source: Figures from PRO CAB 27/2, Report from the CID on War Policy, 30 October 1915, Appendix XIII.

Table 6.5 Industries with largest percentage decreases and increases in employment and their enlistment rates

Industry (class)	Number of workers employed	Number of workers of suitable age and physical standard	Growth/shrinkage in employment	Percentage growth/shrinkage in employment	Enlisted	Enlistment rate (of total)	Enlistment rate (of those fit and of age)
1. Brick, cement (B)	77,800	29,200	−11,100	−14.2	14,600	21.89	68.13
2. Jewellery, watch and clock making (C)	44,300	15,500	−5,600	−12	7,700	19.9	66.49
3. Quarries (B)	98,700	35,800	−10,300	−10.4	14,100	15.95	49.32
4. Tinplate (A)	22,500	8,700	−1,000	−4.4	3,700	17.21	46.25
5. Printing (C)	165,600	63,600	−4,000	−2.4	34,900	21.6	57.4
6. Small arms (A)	6,500	2,200	9,900	152	1,100	6.71	12.05
7. Explosives (A)	6,900	3,200	5,800	84	1,200	9.45	16.53
8. Shipbuilding (A)	163,800	64,100	49,600	30	27,000	12.65	27.32
9. Preserved meats (C)	12,700	6,200	3,700	29	3,100	18.9	35.27
10. Leather/leather goods (A)	66,600	23,700	19,200	29	13,900	16.2	37.43
Total – shrinking industries (nos 1–5)	408,900	152,800	−32,000	−8.68	75,000	19.9	57.52
Total – growing industries (nos 6–10)	243,810	99,400	88,200	64.8	46,300	13.95	28.73

Source: Figures from PRO CAB 27/2, Report from the CID on War Policy, 30 October 1915, Appendix XIII.

Table 6.4 Trade classifications and enlistment rates, August 1914–July 1915

Trade classifications (employment growth)	Total number employed (by July 1915)	Number of men employed (of military age and physically fit to serve)	Number of men enlisted (August 1914–July 1915)	Percentage enlisted (of total)	Percentage enlisted (of eligible and physically fit men)
'A' trades (15.5%)	2,105,000	727,200	368,800	17.52	50.72
'B' trades (4.3%)	2,293,600	841,700	435,200	18.97	51.7
'C' trades (1.7%)	2,394,100	875,400	473,500	19.78	54.09
Total	6,792,700	2,444,300	1,277,500	18.81	52.26

Source: Figures from PRO CAB 27/2, Report from the CID on War Policy, 30 October 1915, Appendix XIII.

Table 6.8 Wage increases and enlistment rates, 1914–1915

Profession	Wages in July 1915 (July 1914 = 100)	Enlistment rate (of eligible men; %)
Compositing	100	38.5
Cotton	103	34.0
Building	103	37.2
Average	**105–110**	**36.9**
Engineering	110	34.3
Agriculture	112	c.32
Coal	113	37.9
Woollen/worsted	115	26.0
Total (below average)	102	36.57
Total (above average)	112.5	32.55

Source: Census figures are in PRO CAB 27/2, Appendix XVIII; agricultural enlistment figures do not seem to be available. However, the Derby Scheme registration found the number of agricultural men of military age remaining in England in August 1915 to be 374,263 which shows an enlistment of 175,000, or 32 %.

The industries in which wages were growing more slowly than average sent 36.6 per cent of their eligible men to the Army. The industries in which wages were growing more quickly sent 32.6 per cent of their eligible men to the Army. This result is exactly what it would be if an economic motivation was one of several reasons that pushed working-class men to enlist. The evidence is not conclusive but does seem strongly suggestive. Economic factors did affect enlistment, exactly as many working-class enlistees said.

Problems with the statistical analysis

There are a number of problems with this analysis. First, the number of workers was adjusted by the government for medical rejections. The War Office assumed that 70 per cent of men between the ages of 19 and 40 would be able to pass the physical exam required for enlistment. There is no evidence to show that that assumption was correct or, more importantly, uniform over all industries. Thus, if workers from growing industries suffered a higher medical rejection rate than did those from shrinking industries, the difference would skew the enlistment rates. For example, a difference of 10 per cent in medical rejections between two industries alters the recruitment rates dramatically (see Table 6.8). If workers from the building trade passed the exam at a 75 per cent rate, while coal miners managed only a 65 per cent pass rate, then their enlistment rates would actually be about the same. The disparity in the unadjusted rates could be an artefact of the different physical conditions of the workers in the two industries. Certainly, with these two examples, an argument could be made for such a disparity. Coal miners, stooped in tiny, underground seams, breathing coal dust for 12 to 14-hour shifts, could have failed the medical rate much more frequently than those in the above-ground trade.

Is there any evidence to suggest that there was such a disparity between various industries?

Table 6.9 Change in enlistment percentages given various hypothetical medical acceptance rates

Industry (one growing, one shrinking)	Workers aged 19–40	Growth/shrinkage in employment	Fit (65 per cent)	Fit (75 per cent)	Enlistments	Enlistment rate (65 per cent fitness)	Enlistment rate (75 per cent fitness)
Building	527,400	−46,000	312,910	361,050	196,400	62.77	54.4
Coal mining	654,300	40,400	451,555	521,025	247,800	54.88	47.56

Source: Numbers carried over from earlier tables.

Pre-war statistics indicate that the government significantly underestimated the general medical failure rate of workers enlisting, but that such rates remained relatively constant across industries. In 1909, the medical rejection rate ran at 299 men for every 1,000 volunteers. Though this is in line with the government's 30 per cent figure, the height and weight standards were raised in 1910 and remained constant through 1914–1916 (excepting the two-month period in late 1914 when Kitchener raised the minimum height). Further, before the war, not all recruits actually underwent an official medical exam. Recruiting officers would 'weed out' potential recruits, rejecting men who would obviously fail the medical exam without letting them in to see the doctor. 'Such cases', one pre-war recruiting officer remembered, 'were not included in the medical rejections as shown in the medical officer's statistics.'[67] In the mad rush of August–October 1914, such screening did not take place. Recruiting sergeants simply did not have the time or the inclination to reject men out of hand for supposed medical deficiencies.

Later figures suggest that the 30 per cent failure rate reported in 1909 and during the war was low. S.T. Beggs, a pre-war recruiting officer, kept records of his enlistees. Of the 1,766 men Beggs inspected before the war, 848 failed the medical exam while 918 passed, a rejection rate of 48 per cent.[68] Since pre-war enlistees were likely to be from the lower levels of the working class, this figure may be higher than a similar one in wartime would be. It nonetheless suggests that the government's wartime figure of 30 per cent might have been low.

Beggs also broke down his figures by industries. Though his categories coincide only roughly with the government's classifications, the differentiation does give a sense of how the failure rate changed from one industry to the next. In essence, the pre-war rejection rate stayed at about the same level across individual industries. In unskilled industries, the rejection rate was 49 per cent while in skilled it was 47 per cent. Miner rejection rates ran at 43 per cent, lower than other skilled industries, but still within striking distance of the average.[69] Thus, in the example used in Table 6.9, there is no indication that the mining industry had an enormously different rejection rate from the building industry. Overall, while it seems that the government probably underestimated medical rejection rates for working-class men, the assumption, by the War Office, that the rejection rate was constant through all industries was justified.

Another factor could change the enlistment figures. The percentages are calculated by dividing those in the service in July 1915 by those working in the industry in the same month. The second figure is reached by adding the amount of growth or shrinkage in the industry to pre-war employment numbers. But that introduces another bias. Of those enlisted by July 1915, the preponderance would be between the ages of 19 and 40 (there was both over- and underage enlistment). There is no way of knowing the age breakdown of their replacements, though it probably contained fewer men within the eligible age range than the overall group of workers. If, as with the physical exams, the age percentages of the replacement workers differed between industries, that too would have affected the enlistment rates. If, for example, all enlisting miners were replaced by men between the ages of 19 and 40, and all enlisting ship workers were replaced by men over the age of

102 '*Money was the attraction*'

40, then by the beginning of 1915 the pool of men available to enlist from each industry would have changed significantly from the official figures. That change would, in turn, alter the enlistment percentages. That the replacement pool would have fewer workers of military age seems likely. Age-eligible men in that pool would also have enlisted in the 1914–1915 period, leaving ineligibles to replace them. But there is simply no evidence to suggest either such a skewing or its absence. Even if skewing did occur, there seems to be no reason to suspect that it would differ significantly across industries.

A final element of distortion in the enlistment figures was a result of government action. Those industries growing at the fastest rates, especially in 1915, were also those from which workers were forbidden to enlist by the government. Thus, for example, the government quickly forbade coal miners to enlist. As a result, part of the difference in enlistment rates may have related to members of a particular industry who attempted to enlist, but were refused. Was this factor responsible for the difference in enlistment rates?

The restrictions did not come into force until the beginning of 1915. Thus, if the limits did cause enlistment rates to skew, such an effect should not be visible in enlistment rates in 1914. Table 6.10 examines the enlistment percentages of ten industries, five 'A' industries and five 'C' industries. The classifications roughly correspond, as they did for economic growth, with industries from which enlistment was forbidden. If the enlistment restrictions had significant effects, then the December 1914 figures for enlistment should be roughly the same between the two sets of industries, while the April–July 1915 figures should show a sharp disparity between the two, with the 'C' industries contributing far more in the way of recruits than did the 'A' industries.

Table 6.10 Enlistment percentages of 'A' and 'C' trades, December 1914 and April–July 1915

Trades	Growth/shrinkage in employment, from August 1914 to July 1915 (%)	Enlisted (as % of men between ages 19 and 40), by December 1914	Enlisted between April 1915 and July 1915 (% of men between 19 and 40)
Building (C)	−4.5	23.8	5.4
Cotton (C)	2.1	18.7	6.8
Printing (C)	−2.4	23.2	7.1
Furniture/upholstery (C)	5.6	25.3	6.5
Bread and biscuit (C)	15.3	20.7	8.4
Engineering (A)	13.0	25.2	3.3
Iron/steel (A)	14.2	24.6	3.2
Shipbuilding (A)	30.3	22.7	2.1
Manufacturing (A)	10.2	26.8	4.4
Cycle/motor (A)	11.3	22.6	4.7
Coal (B)	3.6	24.0	4.8
Total (C)	3.22	22.34	6.84
Total (A)	15.8	23.77	3.54

This, in fact, is exactly what Table 6.10 shows. In December 1914, enlistment from the 'A' trades was slightly higher than that from the 'C' trades: 23.77 per cent versus 22.34 per cent. By contrast, the enlistment percentages from April–July 1915 show almost the exact reverse, with the enlistment rate in the 'C' trades almost double that of the 'A' trades: 6.84 to 3.54 per cent. On an annualized basis, recruiting in the 'C' trades remained at 20.5 per cent, nearly the same as it had been to the end of 1914. By contrast, on an annualized basis, enlistment in the 'A' trades dropped to 10.6 per cent, less than half of the end-of-year figure.

This suggests that the government restrictions did indeed affect the enlistment numbers. Therefore, the disparity between 'A' and 'C' trades noted above may have resulted from the regulation of the 'A' trades, not the economic problems of the 'C' industries. Does this invalidate the statistical evidence for economic motivations?

The effect in Table 6.10 could arise from factors other than government regulations. The most notable of these would be Britain's economic cycle in the first year of the war. It has already been noted that the British economy slumped in the first few months of the war and then began to grow steadily in early 1915. The 'A' trades led the way, fuelled by government contracts. This is reflected in Table 6.10. The 'A' trades in Table 6.10 grew at more than four times the rate of the 'C' trades. The effect seen in Table 6.10 could be produced either by government restrictions or the business cycle. As the economy slumped, all the industries would send a roughly equal number of men into the military. When it began to grow again, those industries which grew fastest would send far fewer men to enlist. Further, as already seen in Table 6.5, when controlled for economic growth, the 'A' industries actually sent a higher percentage of men into the forces, government restrictions or not. This suggests that it was the economic cycle that caused the fluctuation of rates between the 'A' and 'C' industries, not government regulations, though their effect should not be discounted completely.

Conclusion

In the end, the evidence strongly suggests that economic motivations underpinned many working-class decisions to enlist. The personal testimony of volunteers and the statistical testimony of enlistment figures strongly demonstrates such motivations. Outside factors such as age, physical fitness, and governmental restrictions may have affected the overall picture. But the primary influence was an economic calculation that influenced thousands of men. That motivation was not the only one in their minds. The desire to escape and (the subject of the next chapter) allegiance motivations also guided their choices. But economic factors played a large role.

7 'We were being patriotic. Or young and silly'
Enlistment and allegiance

> I was tall for my years. . . . Day after day, I saw men going off to the war and I also saw men coming back from France wounded and read about men who had died in action. My father warned me not to enlist until I was nineteen. All over the country, huge posters, with the picture of Lord Kitchener, and the words 'Your country needs you'. Went to Dundee and enrolled on 7 Jan. 1915.[1]

As is clear from the introduction, this is not a chapter solely about patriotism, though patriotism enters into it. Patriotism as a concept and as an organizational tool is both limiting and dangerous: limiting because it focuses only on allegiance to nation; dangerous because its meaning is deeply contested.

But what to do without 'patriotism' as an organizing label? It is clear that working-class men believed their enlistment served a greater good. Such a motivation was inherently different from the essentially selfish motives of economic gain and adventure. How should we proceed without falling into the conceptual minefield that is patriotism?

The critical distinction is that, while men enlisted for the greater good, that good was only sometimes a national one. Sometimes those working-class men felt that the war was justified to defend their families, their friends, or their region. They had an allegiance to something outside themselves, something they thought worth defending. It could be the British nation; it could be something else. 'Patriotism' was only a part of such allegiances, and thus, for the purposes of this chapter, I will focus on the larger category of 'allegiance' rather than the smaller category of 'patriotism'.

These allegiances effectively justified, in working-class minds, the actions of the British government. The government might have lied, signed secret agreements, and manipulated Britain into war, but fundamentally it was correct in fighting the Germans. 'I'm not at all keen on militarism,' A.R. Reid, an office boy, wrote on 28 August 1914, 'but for the first time, this morning I was forcibly struck with the fact that I ought to do something.'[2] Working-class men argued that something larger was at stake, whether family, friends, or nation. And, whatever the faults of the state, that something was worth defending. In its simplest form, a working-class man might say that 'a country worth living [in], was worth fighting for'.[3]

Some men, certainly, claimed patriotic feelings because they were attracted to the glory and adventure promised by military life, but many, before and during the war, had a deep suspicion of all things military. Their suspicion of the military rested on two main points. For some, the military reflected the skewed spending priorities of the government. Parliament spent money on the War Office, while millions of Britons suffered. James Page, who worked in an electrical engineering firm, thought that military spending could have been better used elsewhere, that the government was 'spending more on the army than they spent on the reduction of the slums'.[4]

For others, the military stood as the last refuge of unemployed or criminal men. Throughout the nineteenth century, few workers aimed for a military career, and few families approved of those sons who did join up.[5] In the 1870s, when William Robertson announced that he was joining up, his mother castigated him: '[The Army] is a refuge for all Idle people. I shall name it to no one for I am ashamed to think of it. . . . I would rather Bury you than see you in a red coat.'[6] Such feelings continued as the new century began.

This feeling seems to have continued even after the Boer War and into the first decade of the twentieth century. Horace Calvert, the son of an ironmonger, remembered that 'it was said that [soldiers] either won't work, or they've got a girl into trouble, or they've got some trouble and they're running away from it, joining the army to get away.'[7] When E. Rolph came home on leave after enlisting in 1908, his parents made their feelings clear. 'There was no emotional outburst, no feelings expressed either way. . . . When my father came home, he showed no signs of pleasure in seeing me, we did not even shake hands.' When Rolph left at the end of his leave, there was 'no expression of sadness'.[8] Even the reform and professionalization of the army by Haldane in the post-1906 period did not make a military career more attractive to working-class men.[9] Most men who joined up before the war disappointed their friends and family and gained neither social nor personal approval for their act.

But the war changed things. Society and, most critically, working-class society now judged that joining the Army was a worthy thing for men to do. Suddenly, the Army became an object of acclaim rather than derision. Now, the working class reacted defensively when the Army was criticized. Bert Chaney said that the 'whole British nation' was now 'so proud' of its regular troops.[10] That change in attitude extended to the individual soldier. E. Rolph, ignored by his family in 1908, came home to a very different reception in August 1914:

> All the people who knew me made a rare fuss and were all most generous towards me. Friends, relatives, and strangers were all contesting to buy me drinks down at the Coach and Horses, where I found a good few old friends of my schooldays.[11]

The working class had decided that Britain was worthy of a defensive effort. As the manifestation of that effort, enlistment was now greeted with approval rather than disdain.

A particular kind of patriotism

The patriotism of enlistees was strange in several ways. It differed from patriotism in other countries. Pre-war Britain, alone among the Great Powers, did not conscript its soldiers. It raised its army through voluntary enlistment. The use of the voluntary method continued when the war started. British men thus had actively to show their support for the war, rather than simply accept it passively, as did men in countries with conscription. W.A. Tucker reported that British voluntarism defied the understanding of foreign soldiers:

> That millions of men, thousands from all corners of the globe, should be volunteering to fight was something most other countries just did not understand. For example, when I was eventually a prisoner in German hands the German soldiers were fond of asking – 'Tommy: du freiwilliger?' (Did you volunteer?) When the answer was Yes, the German soldier would almost always tap his head to imply I was a lunatic.[12]

The British populace acted outside the experience of the rest of the European nations by not merely acquiescing to their government's actions but eagerly participating in them.

Such active participation seems odd, given the state of disenfranchisement of working-class men. The act of voting would seem to parallel the act of enlistment as a fundamental social ritual. Yet, when the war started, only half of working-class men were allowed to vote.[13]

Despite this disenfranchisement, working-class men expressed patriotic feelings before the war.[14] When the war started, such declarations continued and men joined for patriotic reasons. In a November 1914 letter to his family, T. Batty explicitly linked enlistment with the future of the country:

> I am glad to see the recruiting is improving we want as many troops as we can possibly get, the more we have the sooner the war will be ended, and any young fellows hanging back are only prolonging the country's agony.[15]

It was the 'country's agony' Batty was worried about, not his own, or his family's.

Even in towns where there was a great deal of pre-war opposition to the government, people supported the war. Albert Evans, the son of a steelworker, claimed that his hometown in Wales was known as 'Little Moscow' before the war. Nonetheless, he and his friends, as well as many other eligible men in the town, joined up. In Salford, where the army had been stationed in 1911 to prevent riots, the Pals battalion filled up within a week of its creation.[16]

Their support was of a particular kind, however. They would fight, but on their own terms. R. Hunter worked in a cotton factory and was married, with two children. When he went to enlist in August 1914, he was offered only the peacetime enlistment package of twelve years' active service and seven years in the Reserves. He walked out. Not until two weeks later, when Kitchener offered a scheme allowing enlistment for three years or the duration of the war, did Hunter return and enlist.[17] He wanted to fight the war, not just join the military.

Like Hunter, G. Bird, a groom, felt reluctant to serve in the Army longer than needed for the conflict. He wrote to his brother in 1914: 'I may tell you I want no future for the army. If I do my duty that is all I want.'[18] 'My duty', for Bird, was specific to the crisis facing Britain. This seems more a reasoned patriotism, aware of the circumstances, particular about its commitment, and strong-willed enough to reject an offer not to its liking.

Nor, when the volunteers actually entered service, were they any more willing blindly to accept their circumstances. Just as these new volunteers were particular about their terms of service, so too did they have definite ideas about conditions once in the Army. They had chosen to be there and their sense of duty did not extend to accepting the rigid discipline that marked the pre-war BEF. Before the war, James Page related, the Army 'thought more of horses than men. The idea was you could get a new soldier for a shilling but a horse cost £30.'[19] The wartime volunteers were not going to accept such an attitude. They willingly defied the military symbols of authority, with word and deed. R.M. Luther, a miner, challenged his commander on his first day of service:

> [The adjutant] wore a monocle, and after he had looked us up and down, said 'God Help England, if you are the chaps who are going to save her.' . . . Question time arrived, and I jumped up and said, 'Sir, what convinces you that we will all run when we meet gunfire?' He did not answer, but said, 'Take that man's name, for insolence.'[20]

James Dixon Macdonald and his comrades-in-arms tired quickly of their Army diet, resorting to tactics familiar from industrial conflicts to register their unhappiness:

> We had our first unofficial strike, we lined up along the roadside four deep with the full intention of marching to London in protest over getting too much bully beef and very little fresh meat.[21]

The sense is of a shared and cooperative effort, one which entitled volunteers to protest against the words of their officers and the quality of their provisions.

The government recognized that it was dealing with a more prickly group of soldiers than it was accustomed to. A government analysis of the working-class enlistee's motivation outlined the situation:

> Freedom is both an instinct and a passion with him (that is why he is fighting now). . . . He will place himself under discipline if discipline is part of the free contract; he strongly objects being placed under discipline by authority.[22]

Workers joined to defend their country, while remaining sceptical about the military and the government for which they fought. 'The traditional ideas of right, wrong, and duty . . . brought the crowds to the recruiting office,' said an Army officer, 'that point, and no other.'[23]

Finally, the decision to enlist was not a foregone conclusion. G. Ives had joined up in 1899 to fight in the Boer War because 'I don't know. A sort of, you want to fight for your country.' When the war erupted in 1914, Ives considered the situation again, but reversed his 1899 decision. Now a family man, he resolved to sit out the First World War: 'I had had my share of war. I didn't want it.'[24]

But, as already discussed, workers enlisted because of a wider range of loyalties than mere nationalism. The external allegiances that drove men to enlist ranged broadly, but all were, generally speaking, selfless. Men enlisted because they wanted to defend something larger than themselves, and that something was quite frequently not their nation.

Geographic loyalties

Some men enlisted to fight because of loyalty to a geographic area. They talked of a place, whether city, country, or nation, that deserved their service and their defence. That conception led them to join the Army during the period 1914–1916.

The most important of these places – of course – was nation. 'We, England, were confronted with something which was a very terrible matter for us,' said Tom Bromley to explain his enlistment. Such 'Red, White, and Blue patriots', in Francis Anthony's words, 'joined up at the first bugle call.' One of these volunteers said that 'I considered it my duty to join and help my country in her hour of need.'[25] Whatever their later feelings, at the time few working-class men lacked the conviction that Britain deserved defence. Such beliefs led them to join the Army.

The men were not necessarily warlike. Many did not feel the same sort of eager anticipation as did those who joined for escape motives. Some displayed raw scepticism about war even as they joined. But they felt the call of a larger national allegiance. A man by the name of Heptonstall summed up the process that he went through when he decided to enlist:

> When war broke out, a minor battle took place within me. I had no thirst for war, and I loathed the thought of having to kill someone. Yet I felt that I owed a duty to my country.[26]

Not all of this language of national allegiance spoke directly of Britain. Much of the language spoke of things that seemed to represent national allegiance symbolically. For example, much of the language of both working-class enlistees and government propaganda focused on Belgium and its violation. A recruitment poster from 1915 quoted Prime Minister Asquith as saying: 'We shall not sheathe the sword until Belgium recovers all, and more than all, she has sacrificed.'[27]

The plight of Belgium struck a chord among working-class men. Such fears seemed almost to substitute Belgium for Britain in the national consciousness. Belgium became a symbol of Britain. Arthur Ward, a hairdresser's apprentice, said that 'the national response was immediate and remarkable'. Such an event, he believed, 'could never be accepted'. A.J. Gosling, who repaired boots, spoke of the war as a 'just one' which England 'had declared . . . to uphold her honour and the freedom and rights of small nations to live'. The housing of Belgian refugees with British families only deepened that feeling. R. Burns's family, for example, put up a number of Belgian refugees and their stories made Burns think: 'Inwardly as they related their stories I felt that I ought to impress upon them we were doing something to help them get back home.'[28]

The obsession with Belgium seems an odd one. France was Britain's major continental ally. Belgium had remained neutral and uncooperative in the years prior to the war, and the treaty everyone cited dated back to 1839, prior to the unification of Germany. What then led the British people to have such an interest?

The invasion genre I have already discussed suggests one answer. The wide range of books and articles outlining a German invasion of Britain revealed the deep sense of vulnerability to attack many British felt. There is a sense of nervousness in the invasion literature that completely contrasts with, for example, the imperial literature before the First World War. The literature of empire was predominantly optimistic. Britain-in-empire was noble, persevering, and triumphant. The literature of British imperial exploits followed a certain form. British forces faced seemingly overwhelming odds but normally triumphed. The works of Rudyard Kipling and H. Rider Haggard spoke of imperial experiences that redeemed and revitalized Britain.[29] By contrast, the literature concerned with Europe emphasized British vulnerability, rather than her strength. The entire genre of invasion literature revealed an abiding British worry about her vulnerability to a European opponent.[30] The fears of vulnerability permeated both official Britain and the working-class population.

When the war began, it is not surprising that the attack rolling through Belgium in August and September 1914 reminded many Britons of their pre-war fears. J.H. Dible spoke of the conflict in Belgium in apocalyptic terms on 25 August 1914:

> [The Belgian town of] Namur has fallen. Namur which we believed could hold out for weeks against any odds. The clouds are gathering up for the thunder burst. For us the decision of the struggle in Belgium, and on the left of the allied position, will be of enormous moment.[31]

Once Belgium fell, could Britain be far behind? S.T. Kemp, a farm labourer, did not think so. The Germans would not stop with Belgium or even France. She was determined to 'come through Belgium . . . attack France, conquer them and then go for Britain'.[32] Kemp saw Belgium as the first domino in a row including Britain and France. Belgium's fate prophesied Britain's.

Belgium was not the only symbol that working-class men used when talking of their allegiance to nation. Many personalized the war by focusing on individuals. D. Stephen transferred his personal experiences with the Germans to the larger conflict as a justification for joining up:

> As young apprentices we were engaged often working on repairs on German trawlers round the Fish Docks. It was here that I, along with most of my pals,

developed an extreme dislike for the German fishermen we met. Some of us knew a little German and knew that they called us the Scotch B...s and English swine. Aboard one German trawler called the Olbers, when we were working all night we had a 'free-for-all'. They were all big men [German Naval Reservists]. I hit a big one so hard that I dislocated my right hand; this settled me. The war clouds were gathering. I had one burning ambition – if we were to fight the Germans, I was to be in it![33]

Stephen's attitude is of personal hatred for Germans, but he clearly connects this animosity to the larger country. The fishermen who enrage him are distinguishable only as Germans. Their characteristics, for Stephen, are national characteristics. They were bad and they were German; the two traits were indistinguishable.

But, of course, there were individuals ready-made for such symbolic use: the respective royalties. Many used the shorthand of the British King and the German Kaiser to stand in for the larger nations, both as symbols and as explanations. For B.W. Chenery the war came about because the 'Kaiser was very jealous of our King Edward VII'. The war itself was thus, Chenery thought, a personal betrayal of the friendship between the King and the Kaiser. Though 'the Kaiser would very often invite Edward VII over to Germany on shooting missions, he was really plotting to overthrow him and his Empire'.[34] By personalizing the war, Chenery used Britain's symbolic leader to make abstract issues concrete.

More importantly, it was not the Cabinet that was the focus of Chenery's beliefs, but the King. It was the symbolic as opposed to the actual ruler. This focus fits in with the 'sacred geography' of England, a 'closely held iconography of what it is to be English'.[35] By focusing on the King, the working-class volunteers asserted an investment in such Englishness. Such a claim was, in its own way, an assertion of belonging and power on the part of the workers. These traditions belong to us as well, the workers were saying, and that the elites of Britain can no longer exclude us. In the crisis of war, working-class enlistees could, just as well as the British upper classes, appropriate and alter England's sacred geography.

Perhaps the best example of this is found in the one leader who occupied a both symbolic and actual position in British life, the Secretary of State for War Herbert Kitchener. Kitchener occupied a symbolic space in both Britain and empire. Because he had spent almost all of his career outside Britain, he, unlike the King and Cabinet members, had not been caught up in the partisan political battles that led many to have mixed feelings about their government.[36] He was known to the populace only through the reports of his exploits. In the children's games of the generation of men who volunteered, Kitchener had been the plum role. R.J. Carrier remembered that his best friend Georgie had always had a 'fanatic' regard for Kitchener, 'and in our game sadly wanted to play that part; but no, I must always be Kitchener and he would have to take a lesser part'.[37] Kitchener appeared as an untainted exemplar of Great Britain and empire who had returned to Britain to save the nation.

Kitchener's image loomed over the British recruiting efforts, standing as a singular representation of the war effort. The poster of him, 'a huge face . . . a stern moustache and a pointing finger with the accusing slogan "Your King and Country needs you"', first issued in September 1914, proved particularly potent. A.W. Askew, a farm worker, said 'every time I saw the poster, with the finger pointing, Kitchener wants you, I felt I ought to go'.[38] It overstates the case to call the poster the 'most effective recruiting propaganda ever devised' as it did not appear until late October 1914, after the greatest rush of enlistment.[39] It nonetheless revealed the almost personal relationship many volunteers felt with Kitchener. G.E. Dale, for example, wrote of the situation this way:

> I was no hero, brass-hat, or even a golden boy. Just an ordinary bloke who volunteered for the New Army and had to go where sent, and do what he was told – more or less. But I like to think that, but for me, the great Kitchener would have been one short of his First Hundred Thousand – and I'm sure he would not have liked that.[40]

Dale had never met and would never meet Kitchener, but he felt a personal sense of the man, and did not want to disappoint such a living avatar of the British Empire.

But if the national allegiance drove many, it was not the only geographic loyalty that spurred men to enlist. Regional loyalties were also important. The four nations within Britain sent thousands to the Army, and many of them fought not for the honour of Britain, but for the honour of their homeland. W.J. Lynas wrote home to Ireland after the battle of the Somme had started in July 1916 and talked of the Ulster Brigade. His allegiance was not to Britain but to Ulster:

> They [the Brigade] did not disgrace the name of Ulster or their Forefathers little did you think as you sat writing that letter on the first day of July that our boys had mounted the top and made a name for Ulster that will never die in the annals of history.[41]

The Irish case was, naturally, somewhat special. As D.G. Boyce has pointed out, the Irish were never more than 'marginal Britons, included only peripherally in the British national image'.[42] The lengthy political struggle over Ireland's position within Britain meant that Irish allegiance was particularly conflicted. The infighting over Home Rule in the pre-war years had only exacerbated that sense of apartness.

The meaning of regional loyalty in Ireland was further complicated by the different religions. The Ulster Brigade held only Irish Protestants, men loyal to the British Crown and to the concept of a Great Britain which included Ireland. When the Liberal government tried to bring in Home Rule in the pre-war years, E.J. Brownlea had run guns into Ireland to 'delay' it. When the war started, he enlisted to serve under the same Liberal government because of his 'loyalty to the crown'.[43] David Starrett had been a member of the Ulster Volunteer Force before the war. At the beginning of 1914, he was ready:

> 1914 found me, like many another Belfast lad, all keyed up to fight. We in Ulster were ready and eager for fighting – drilling day and night. Outposts

were scattered over the length and breadth of Ulster and pickets were posted at every place of importance, particularly of course where we had our guns hidden. Yes, the lads of Ulster in 1914 were ready to fight. We were the Ulster Volunteer Force of Carson's Army. But little did we think we were drilling to fight not our own countrymen but the Germans.[44]

Protestant Irishmen clearly conceived of themselves as part of a larger Britain.

Catholic Irishmen, on the other hand, had much more mixed feelings about the British and the war. On one hand, John Redmond, the leader of the Catholic Irish Parliamentary Party, called in September 1914 for Irish Catholics to fight for Britain and thus prove their right to Home Rule. Over 140,000 Irish Catholics followed his advice.[45] On the other hand, there remained a great deal of scepticism among Irish Catholics about the war. One Republican, Ernie O'Malley, remembered that at many recruiting meetings when the British officer spoke of 'poor little Belgium', Irish Catholics spoke up to ask about the 'freedom of Ireland' and were promptly arrested.[46] Working-class Irish Catholics, unlike British workers, seem to have been surprised that the British wanted them to enlist. David Starrett, who after his enlistment spent some time as a recruiting officer, was told by the men he recruited that 'up to now no one had told them that [the British] recruited Catholics as well as Protestants'.[47] The sense of alienation from the British nation was profound.

Local loyalties on a smaller scale than individual countries such as Ireland also played a role. Loyalties to town and county influenced men to join up. The structure of Kitchener's Army played on such local loyalties. New Army units drew on a specific catchment area and became service battalions to Regular Army regiments, emphasizing their local nature. The Pals battalions continued that process by making organization and training almost completely a local affair. The 'Pals' battalions thus exploited regional loyalties and regional beliefs.[48]

The Pals battalions emphasized their local basis to induce enlistment. One technique was to put a local war hero up on the stage at a recruiting meeting. William Tucker attended a recruiting meeting at which a 'retired Colonel' from the area spoke. Tucker, as a result, was unable to 'resist the blandishments of "Your King and Country"'.[49] Another technique was to play on a sense of competition between localities. A recruiting meeting at Sunderland, reported by A.W. Askew, a farm worker, nearly ended in a riot after such tactics:

> The Earl of Durham was giving out the figures of recruitment of different towns and when he gave the Sunderland figures out he said, 'you men of Sunderland are not doing your duty.' I thought there was going to be a riot; the miners up and dashed towards the stage if they had got hold of his Lordship, I don't know if he would have got out alive.[50]

Personal loyalties

But if geographic loyalties to town, country, and nation played a large role, personal loyalties did as well. Men joined because they felt an allegiance to a specific person, or set of persons. For some, personal loyalties meant defending the objects of their loyalty. Men enlisted because, by doing so, they felt that they were defending either family or friends. For some, personal loyalties meant joining the objects of their loyalty. Men enlisted because others were joining or had already joined. Men enlisted to stay with their friends. Although some of these motives may have shaded into social pressure, for the most part, in the minds of the volunteers, the motives were selfless.

Workers often spoke of their allegiance to other people in non-specific terms. They enlisted because they felt a sense of duty to others, even people they did not know. A. Clayden, a saddler, joined up because he wanted Britain to be 'better for everyone' when the war was over. E.V. Crumpton thought that, 'although I wasn't particularly patriotic, from the angle of fellowship with the people, with the soldiers at Mons, I decided to join the army'.[51]

But for the most part, personal loyalties were to those the men knew already. Some of these loyalties were to friends. Such motives were particularly useful to the Pals battalions. A man enlisting in a Pals battalion entered not only an organization representing his city or region but, most likely, one that contained friends. Many joined the battalions to be with those friends. George Pollard, an apprentice, put it straightforwardly: 'I joined the Pals because my mates did.' Working-class enlistees often self-consciously created such a group by going *en masse* to the enlistment centre. G.E. Dale discussed the situation with several of his friends and decided that it was best 'to stay together like brothers'.[52]

Personal motives frequently centred on the families of volunteers. At the most basic, men with relatives already serving felt a lure into the army. Joseph Murray, the son of a miner, adored his older brother, Tom, who was in the Naval Brigade: 'To me, everything that Tom did was manly, and honest, I worshipped him though he did not know it.' When the war started, Joseph acted promptly to join his brother, walking 8 miles to enlist in the Naval Brigade.[53]

Even if no family members currently served, a history of military service could do the trick. For many young men, their earliest memories were of the victory parades for the Boer War. The marching soldiers marked many a child's mind indelibly. If a relative marched with them, it made the impression that much stronger. E. Buffey, a labourer, remembered:

> [The] martial desire [was] instilled into me when as a wee bairn my father hoisted me up onto his shoulders to enable me to have a good view of the victorious troops as they paraded through my home town on their return from the Boer War in South Africa. As the cavalcade neared my point of vantage, I was thrilled when a Sergeant reined in his fiery steed and pulled across to us, it was my uncle, my father's brother. For ever after whilst still a boy, I would always say that when I grow up I am going to be a soldier, ride a war horse, and carry a lance.[54]

Many working-class men saw an implicit connection between the war on the continent and their families. This feeling, in a sense, paralleled the personalization of the war noted earlier; just as many working-class men personalized the enemy, 'the Kaiser and his henchmen', so too did they personalize what that enemy threatened.[55] The conjunction of the threat of the Germans and family life occurred in many working-class memoirs. Family allegiance was simple, close to home, and easy to explain. It made the general specific. G. Bird spoke of this feeling in a letter to his mother. He fought because 'it is a matter of duty this war. I am out to save our home and you the same as millions more are doing.' J.G. Mortimer, a factory worker, decided three months after the beginning of the war 'that it was time for me to do my little bit towards protecting my family from the Germans (noble thought)'. Mortimer's cynical post-mortem ('noble thought') suggests a retrospective sense of the futility of such a personal, small-scale motive in such an impersonal, large-scale war.[56]

Some men believed that each family owed a duty to the nation. If one member could not go, then another must go in his stead. Rather than protecting the family from the Germans, these men fulfilled a responsibility. W. Potts, 'fired by patriotism', looked at the situation in 1915: 'War was still going on, so being the eldest of seven and Dad unable to go, I said to myself "Well here goes" . . . and [I] set off to join up.'[57]

But family allegiance did not always push a man towards enlistment. Some men felt that they should stay with their families rather than enlist. James Gerrard presented enlistment as the abandonment of family for little reward: 'Men who had enlisted to save Great Britain left their parents and jobs to risk their lives for 1/ per day.' Albert Attwood's brother was in the Army when the war started and Albert, a domestic servant, refrained from joining because he was worried about his mother: 'My eldest brother was already in the army, and for a while, thinking of leaving Mother behind, I held back.'[58]

Further, family allegiance was often presented by the parents themselves as a reason *not* to enlist. They objected for reasons ranging from religious conviction to an unwillingness to let an underage son go to war. D.A. Hodge, a printer's apprentice, found himself in the first category:

> My parents were Methodists and the thought of violence would appal them, so it meant quite a long mental struggle before I decided to offer myself 'for the duration'. I think my dear mother had a special dread that any of her three boys should be a soldier.[59]

J.R. Hart managed to compromise between his family's opposition to killing and his brother's and his desire to serve their country. He enlisted in the Territorial Field Ambulance because his 'family had reservations about destroying human lives and prepared its sons to work rather for the saving of life'.[60]

The mother of a man named Carr reacted violently when he enlisted underage:

She said you little bugger I will scald you for that and she picked up the kettle of boiling hot water off the hob and my mates ran out of the house. I didn't see them again until I got to Sunderland and I ran into the toilet and my Mother brayed that door down with her fists and shouted out come out here and I will teach you to enlist.[61]

Families, in the end, proved a mixed allegiance. For some, family loyalty meant enlistment. They wanted to defend their family. They believed their family owed a duty to the nation. They wished to imitate a relative who had served or was serving. For others, family allegiance made enlistment more difficult. Parents might object for a variety of reasons, or the son might have to stay home to deal with illness or impoverishment. If there is a common theme between the two sets, it is that, in both cases, family allegiance proved the dominant one. Men made decisions based mostly on their personal loyalty to their families. They might be to enlist. They might not. Both, in their own way, put their families first.

How much were such motivations self-generated and how much were they the products of external pressure? Changing the label of such motivations alters them significantly. Calling them 'allegiances' to family and friends locates them in a larger body of motivations that can be labelled selfless. Calling them 'giving in to peer pressure' puts them into a realm of external societal pressure. Which of the two is correct?

This is not necessarily an either/or question. A more sophisticated analysis would locate the motivations along a spectrum. Some felt they were joining for selfless, voluntary reasons, without too much pressure from outside. Others, like Arthur Groves, a piano-maker, felt that (though he joined up under the Derby Scheme) because of the social pressures upon him he was 'more or less conscripted'. Many may have felt such pressure, as Albert Barker suggested: 'Everybody was joining. Thousands upon thousands, so we all went, of course.' Clearly, his allegiance was mainly the result of duress. T. Leithead experienced similar duress. He eventually signed on because his mates pressured him and not without a fair amount of resistance: 'I was the same as the rest. My mates joined up and I followed them. They used to plague my life asking me to join with them and I eventually did.'[62] His language indicates a reluctant enlistee, one going only because he felt the pressure of his peers.

But not all who joined up for their friends echoed Leithead's attitudes. W.J. Barker, a paperboy, felt more enthusiastic: 'I joined up when I was old enough, because all my friends were joining up. I thought I had better get a move on and join up too, to give them a hand.'[63] 'To give them a hand.' Such words speak of a vastly different sentiment from Leithead's, a difference more of kind than degree. Barker's emotion seems to have been an allegiance to his friends and peers, a commitment to supporting and sharing their experiences. P. Morgan felt similarly; he joined because he thought that doing so would help protect 'the security of my friends'.[64] As with family, the impulse was one of protection, this time focused on a different group.

Perhaps in between Leithead's reluctance and the Barkers' enthusiasm lay A.J. Heraghty, who worked on top at a coal mine. Though he enlisted because he wanted to be with other friends who had already joined up, his behaviour after enlisting clearly suggests that the reward of society's good graces had not been far from his mind. He and his friends were 'real proud' of themselves for joining and they wasted no time in letting the rest of their neighbourhood know that they were going 'to fight for King and Country'. But, 'most of all', they told their girlfriends, who were 'part glad and part sorry'.[65] Heraghty's account seems to have mixed his own feeling with a desire to prove to his neighbours and his girlfriend that he was fulfilling his duty.

External pressures

But that does not deal with the entire issue of social pressure. I should deal with the question of external demands. How much did they shape enlistment?

The short answer is that there was certainly outside pressure on men to enlist. Perhaps the most straightforward example of external pressures was in employer/worker relations. Many men joined at their employers' behest. Sometimes, it was a simple financial transaction. Some employers rewarded employees who joined up. Arthur Cave's firm gave him £2 when he enlisted.[66]

Sometimes, it was more coercive. Many labourers were forced, in one way or another, to sign up. W. Orchard spoke of the situation faced by many young male employees, in a letter to his mother in September 1915:

> Large employers are sacking their young employees in order that they should be compelled to do their duty and enlist and those who [don't] enlist for whatever reason are looked upon as funks and shirkers, so you can imagine my feelings, as I can't bear to be thought a funk. . . . I told Phil when I left him that I shouldn't join unless forced to but I simply must.[67]

Orchard joined soon after, with little enthusiasm.

Not that employer pressure to enlist was always obeyed or greeted with particular favour. In Great Leighs, just north of London, the local lord found resistance when he tried to push his footmen into the military: 'Village lads are not very pleased at pressure put by the Squire to compel his two footmen to enlist. To use the phrase of one of the lads, the "idle sons" of the house ought to have set an example of going.'[68] Note the interesting phrasing, though. The resistance is constructed not to the war itself, but to the 'idle sons' of the squire, who were supposed to set an example.

On the other hand, many employers insisted equally as vehemently that their workers stay. F.J. Jarrod's employer begged him to remain when he mentioned enlisting:

> He [my boss] said stay with me, we have a large quantity of stock for the market and unless we get our stock out soon it will be too late. So I said I would stop and help out the goods we had for Christmas trade.[69]

S. Bradbury's boss even threatened him with retribution should he enlist:

> Many times, [I] requested my employer to release me in order to join up but he insisted on my staying with him. . . . The hint however was constantly given to me that it would not be to my future benefit to act in opposition to my Employer's wishes.[70]

When the government attempted to conscript Bradbury, his employer aggressively fought it. In late 1915, as part of the Derby Scheme, Bradbury found himself in a group about to be called up. His employer made 'desperate attempts' to prevent his enlistment and succeeded in holding Bradbury until 1 April 1916. 'I must have been an indispensable sort of chap' was Bradbury's final comment.[71] Bradbury did not seem to have been terribly distressed about missing the war. He may have exaggerated his employer's efforts to keep him out of service. Nonetheless, it seems that some employers did try to prevent some of their employees from joining.

Employer pressure was not the only coercion. Early in the war, elements within society put intense pressure upon eligible men. A.W. Riley gave an indication of the fevered atmosphere of the first few months. Working on 7 August 1914, he said that there were:

> Posters all over corner of streets, Your King and Country Needs You. The Call was heeded, Men were leaving work at all hours joining up and recruiting officers were everywhere.[72]

Peer pressure also influenced men like E. Hunter, the foreman in a mineral water factory:

> We always used to make a presentation for anyone that joined up and of course the girls started to sing you won't enlist, someone wants you and it got on my nerves. . . . So, therefore, I thought to myself, well here it goes and I went up to the attestation office and enlisted.[73]

The sexual pressure felt by Hunter, as represented by the singing girls, has become a fundamental part of First World War iconography. One of the prevalent legends emerging from the First World War was that of the 'white feather', given by British women to men not in uniform to shame them into their country's service. Instances of this undoubtedly happened. J.A. Wilkinson, an office boy, remembered: 'There was a lot of criticism of men not in the services and it was not unknown for women to hand out white feathers to men out of uniform. . . . This harassment was so prevalent that we used to sing a parody [about it] on the song "Broken Doll".'[74] But its frequency and effect remain open to question. Most of the white feather incidents reported by men fall into two categories. In one, the men reported that the white feather had been given to someone else: a friend, an acquaintance, the friend of a friend. In the other, the men received the feather themselves, but managed to turn it around on the giver, either by already being in the military and merely in civilian clothes for the day, or by being physically damaged in some way that made it impossible for them to serve. In either case, these stories have the air of myth.[75] Further, out of the 1,415 records examined for this book, only fifteen mentioned white feathers, and only five men recalled being personally given a white feather. Such figures suggest that white feather giving was much rarer than has been assumed.[76]

Though societal pressure existed on men to fight, as with employers, much pushed in the opposite direction. A Chief Constable in Lincoln reported to the Home Office that while one of his 'senior officers' was trying to convince two eligible men that 'it was their duty to enlist', he was interrupted by another man who urged them 'not to listen to such advice and that there were plenty of other things to think about besides soldiering'.[77] W.W. Ashton experienced a more subtle societal pressure that disapproved not of enlistment, but of killing:

> On the tube train which we boarded at the Terminus (Finsbury Park) were a couple of old ladies. One leaned across to me and said, in a way that I thought patronizing 'And who are you going to fight?' I promptly replied, 'I'm not going to fight anyone', and drew attention to the red cross on my sleeve. At this there were satisfied mutterings of 'Ah, Red Cross, Red Cross' and no more was said.[78]

Again, there is no clear indication which way the preponderance of societal pressure pushed. The assumption has been that most aimed at making men volunteer, but conclusive evidence is lacking.

Official government policy, whether local or national, put pressure on men. An extreme example of local pressure came in Birmingham, where the *Daily Post* printed the names of thousands of men of military age, and invited them to enlist. F.J. Field was one, and the invitation led to him joining up.[79] Somewhat more subtly, the government began a series of advertisements in the national media encouraging enlistment in 1914 and W.R. Thomas, a labourer in North Wales, responded to it:

> I enlisted in Kitchener's Army as the urgent call went out in the only media that existed in those days of August 1914, i.e. the National Press, Posters, Meetings as soon as war was declared.[80]

This has been called 'an unrelenting barrage of recruiting propaganda', an evaluation that seems somewhat overstated.[81] The advertisements in the first few months were small and restrained. Kitchener would not, in fact, allow the War Office to change the one-eighth of a page advertisement that they had mocked up in a hurry early on. Small and without a picture, it hardly fits into the conception of overwhelming social pressure.[82] A concerted campaign of government propaganda did not begin until late 1914 after the greatest wave of enlistment and remained 'ad hoc, decentralized, and ultimately chaotic until the last year of the war'.[83]

'Patriotic. Or young and silly' 119

Conscription, a fairly compelling social pressure, did become an issue in the autumn of 1915. Lord Derby emphasized that forced induction would result if his enlistment campaign in late 1915 failed. He thus played on social fears of conscription. Evidently, volunteering was socially more acceptable than being drafted. Percy Hall did not want to be conscripted. He joined in late 1915, during the Derby campaign, because it 'allowed one to volunteer to serve . . . so that one was not classed as a conscript'.[84] Even men who 'abhorred' soldiering feared being conscripted more than joining voluntarily: R. Knabbit, the son of a tram conductor, 'dreaded' enlisting. Nonetheless, because 'war and conscription came [and] my age group call-up was near and much on my mind', he volunteered.[85] Neither man specified the consequences of being labelled a conscript, but clearly there were some.

Again, though this suggests that external pressure was important, it does not fully answer the question of how important. How much did external pressure influence enlistment? Here again exists a necessity for caution. Abe Moffat might claim that it was the propaganda that persuaded him to enlist:

> When the First World War broke out, I was, like many other young lads at that time, carried away with the imperialist propaganda about the need to defeat the Prussian militarists, and that this was the war to end wars and to make a country fit for heroes to live in. During the war miners were exempted from conscription owing to the importance of coal, but after several attempts I was accepted as a volunteer into the British Army.[86]

But note that he was so 'carried away' by the propaganda that – since conscription did not arrive until January 1916 – he waited at least a year and half after the start of the war to enlist.

R.M. Luther may serve as a useful case study, for he analysed his own situation at some length and spoke of the range of pressures that men encountered:

> Huge posters appeared on the hoardings, with a picture of Lord Kitchener, with a finger pointing directly at the onlooker, and the caption: 'I WANT YOU.' Then other posters appeared, of depleted ranks of soldiers, artillery gunners and drivers with empty saddles, urging, 'HERE IS A PLACE FOR YOU. FILL IT.' Very inviting indeed. . . . [author's ellipsis] I looked hard at those pictures. But the crowning glory was yet to come – beautiful ladies, the Marchioness of Bute and her entourage giving out handbills: 'FIGHT FOR THE LAND OF YOUR FATHERS. JOIN THE WELSH HORSE REGIMENT. COME TO GLORY. PROTECT YOUR HOMES, PROTECT YOUR MOTHERS, WIVES AND CHILDREN. YOU ARE GALLANT MEN – FIGHT FOR THEM AGAINST THE HORRIBLE HUN.'[87]

Luther's summary touched upon perhaps all the motivations examined in this chapter. He identified the propaganda invoking Kitchener's popularity, sympathy for the BEF, regional loyalties (Wales, in this case), family, and hatred of Germany. Note also the gendered nature of his remembrance: 'your mothers, wives, and children', 'gallant men', 'beautiful ladies'. Such words reinforce the idea that sexual pressure carried weight in influencing men to enlist.

But Luther did not actually enlist until several weeks after he first encountered this pressure, and his memoirs indicate that other events affected him more:

> Now the heat was turned on. Namur, Liege, Belgium and Tours were in flames. Cruel German soldiers were cutting off women's breasts, and carrying their babies on bayonets. . . . That did the trick. Young men flocked to join the army. Our soldiers had fought a big battle at Mons, and were now in retreat against superior numbers. Recruiting offices were opened up. I joined up on the 9th September – height: 5'4", weight: 130 pounds, regiment: the Welsh Fusiliers, pay: 1/- per day.[88]

The external pressures certainly affected Luther. The information he received about Namur, Liège, Belgium, and Tours was shaped to accentuate the terrors reportedly inflicted by the 'Horrible Hun'. Note also that the frightful events he remembered about Namur are gendered themselves, suggesting a more subtle sexual pressure than the handing out of white feathers. The cutting off of women's breasts struck him as worthier of anger than events he did not mention, such as the deaths of thousands of Belgian men.[89] But mixed with that remembrance was also his concern for the British Expeditionary Force. Further, note that his last comment is on the pay he would receive, hardly the thoughts of a man overwhelmed by society's demands. Luther's enlistment emerged from a welter of events and pressures, some external, some not. All clearly affected him. Perhaps more important than specific external pressures was the climate they created, one in which enlisting was an acceptable and lauded choice. But it seems unlikely that external pressures created a desire to enlist, or were the sole factor in causing a man to volunteer. The working class had demonstrated strong scepticism about government propaganda before the war. That scepticism endured into the war. The factor that changed between the two was not the government's actions, but the workers'; not the external pressures, but the internal decisions.

Representative?

Can the speakers cited so far be taken as representative of the working class? Given that men who wrote diaries and memoirs were a self-selected class and that those interviewed were recounting episodes long in the past, what can be inferred from their evidence? Did they speak for the entire working-class population? Is there hard evidence against which to measure their testimony? Enlistment statistics might say something about motives of allegiance. If men felt duty-bound to defend country, region, family, then they might be expected to enlist most numerously when the object of their loyalty appeared directly threatened. P. Nimmo wrote to a brother from training camp in October 1914: 'You will have seen the war news in the papers; it does not look very promising for us, we will need all the men we can get into good fighting order.'[90]

'Patriotic. Or young and silly'   121

If the feelings of allegiance were general, then enlistment figures should increase as bad 'war news' spread around the country, with the urban areas, well-served by newspapers and recruiting centres, leading the way, followed by the more distant rural areas.[91] For example, when J.T. Jenkins read about the bombardment of Hartlepool, on the east coast of Britain, by German cruisers in November 1914, he promptly left his mine and joined up.[92] He reacted to negative war news by enlisting. He did not claim that allegiance to nation, family, or region led him to enlist, but clearly he felt that something was threatened by the German attack.

Thus examining an example of such negative war news to see what enlistment rates did afterwards should reveal whether allegiance motivations were general to the public or merely anecdotal. In 1914, the singular event which shocked the British public out of its complacency was the rapid retreat of the BEF in late August 1914 and the consequent realization that this war was unlikely to be over by Christmas. Suddenly, not only Belgium but Britain seemed threatened. T. Batty remembered the stand of the BEF in a letter home to his family from enlistment camp on 16 November 1914:

> The army has acted beyond all expectation, to be shelled all day by those terrible shells and afterward to shoot straight and resist superior numbers, to keep steady and never budge is to be candidates for highest honours in this or any other age, or country.[93]

As we have already seen in Chapter 2, enlistment figures surged immediately after the article appeared. But was that surge the result of the article? Did men see something they felt an allegiance to threatened and react by joining up?

There is anecdotal evidence that the article had a galvanizing effect. E.V. Crumpton, a railway porter, joined in early September 1914 because of the situation at Mons. The article made D.A. Hodge, a printer's apprentice, realize that the war 'might after all concern me'.[94]

There is also statistical evidence. On 30 August, the day *The Times* article appeared, 6,693 men enlisted, twice the number of any previous Sunday. Notably, a higher percentage of those enlistees came from London than average.[95] London men must have had the first chance to hear and act on the news, especially on a Sunday, before those in other cities or in the countryside. On Monday, 31 August, the tumult began. Enlistment nationwide surged to 20,909 men that day; Londoners again made up a more substantial proportion of the overall number than previously. On 1 September, enlistment increased to 27,914 men. Now, however, the regional imbalance reversed itself. Recruits from London made up a smaller proportion of the national figure than before, a trend which continued as recruitment continued to increase, to 31,947 on 2 September, to 33,204 on 3 September. Thereafter it levelled off at between 25,000 and 30,000 per day, with the exception of Sunday, 6 September, when 11,472 men joined and 10 September when the number was 17,616.[96] On 11 September, his training system nearly destroyed by the masses of volunteers, Kitchener announced a raising of the physical standards required for entry to the military.[97] This effectively ended the rush, depressing recruitment back to mid-August levels. The week of 12–19 September saw 44,679 men join up, the week after 27,589.[98]

Historians have suggested that this end-of-August rush was the result of initial 'hesitation' over 'moral or intellectual' misgivings on the part of British men.[99] But the pattern of the recruiting figures seems to challenge this interpretation. The recruiting figures apparently reacted to the tidings from France in a way that mimicked the dispersal of that news. The article and its news would have spread fairly quickly around Britain. The major cities would have received *The Times* the same day, and even rural areas like Hertford would have received a shipment of the newspapers on the evening train or, at the latest, the morning train. Even small towns in the north of England, like Keswick, where R.T. Wallace grew up, would have received the London papers in the afternoon of the following day. The Reverend Andrew Clark, who lived in the north of England, wrote that the news reached him on 31 August, the day after publication.[100]

While the news spread rapidly and fairly evenly around the country, the same could not be true of people responding to it. London and the major industrial cities teemed with recruiting centres. No matter where you lived in London or Manchester or Liverpool, it took no more than an hour or two to get to a recruiting centre. In the rural areas the situation was different: the nearest recruiting station could be many miles away, accessible for a worker only by walking. R. Hunter, living in rural Yorkshire, found himself in exactly that situation:

> The nearest recruiting office was at Barnsley (11 to 12 miles away). I walked there and had no difficulty finding the place as it was besieged by a large crowd of men young and otherwise.[101]

Thus, one would expect the wave of recruitment to start in London and the major cities and then spread to rural areas.

That is very nearly what happened. As mentioned above, the percentage of London enlistees in the overall recruitment figures jumped to above average in the first four days after the article had appeared, suggesting that the first wave of enlistees appeared in the capital. Similarly, Liverpool's percentage contribution to the overall enlistment figures jumped. After those four days, however, both cities' numbers dropped to a below-average percentage of the overall figures, consistent with the spread of the enthusiasm to the rest of the country and its reaching a plateau in the centre. In rural Hertford, a different pattern emerged. An initial jump, starting on 30 August, took its figures to triple their previous percentage of the national average. By 2 September, however, they had dropped back to the mid-August level, only to jump back up to quadruple that level on 3 and 4 September. The pattern suggests that men read the article about the defeat of the BEF and reacted by enlisting.

Was this an isolated incident? Certainly, Mons could have been unusual. It was early in the war, it was a particularly bad defeat, and the initial war enthusiasm was still running high. But similar surges occurred after British defeats throughout 1914 and 1915. After the bombardment of Hartlepool by German warships on

'Patriotic. Or young and silly' 123

3 November 1914 (mentioned above), recruiting again surged. In the period from 6 November (allowing the news to spread throughout the country) to 13 November, 38,849 men enlisted, compared to 21,262 in the week ending 3 November. Enlistment for the whole month of November jumped to 169,862, more than either October (136,811) or December (117,860) 1914.[102]

Another event remarked on by some volunteers was the sinking of the *Lusitania* by a German U-boat on 7 May 1915. R.L. Venables, a labourer, remembered that it was 'this episode led me and my friends to consider that it was time we took a more active part in the war'.[103] Venables and his friends do not seem to have been alone in this feeling; the sinking preceded an increase in enlistment. The figure for the month of May was 135,263, an increase on the March and April figures, which were 113,907 and 119,087 respectively.[104]

Again, the figures strongly suggest that the allegiance motives expressed early in this chapter by working-class volunteers were genuine. British men reacted to war difficulties by supporting the war effort in the most obvious of ways, enlisting. They saw something that they felt allegiance to and took the path that enabled them to act in its defence. The evidence is not absolute, certainly, but it does suggest strongly that the working-class volunteers quoted in this chapter did speak for the larger group, that the British working class did feel and act upon allegiances outside themselves. 'We have done our bit for England,' R. Thompson, a factory worker from Bermondsey, wrote home after the battle of Neuve Chapelle in April 1915, 'but cheer up we are not dead yet'.[105]

Conclusion

Oddly enough, the government seems to have understood the attitude of the working class better than its titular representatives. The Independent Labour Party raged against the government in a pamphlet published and distributed in Wales in 1914. The war, the ILP felt, was the fault of all of Europe's governments. Each government's diplomacy, Britain's included, 'has been underground, secret, deceitful, each Power endeavouring by wile and stratagem to get the better of its neighbour'. To support the war would be folly.[106] A Home Office civil servant reacted to the ILP's anti-war pamphlet with these dismissive words: 'I do not see much harm in the pamphlet – some parts are excellent. I do not think it will do much damage to recruiting.'[107] He was right.

The workers did not so much disagree with the ILP's analysis as find it beside the point. The government may well have signed secret covenants with France, ones concealed from Parliament and the public. Or they may have ignored the impending German threat. But the government was not Britain. Britain had known of the threat, even if the politicians had not: 'For years England, the politicians excluded, has known of this [German] menace,' J.H. Dible confided to his diary in August 1914.[108] The working class understood that the larger issue of defending the objects of their loyalty, whether nation, region, family, or friends, and destroying the German state, was more important than the culpability of their government. R.W. Farrow, a labourer and a socialist, summed up this attitude in August 1914:

> At a public meeting I strongly denounced the war mongers who had stumbled into this terrible situation; 'but,' said I, 'we are actually in it; we shall have to see it through; all of us must help.'[109]

They may not have cared for those who ruled them, but they cared about what was ruled:

> I would not salute any damned King that was ever bred. I will salute the British people, I will salute the French people, and if need be against the Germans I will fight – and a damned sight better than you.[110]

Workers looked past their suspicions of the government to their own allegiances, and enlisted. They felt and reacted to external pressures but the true impetus came from within themselves. They were doing what they wanted, if sometimes uncomfortably, unhappily, or doubtfully. They surveyed their world and found it worth defending. J.A. Wilkinson wrote to his sister: 'Then when I come home again you can say well I had a brother too who was not frightened to go and fight for his country I know it is a bit hard for you but these things will happen.'[111]

8 Conclusion

The neglect of the British volunteers has continued to the present day. Just recently, Niall Ferguson argued that 'British soldiers . . . were unsure what they were fighting for.'[1] For some men, that may have been true. But to project it as a general case ignores the varied motives that volunteers expressed. Perhaps the enlistees, especially the working-class enlistees, did not explain their reasons in the language that a 'self-consciously clever, confrontational young don' would recognize easily.[2] Nonetheless, the motives did exist and the workers did talk about them. But Ferguson at least acknowledged that the working-class soldier existed as an individual. Too many historians have not.

There is a historiographical obsession with the carnage that drives this ignorance. Historians have been fixated on the casualties suffered by the British on the Western Front, most particularly at the Somme. Stepping forward to the attack on 1 July 1916, Kitchener's Armies, the Regulars, the Pals battalions, and the Territorials, found not the ruined German defences promised them but massed machine-gun nests, fields of fire neatly interlocking, supported by heavier guns already ranged on the approaches to the German trenches. Thousands of men fell together in No Man's Land, organized neatly into rows as if to be more easily counted. The baptism of the new British Army decimated entire units. Fifty-seven thousand casualties in that one day: 1 per cent of the total wartime fighting strength of the British military, 8 per cent of the total wartime casualties. 'It was the biggest battle her army had ever fought, or probably would ever fight, in a single day.'[3]

Those singular 24 hours, 'the middle day of the middle year of the war', cast a long shadow.[4] It stretched back to Britain and into working-class homes across the nation. Of the ten battalions suffering the highest casualties, seven were from Kitchener's Armies. Of the thirty-two battalions losing more than half their original strength (i.e. 500 men), twenty were from Kitchener's Armies.[5] All the hard work done over months was destroyed in less than an hour. Joseph Murray, a miner, remembered: 'It took maybe twenty months to organize, recruit, train and dispatch [them] overseas and less than twenty minutes on the Somme to annihilate them.'[6] The strength of Kitchener's Armies – the Pals battalions with their geographic bond and close-knit social grouping – now stood revealed also as a weakness. Entire neighbourhoods lost their sons in an instant, as the machine guns opened fire on the morning of 1 July. Entire neighbourhoods were visited by postmen carrying letters of condolence.

And while the first day stood alone in its absolute size, it served as an omen for the scale and intensity of casualties to be experienced by the British Army through the rest of the war. The Somme battle, which lasted until November 1916, proved only the first of a series of sanguinary battles that chewed up a large part of a generation of British men. After the Somme, came Arras, and Third Ypres, and Passchendaele. After the Somme, the letters never ceased coming.

Nor, after the war, did the battle lose its power. British cities and towns adopted French villages closest to where the men of their battalion had fought and fallen. Thus Sheffield adopted Serre, and Wolverhampton, Gommecourt. In the years after the war, those British communities sent money and assistance to help rebuild the ruined French communities.[7] So general was the suffering that everyone felt it. The Somme and Verdun occupied equal spaces in British and French memory. In almost every town in France and Britain, there is a memorial to those who died. The Somme became part of what historian Jay Winter calls a 'universal history' of bereavement.[8]

The Somme also shaped the historiography of the war. The events of the Somme and the battles that followed have become solidly entrenched in the imagination of historians, and treated not just as battles, but as a transition from one era to the next. It was, John Keegan remarked, 'the end of an age of vital optimism in British life'.[9] This 'caesura in the history of modern warfare' must, many historians believed, have great meaning, for good or ill.[10] Such sacrifice demanded nothing less:

> Yes, these millions died for their country, but to say so was merely to begin, not to conclude, the search for the 'meaning' of the unprecedented slaughter of the Great War.[11]

But, by searching for such meaning, historians demanded that everything live up to the 'unprecedented slaughter'. Historians sought justification in place of explanation. As a result, many elements of the war were weighed against the slaughter and found wanting: most obviously, the generals and the war leaders who have long been found guilty of arrogance, stupidity, and inflexibility.[12] But, in a more subtle way, the same has happened to enlistment motivations.

Because the motivations often do not seem to be equal to the slaughter, historians have, in different ways, diminished or belittled the motives. Some have simply found themselves unable to understand the motivations. They treat the Edwardian period and the beginning of the war as a simpler age, in which motives were both purer and more suspect:

> It is difficult to comprehend what made [patriotism] a force so powerful that it could propel so many men into one of the bloodiest wars ever fought without anything in the way of legal compulsion.[13]

This lack of comprehension effectively precluded analysis. Other historians have acted as if they understood the workers too well. Ferguson's assertion that the workers did not understand their own motives is one example. Further on, he responds to a working-class volunteer who talked about wanting to fight the Germans to protect Britain by saying 'this was almost plausible, though wrong: as we have seen, there was no German plan to invade Britain'.[14] This dismissal of a working-class motive using knowledge that no Briton could have had in 1914 allows a comfortable paternal distance from the events and meanings of 1914, but it is not good history.

It is wise to remember Jay Winter's point. At the beginning of the war, Winter reminds historians, 'no sombre thoughts of trenches and gas masks troubled the clerks and greengrocers, teachers and farmers, manufacturers and publicans who joined up by the thousands'.[15] It is an obvious point, but one which some have clearly lost. Certainly, in retrospect, some of the enlistees' decisions look foolish. Joining to escape a dreary home life and experience adventure seem almost trivial in relation to the horror awaiting most at the front. Joining to find a steady job and support a family seems small reward for the opportunity to die in the fields of Flanders. Joining to defend a family assumed that that family was in actual danger, which was not true for most. Joining to defend the city, county, or country assumed the same. But this sort of retroactive evaluation slips worryingly into the ahistorical. If we judge them by the consequences of their actions, then we lose those actions in the larger picture. We ignore the individual to indict the mass.

For, ultimately, the rush to colours boiled down to hundreds of thousands of individual decisions. Certainly, the workers had been trained for it. They had grown up in an era of British dominance and British imperialism. They knew that the empire was supreme. They knew that Germany was the enemy. Their education had stressed both facts. The newspapers they read in school and afterwards had reinforced those messages. But, after 4 August 1914, each man approached his choice on his own. Influenced however much by family, by society, by propaganda, each man nonetheless decided for himself. They decided according to their estimations of their own and society's needs.

When the war started, working-class men who might otherwise have protested against British involvement weighed their options and responded by joining up. Some may have seen this as a way to earn money for themselves and their families. Some may have seen it as a chance to escape their lives, either temporarily or permanently. If they did not understand what they were getting themselves into, neither did the politicians, generals, or lords above them.

The surge was initially checked, as a result of the government's mixed messages. Though Kitchener publicly called for 500,000 men and was backed by Parliament, Cabinet insistence on 'business as usual' seems to have dampened the enlistment rates slightly. The figures dwarfed those of pre-war years, but they did not overwhelm the recruiting structure completely. For most of August, it seemed that Britain could rely on her Regulars and her Navy quickly to fight and win the war against Germany. The war, most believed, would be over by Christmas. Thus many stayed at home, worried about their families, about their jobs, and about their positions. Employers sometimes proved less than eager to lose men to the military. Though the sources are not numerous enough to substantiate this, it is possible that, during the initial month, those seeking adventure and economic benefits formed the largest part of the working-class enlistment.

By the end of August, public confidence in the government broke down. The near destruction of the BEF, published by *The Times* (London) on 30 August and picked up by newspapers around the country, galvanized popular opinion. The war stopped being something distant that would end quickly. Now it was immediate, and apparently threatening. That the soldiers fighting in the BEF came from the working class added a particular urgency to the matter. Though they might have been looked down upon for enlisting, they nonetheless shared a common heritage with the men back in Britain reading about them.

As a result, the enlistment surge became a tidal wave. The British people read *The Times* report and reacted to it. They enlisted to support the Army and support the nation. They could have chosen otherwise. They could have chosen to see the British commitment to the continent as a losing cause, one out of line with British history, and one that was of no concern to an oppressed working class.

But they did not. Instead, the British volunteered in such numbers that the enlistment infrastructure was inadvertently destroyed. Nearly 10 per cent of the total number of British wartime volunteers joined in the two weeks after the first newspaper article. Many stepped forward. They included local power brokers like Lord Esher and Lord Derby, who created their own organizations to enlist and train the volunteers. But, most critically, they included hundreds of thousands of working-class men.

The individual who personalized the war for many was Kitchener. Workers believed themselves to be personally assisting Kitchener. They distinguished him from the rest of the Cabinet and made him an avatar of Britain. They made the nation concrete in one person. In effect, by separating that person from the government, they separated state from nation. Thus workers defended the British nation without having to justify or atone for the British state.

It was Kitchener, however, who reduced the flow of recruits. His raising of the standards in the middle of September 1914 effectively ended the tidal wave. That rejection seems to have depersonalized the war for many. The raising of the standards announced that Britain did not need so many men, that the war was not urgent. It did so at a very personal level, and one at which working-class men were particularly vulnerable. As a result, the number of volunteers returned to a point slightly below that of the early August average. The reduction spared the depots and the training camps further overloads, but put a final end to the mad rush of enlistees.

But that rush had become fixed in the minds of the Cabinet and the War Office as the norm. They expected to switch it back on when the enlistment system had been repaired and enlarged. Because the enlistment numbers never reached their August/September high, they were seen as a disappointment by the decision-makers. By any other measure, weekly enlistment figures remained high enough to replace casualties and simultaneously allow expansion of the Army. Nonetheless, the Cabinet and the War Office felt otherwise. The perceived drop-off in numbers suggested to them that there was a pool of men avoiding service. These 'shirkers' were thought to be working-class and single, and, as early as the middle of 1915, the government began to think of ways to bring them into the military. Compulsion seemed the best route.

At the same time, the government realized that the heavy enlistment of industrial workers handicapped the war effort. The preponderance of urban factory workers volunteering hampered the production of war material. The loss of coal miners to the Army reduced coal output at a time of high civilian and military demand. 'Business as usual' could not continue. Britain could not build a mass Army under voluntarism and create industries to equip that Army at the same time.

At first, the government forbade workers in important industries from enlisting, but volunteers got around the ban by lying. Finally, to manage the problem, Lloyd George pushed to have a Ministry of Munitions created. Appointed its head, he managed to set up controls fairly quickly. Both the unions and the manufacturers were responsive to, if wary of, his calls for tighter industrial control. By the autumn of 1915, he had moved a long way towards managing Britain's industrial production. But the problem of enlistment remained and the solution seemed to be control over who could enter the military.

The need for industrial control and the belief in 'shirkers' reinforced each other. State control of the war industry required the management of who entered the military. The campaign to move 'shirkers' into the Army required the same control. Again, conscription seemed the answer. The only thing preventing the government from introducing conscription by late 1915 was residual resistance within the Cabinet and worries over the reaction of Parliament and the people. Asquith and Lloyd George thus created a test. Lord Derby would run a campaign that would be understood to be the last gasp of the voluntary system. If it did not succeed in enlisting the 'shirkers', then conscription was guaranteed. The Derby campaign increased enlistment numbers, but not sufficiently to satisfy the pro-conscription forces. In January 1915, Asquith introduced a bill for conscription in Parliament. The outcry was less than expected and the bill became law by the end of the month.

Conscription fixed one of the two problems facing the government. It prevented workers in critical industries from enlisting. But getting a sufficient number of men remained difficult. The bill applied only to single men because they supposedly made up the majority of the pool of 'shirkers', but it quickly became clear that few, if any, shirkers existed. The enlistment numbers under conscription came nowhere near the numbers under voluntarism. By May 1916, conscription was extended to married men. Conscription now affected all males between the ages of 19 and 40 in Britain, except those in Ireland. But even so the Army complained about manpower shortages throughout 1917–1918. There simply were not enough men to keep the war industries running and maintain the Army, no matter what system was used.

130 Conclusion

In essence then, it is clear that voluntarism provided enough men to fight the First World War during 1914–1915. What would have happened in the sanguinary years of 1916–1917 is not clear, but up to January 1916, voluntarism provided enough men to replace British casualties and build up the Army. That the British generals and politicians did not agree had more to do with two other factors than with lack of enthusiasm on the part of the populace. The first factor has been explored above. The wrong people were enlisting. The enthusiasm in urban, industrial centres meant that those men most needed to stay at home and build war equipment, or to dig coal from the mines, made up the largest group of volunteers. Britain needed to control who entered and who stayed at home. They could not do that under the voluntary system.

Second, at root, the politicians and generals had very little idea what to expect. Neither the Cabinet nor the military understood the war they were fighting.[16] Their pre-war plans were in tatters, no breakthrough appeared likely on the Western Front, and, by autumn 1915, the attempted flank attack at Gallipoli had failed disastrously. Under Lloyd George's pressure, they moved away from 'business as usual' in May 1915, but the end results of his policies were far from clear. By autumn 1915, there seemed few opportunities for action available. The Home Front, in fact, seemed the only place where the ministers could still make a difference. Thus, I suggest, they seized upon conscription. They could bring about change, be seen acting against supposed 'slackers', and perhaps speed the end of the war. This would give them control over something in the swirling chaos, even if that control was not absolutely necessary.

For the ruling elites still did not understand the willingness of the working class to fight the war. They had viewed the initial rush with some surprise and had not fathomed its depths. They did not grasp the mind-set of the men who volunteered. The workers understood the world around them to a large degree, and made their decisions based on that understanding. They certainly did not understand the war better than the generals and the ministers. The volunteers certainly did not have some mystical insight into what was to come.

But they did have an insight into their own beliefs. Those beliefs included a hierarchy that located them not merely on an economic or political level but also on a national, European, and imperial level. They conceived of themselves as part of a larger whole. They conceived of themselves as part of a unit that included Britain, that included Europe, and that included empire. They had a national conception of themselves, as well as a class conception. The decisions they made to enlist, whether for reasons of economy, adventure, or allegiance, arose out of that understanding. Nor were those who did not or could not enlist ignorant. They too grasped that the world around them was larger than their neighbourhood, their factory, or their city. J.W. Roworth's greeting when he returned home a soldier was enough testimony to that understanding. His family and neighbours greeted him as a hero not out of a simple reverence for the uniform but because they understood and approved of his actions. No one, at that point, knew what faced the soldiers. The long casualty lists of later years were yet to come. But if they did not yet understand the full price of their choice, they discerned a fundamental distinction that perhaps the elites did not. They separated the state from the nation. While criticizing the British state for its missteps before and during the war, they felt, in 1914 and 1915, a duty to defend the British nation, in whatever form they conceived it. The education of slaughter would come later.

Notes

Abbreviations in the notes are as follows:

BL = British Library
IWM = Imperial War Museum
    IWM CON/SHELF = Cataloguing ID
    IWM DS/MISC = Cataloguing ID
    IWM P = Cataloguing ID
    IWM PP/MCR = Cataloguing ID
    IWM SR = Sound Recording
LA = Liddle Archive
    LA W/F = Western Front
NAM = National Army Museum
PRO = Public Records Office
    PRO CAB = Cabinet
    PRO HO = Home Office
    PRO MUN = Munitions
    PRO NATS = National Service
    PRO RG = National Register
    PRO T = Treasury
    PRO WO = War Office

1 Introduction

1. Imperial War Museum (IWM) 80/40/1, Roworth, John William, 'A War Story, 1914–1918', b. 1897. Where possible for the IWM records, a date of birth is given. Otherwise, the date listed is as in the museum catalogue: 1914–1918.
2. Ibid.
3. J.M. Winter, *The Great War and the British People* (Cambridge, MA: Harvard University Press, 1986), 27.
4. Ibid., 25.
5. H.H. Asquith to the railwaymen in 1911. Quoted in David Powell, *The Edwardian Crisis: Britain 1901–1914* (London: Macmillan, 1996), 126.
6. Ypres, for example, became 'Wipers' to most British soldiers. See IWM 82/22/1, Beall, R.E., 'The Green Fields Beyond', 1914–1918.
7. Michael Howard, 'Total War in the Twentieth Century: Participation and Consensus

in the Second World War', in *War and Society: A Yearbook of Military History*, ed. Brian Bond and Ian Roy, vol. 1 (London: Croom Helm, 1975), 216–226.
8 Michael Howard, 'British Grand Strategy in World War One', in *Grand Strategies in War and Peace*, ed. Paul Kennedy (New Haven, CT: Yale University Press, 1991), 31–41. Also Gerd Hardach, *The First World War* (London: Penguin, 1987), 174.
9 For example, see D.J. Goodspeed, *The German Wars, 1914–1945* (Boston: Houghton Mifflin, 1977). G.D.H. Cole and Raymond Postgate refer only to the 'drain of workers for military service', in G.D.H. Cole and Raymond Postgate, *The British People, 1746–1946* (London: Methuen, 1961), 510; Peter Clarke, *Hope and Glory* (London: Allen Lane, 1996), 73, spoke of 'volunteers flooding in', but not why. John Terraine, *The First World War 1914–1918* (London: Macmillan, 1965); Ernest Llewellyn Woodward, *Great Britain and the War of 1914–1918* (London: Methuen, 1967); and Paul Guinn, *British Strategy and Politics 1914–1918* (Oxford: Clarendon Press, 1965) simply ignore the question.
10 Gerald J. DeGroot, *Blighty* (London: Longman, 1996), 49.
11 Trevor Royle, *The Kitchener Enigma* (London: Michael Joseph, 1985), 257; Cyril Falls, *The Great War* (New York: G.P. Putnam's Sons, 1959), 94. Mark Girouard, *Return to Camelot: Chivalry and the English Gentleman* (New Haven, CT: Yale University Press, 1981); Michael C.C. Adams, *The Great Adventure: Male Desire and the Coming of World War I* (Bloomington, IN: Indiana University Press, 1990); W.J. Reader, *At Duty's Call: A Study in Obsolete Patriotism* (Manchester: Manchester University Press, 1988). For a discussion of this argument, see Clive Hughes, 'The New Armies', in *Nation in Arms* (Manchester: Manchester University Press, 1985), ed. Ian F. Beckett and Keith Simpson, 99–126; Basil Liddell Hart, *The Real War, 1914–1918* (Boston: Little, Brown, 1964 [1930]), 69–70; Peter Dietz, *The Last of the Regiments: Their Rise and Fall* (London: Brassey's, 1990), 158–159. Oddly enough, historians have been more sophisticated about the Napoleonic wars. They have been much more willing, as J.E. Cookson points out, to grasp the 'opportunistic, interested, and conditional' nature of working-class voluntarism from 1793 to 1815 than they have for 1914–1918. See J.E. Cookson, *The British Armed Nation* (Oxford: Clarendon Press, 1997), 9.
12 Quote from Peter Simkins, *Kitchener's Army: The Raising of the New Armies, 1914–1916* (Manchester: Manchester University Press, 1988), 49. A.J.P. Taylor, *English History, 1914–1945* (Cambridge: Cambridge University Press, 1965), 18. See also Basil Williams, *Raising and Training the New Armies* (London: Constable, 1918), 19; Victor Germains, *The Kitchener Armies: The Story of a National Achievement* (London: Peter Davies, 1930), 39; Howard Green, *The British Army in the First World War: The Regulars, The Territorials, and Kitchener's Army* (London: J. Trahern, 1968), 61; Keith Robbins, *The First World War* (Oxford: Oxford University Press, 1984), 18; Hart, *Real War, 1914–1918*, 69–70; Jay Winter, 'Army and Society: The Demographic Context', in *Nation in Arms*, ed. Beckett and Simpson, 193–209; Ernest Llewellyn Woodward, *Great Britain and the War of 1914–1918* (London: Methuen, 1967), 59–60; Martin Gilbert, *The First World War* (New York: H. Holt, 1994), 187; Arthur Marwick, *Britain in the Century of Total War* (Boston: Little, Brown, 1968), 58. A useful discussion of what is meant by 'nationalism' in the context of First World War historiography comes in L.L. Farrar, Jr, 'Nationalism in Wartime: Critiquing the Conventional Wisdom', in *Authority, Identity, and the Social History of the Great War*, ed. Frans Coetzee and Marilyn Shevin-Coetzee (Oxford: Berghahn Books, 1995), 133–152.
13 Bernadotte E. Schmitt and Harold C.L.B. Vedeler, *The World in the Crucible* (New York: Harper & Row, 1984), 477.
14 Note, for example, that of the five main works on the creation of the British Army in the First World War, four are exclusively focused on Herbert Kitchener, the Secretary of State for War. They thus look from the top down at the rush to colours.

This is not to argue that this method is not useful, but it is to suggest that such a unanimity of focus leaves other critical issues, most importantly working-class reaction to the war, unexplored. See Philip Magnus, *Kitchener: Portrait of an Imperialist* (London: John Murray, 1958); Green, *The British Army in the First World War: The Regulars, the Territorials, and Kitchener's Army*; Peter Simkins, *Kitchener's Army: The Raising of the New Armies, 1914–1916* (Manchester: Manchester University Press, 1980); A.J. Smithers, *Fighting Nation: Lord Kitchener and His Armies* (London: Leo Cooper, 1994); John Morton Osborne, *Voluntary Recruiting Movement in Britain, 1914–1916* (New York: Garland Publishing, 1982).

15 The General Strike of 1926 involved 2.7 million workers, roughly the same number as volunteered during the First World War. See Thelma Liesner, *Economic Statistics: 1900–1983: United Kingdom, USA, France, Germany, Italy, Japan* (New York: Facts on File, 1985), 26. The historian Christopher Hill has suggested that social historians have been too narrow in evaluating the triumphs of the British people. The celebrated achievements, Hill believed, had been limited to movements or organizations set up to oppose or defy the capitalist economy: trade unions, the Labour Party, and strikes. But Hill argued that other things should be seen as working-class successes, things such as railways, bridges, shipyards, and what he calls the 'British people's gift for forming voluntary associations'. See Christopher Hill, 'History and Patriotism', in *Patriotism: The Making and Unmaking of British National Identity*, ed. Raphael Samuel, vol. I (London: Routledge, 1989), 6. But he did not include, or even acknowledge the voluntarism in 1914–1915, the largest working-class voluntary association to that point in British history. The same flaw was on display in Mary Langan, '"A Safe and Sane Labourism": Socialism and the State, 1910–1924', in *Crises in the British State 1880–1930*, ed. Mary Langan and Bill Schwarz (London: Hutchinson, 1985), 126–151.

16 Gareth Stedman Jones, *Languages of Class: Studies in English Working-Class History, 1832–1982* (Cambridge: Cambridge University Press, 1983), 2. By contrast, the historiography of the elites in the pre-war years has been less fractured. After 1918, opinions diverge about the position of the elites in Britain. Before 1914, there is still a reasonable consensus. The elites up to 1914 consisted of three main bodies. First was the aristocracy, whose power arose out of its land holdings and hold on the House of Lords. Second was the newly growing industrial elite of northern England. They controlled the structure and products of the Industrial Revolution, which equipped them with wealth, if not initially the power to go with it. Finally, there was a commercial and financial elite, based in London and southern England, who dominated British trade and finance. These three groups fought for dominion within the British political system. By the beginning of the twentieth century, the industrial and commerical/financial elites had begun to gain influence over the landed aristocracy, as best evidenced by the curtailing of the power of the House of Lords in 1911. Though, as historian David Cannadine points out, this is something of a 'monstrous oversimplification', it is nonetheless roughly accurate. See David Cannadine, *The Decline and Fall of the British Aristocracy* (New Haven, CT and London: Yale University Press, 1990), 10. Also useful is W.D. Rubinstein, *Elites and the Wealthy in Modern British History* (New York: St Martin's Press, 1987).

17 For Marx's thoughts on class, see Karl Marx and Frederick Engels, *The Communist Manifesto: New Interpretations*, ed. Mark Cowling (New York, New York University Press, 1998); E.P. Thompson, *The Making of the English Working Class* (New York: Vintage, 1963).

18 Jones, *Languages of Class*.

19 Trevor Lummis, *The Labour Aristocracy: 1851–1914* (Aldershot, UK: Scolar Press, 1994), ix. See Hobsbawm's work on the labour aristocracy in Victorian England. The labour aristocracy thesis posited that Britain had not witnessed a proletarian revolution because the top level of the working-class had become economically

secure in the mid-nineteenth century and was thus co-opted by the elites. Without their support, a revolutionary consciousness could not develop. See Eric J. Hobsbawm, *Labouring Men: Studies in the History of Labour* (London: Weidenfeld & Nicolson, 1964); Eric J. Hobsbawm, 'Artisan or Labour Aristocrat', *Economic History Review* 37 (1984): 355–372; and Eric J. Hobsbawm, 'The Aristocracy of Labour Reconsidered', in *Worlds of Labour: Further Studies in the History of Labour* (London: Weidenfeld & Nicolson, 1984). Gareth Stedman Jones essentially dismantled this thesis by pointing out that such a labour aristocracy had existed throughout much of English history and that the mid-nineteenth century was in no way unusual in this regard. See Gareth Stedman Jones, 'Class Struggle and the Industrial Revolution', in *Languages of Class*, 25–76. Another take on the labour aristocracy, focusing mostly on the exclusionary definition of 'skilled workers', is Charles More, *Skill and the English Working-Class, 1870–1914* (New York: St Martin's Press, 1980).

20 The works in which they laid out this interpretation are Patrick Joyce, *Democratic Subjects: The Self and the Social in Nineteenth-Century England* (Cambridge: Cambridge University Press, 1994); Patrick Joyce, *Visions of the People: Industrial England and the Question of Class, 1840–1914* (Cambridge and New York: Cambridge University Press, 1991); Jones, *Languages of Class*. The debate over the 'linguistic turn' has been fierce. The latest exchanges can be followed in David Mayfield and Susan Thorne, 'Social History and Its Discontents: Gareth Stedman Jones and the Politics of Language', *Social History* 17 (1992): 165–187; J. Lawrence and M. Taylor, 'The Poverty of Protest: Gareth Stedman Jones and the Politics of Language – A Reply', *Social History* 18 (1993): 1–18; Patrick Joyce, 'The Imaginary Discontents of Social History: A Note of Response to Mayfield and Thorne', *Social History* 18 (1993): 81–85; Patrick Joyce, 'The End of Social History?', *Social History* 20 (1995): 74–91.

21 Charles Booth, *Life and Labour of the People in London* (London: Macmillan, 1902).

22 Ibid.

23 J.A. Banks, 'The Social Structure of Nineteenth-Century England as Seen Through the Census', in *The Census and Social Structure: An Interpretive Guide to Nineteenth-Century Censuses for England and Wales*, ed. Richard Lawton (London: Frank Cass, 1978), 179–223.

24 Mike Savage and Andrew Miles, *The Remaking of the British Working Class* (London: Routledge, 1994), 30–40.

25 Liddle Archive Western Front (hereafter LA W/F) RECOLLECTIONS, Sloan, James Alexander Cameron.

26 IWM 88/52/1, And Truly Serve – Memoirs of Frederick Hunt, Sheriff of Lincoln 1959–1960, High Constable 1960–1961, 1914–1918.

27 Allen Clarke, *The Effects of the Factory System* (London: G. Richards, 1899), 26–34. Joyce makes a similar point. Joyce, *Visions of the People*, 157.

28 See, for example, Judith L. Newton, Mary P. Ryan, and Judith R. Walkowitz, 'Introduction', in *Sex and Class in Women's History*, ed. Judith L. Newton, Mary P. Ryan, and Judith R. Walkowitz (London: Routledge, 1983), 1–17; Joanna Bourke, *Husbandry to Housewifery: Women, Economic Change, and Housework in Ireland, 1890–1914* (Oxford: Clarendon Press, 1993), 4–8; Anna Davin, 'Feminism and Labour History', in *People's History and Socialist Theory*, ed. Raphael Samuel (London: Routledge & Kegan Paul, 1981), 176–187.

29 Sloan remembered:

> My father, who might have been described as a martyr to insolvency, never went out without a clean stiff collar, starched front and cuffs and spats even if his underwear were frayed and his shoes leaking water through the soles.

See LA W/F RECOLLECTIONS, Sloan, James Alexander Cameron, 1979. Where possible for the Liddle Archive documents, the date of birth and the date of interview are given. Some interviews have neither, but all the interviews occurred after 1970.
30. IWM PP/MCR/283, The First World War Journal of B.J. Brookes.
31. IWM 79/17/1, Skelton, G. (Papers). Skelton was not working-class, having attended a public school.
32. Very large for some. G. Ives was interviewed in 1991, when he was 110 years old. See LA TAPE 855, G. Ives.
33. IWM 73/150/1, Papers of H.C. Parker, 1914–1918.
34. *Statistics of the Military Effort of the British Empire during the Great War, 1914–1920* (London: HMSO, 1922), 363.
35. Ibid.
36. Figures for London are from Stephen Inwood, *A History of London* (London: Macmillan, 1998), 411–413, 708.
37. Census Office, *Census of England and Wales, 1911*, vol. 2 (London: HMSO, 1912).
38. Dr Peter Liddle, interview with author, 14 December 1996, Leeds, England.
39. Though some did not. IWM 67/7/1, Taylor, J.E. (Papers), 1914–1918 died in a POW camp; IWM 86/19/1, Gautier, F.H. (Papers), 1914–1918 died in a British hospital in France; IWM 86/57/1, Nettleton, G.E.H., 1914–1918 died of influenza in 1918; IWM 90/1/1, Payne, 2nd Lt H.S., 1914–1918 died of his wounds in 1919; IWM 93/25/1, G.S. Smith (Papers), 1914–1918 was killed in 1915.
40. LA TAPE 24, Aitcheson, Mr, b. c1896.
41. LA TAPE 139, A. Whiteley, b. 1897.
42. LA GALLIPOLI RECOLLECTIONS, Attwood, J.C., interviewed 1972.
43. Quoted in IWM 81/28/1, Papers of C.K. Ogden, 1914–1918. It should be noted that this account may well be straightforward; it may also have been the dismissive reaction of a working-class soldier to an officer asking annoying questions.
44. Raphael Samuel, 'Preface', in *Patriotism*, ed. Samuel, xv.
45. Hugh Cunningham, 'The Language of Patriotism,' in *Patriotism*, ed. Samuel, 78. See also Linda Colley, 'Radical Patriotism in Eighteenth-Century England', in *Patriotism*, ed. Samuel, 169–187.
46. C.H. Norman, *Nationality and Patriotism* (Manchester: National Labour Press, 1915), no page numbers.
47. LA W/F RECOLLECTIONS, Hare, Walter, no date (hereafter nd).
48. IWM 74/61/1, First World War Recollections of H.D. Watson, 1914–1918.
49. Quotes from Jeremy D. Popkin, 'Historians on the Autobiographical Frontier', in *American Historical Review* 3 (June 1999): 725–726; see also Jerry White, 'Beyond Autobiography', in *People's History and Socialist Theory*, ed. Raphael Samuel (London: Routledge, 1981), 33–42.
50. See Daniel James, 'Doña María's Story', in *The Gendered Worlds of Latin American Women Workers*, ed. Daniel James and John French (Durham, NC: Duke University Press, 1997), 31–52; and John D. French and Daniel James, 'Oral History, Identity Formation, and Working-Class Mobilization', in *Gendered Worlds*, ed. James and French, 297–314.
51. LA ROYAL NAVY/MERCHANT NAVY RECOLLECTIONS, Struidiron, Mr, interviewed 1971. Others using similar phrasing include: IWM 85/22/1, Papers of T.H. Edmed, 1914–1918.
52. Anne Summers, 'Edwardian Militarism', in *Patriotism*, ed. Samuel, 236.
53. Cunningham, 'The Language of Patriotism', in *Patriotism*, ed. Samuel, 78.
54. Peter Liddle, 'British Loyalties: The Evidence of an Archive', in *Facing Armageddon: The First World War Experienced*, ed. Peter Liddle and Hugh Cecil (London: Leo Cooper, 1996), 523–538.
55. Anthony Bennett, 'After Nationalism', in *Patriotism*, ed. Samuel, 140–155 (141).

56 Laurence Senelick, 'Politics as Entertainment: Victorian Music Hall Songs', in *Victorian Studies* 19 (December 1975): 149.
57 Alan Clark, *The Donkeys* (London: Hutchinson, 1961). For a less polemical analysis, although more limited, see Correlli Barnett, *The Swordbearers: Studies in Supreme Command in the First World War* (London: Eyre & Spottiswoode, 1963); for an argument against it, see Gary Sheffield, *Forgotten Victory, the First World War: Myths and Realities* (London: Headline Books, 2001); Samuel Hynes, *A War Imagined* (New York: Collier Books, 1990), xi; Paul Fussell, *The Great War and Modern Memory* (London: Oxford University Press, 1975).
58 IWM 73/150/1, Papers of H.C. Parker, 1914–1918.
59 Anonymous quote from *Narrow Waters: The First Volume of the Life and Thoughts of a Common Man* (London: William Hodge, 1935), 205; for Shaw quote, see IWM 81/2/1, Memoirs of J. Shaw, b. 1903; 'Mistaken mentality' from IWM Sound Recording (hereafter SR) 13842/2, Bennett, James (Interview), b. 6 June 1898.
60 John Burnett (ed.) *Destiny Obscure: Autobiographies of Childhood, Education, and Family from the 1820s to the 1920s* (London: Routledge, 1994/1982), 89.
61 LA GENERAL SECTION, Carrier, R.J., Memoirs, 1978.
62 LA MIDDLEBROOKE: SOMME, Allsop, John, nd.
63 LA W/F RECOLLECTIONS, Smith, Norman, nd.
64 LA GENERAL SECTION, Ames, John, nd.
65 IWM SR 8323/6, Beeton, Arthur George (Interview).
66 IWM 76/225/1, Memoirs of R.L. Venables, 1914–1918.
67 IWM SR 8867/3, Dawson, Claude (Interview), b. 30 May 1896.
68 Quoted in Taylor, *English History*, 20, fn.1.
69 For H.G. Taylor, see IWM 73/206/1, Papers of H.G. Taylor, b. 27 September 1896; For Pitkeathly, see LA SEVERAL FRONTS RECOLLECTIONS, Pitkeathly, David, nd.
70 Or, as the historian Bruce Porter put it, the nation became the 'supreme claimant on human loyalty'. See Bruce Porter, *War and the Rise of the State* (New York: Free Press, 1994), 170.
71 Bernard Waites, *Class Society at War: England, 1914–1918* (Leamington Spa, UK: Berg, 1987), 275.
72 Ibid., 5.

2 The rush to colours, business as usual, and the coming of conscription: August 1914 to May 1916

1 The historiography of Britain's experience in the First World War is voluminous; too much so for it to be worth re-examining at length here. A useful entry point into that historiography is Stephen Constantine, Maurice W. Kirby, and Mary B. Rose, eds, *The First World War in British History* (London: Edward Arnold, 1995). James Joll sums the historiography of the causes of the First World War quite well in James Joll, *Origins of the First World War* (London: Longman, 1984).
2 V.R. Berghahn, *Germany and the Approach of War in 1914* (New York: St Martin's Press, 1973), 212. See also Michael R. Gordon, 'Domestic Conflict and the Origins of the First World War: The British and German Cases', *Journal of Modern History* 46 (1974): 191–226. For a counter-argument, see David E. Kaiser, 'Germany and the Origins of the First World War', *Journal of Modern History* 55 (1983): 442–474.
3 Good on the critical period is John Albert White, *Transition to Global Rivalry: Alliance Diplomacy and the Quadruple Entente, 1895–1907* (Cambridge: Cambridge University Press, 1995). A usefully short analysis of the British and German arms race comes in Michael Howard, 'The Edwardian Arms Race', in *Edwardian England*, ed. Donald Read (New Brunswick, NJ: Rutgers University Press, 1982), 145–161.

4 Quote in C.H. Rolph, *London Particulars* (Oxford: Oxford University Press, 1980), 88. The growth of enmity between the two countries is exhaustively explored in Paul Kennedy, *The Rise of the Anglo-German Antagonism* (London: George Allen & Unwin, 1980).
5 LA SEVERAL FRONTS RECOLLECTIONS, Baker, W.E., Military Medal, 1977.
6 For German bands, see LA GENERAL SUBJECT, Cripps, H.J., 1970, b. 1895; IWM 78/59/1, Papers of G.E.E. Williamson, 1914–1918; Hunt's account of his countermeasures is in IWM P/268, Hunt, H.E. (Papers), 1914–1918.
7 For a case study of British reaction to German moves, see Kenneth L. Moll, 'Politics, Power, and Panic: Britain's 1909 Dreadnought Gap', *Military Affairs* 21 (Fall 1965): 133–144. Sometimes she built more than she could afford. See Winston Churchill's take on the 1909 Dreadnought building programme: 'The Admiralty demanded six ships; the economists offered four: and we finally compromised on eight.' In his *The World Crisis*, vol. 1 (New York: Charles Scribner's Sons, 1923), 33.
8 They did not, however, go to conscription, for a number of reasons. Primary among them was the long-standing antipathy of the British towards conscription and large standing armies. By the end of the nineteenth century, the government also worried about training and arming a potentially rebellious working class. See V.G. Kiernan, 'Conscription and Society in Europe before the War of 1914–1918', in *War and Society: Historical Essays in Honour and Memory of J.R. Western, 1928–1971*, ed. V.G. Kiernan and M.R.D. Foot (London: Paul Elek, 1973), 141–158. There is a useful study of the military reforms in Jay Stone and Erwin A. Schmidl, *The Boer War and Military Reforms* (New York: University Press of America, 1988), 3–163. For a working-class perspective on it, see Richard Price, *An Imperial War and the British Working Class: Working Class Attitudes and Reactions to the Boer War 1899–1902* (London: Routledge & Kegan Paul, 1972).
9 Quote from John Gooch, 'Haldane and the "National Army"', in *Politicians and Defence: Studies in the Formulation of British Defence Policy 1845–1970*, ed. John Gooch and Ian Beckett (Manchester: Manchester University Press, 1981), 77; for an account of Haldane's reforms, see Franklyn Johnson, *Defence by Committee: The British Committee of Imperial Defence 1885–1959* (Oxford and London: Oxford University Press, 1960).
10 Quote from Anna Davin, 'Imperialism and Motherhood', in *Patriotism: The Making and Unmaking of British National Identity*, vol. I, ed. Raphael Samuel (London: Routledge, 1989), 204. For a discussion of the reaction to racial health issues, see Richard Allen Soloway, *Birth Control and the Population Question in England, 1877–1930* (Chapel Hill, NC: University of North Carolina Press, 1982), 31–65.
11 The entire situation is well analysed in G.R. Searle, *Quest for National Efficiency: A Study in British Politics and Political Thought, 1899–1914* (Oxford: Basil Blackwell, 1971). For working-class boys' associations, see John Springhall, *Youth, Empire and Society: British Youth Movements, 1883–1940* (London: Croom Helm, 1977), 71–74.
12 IWM 77/113/1, E. Buffey, 1914–1918. Walter Guthrie, a labourer, said:

> The Army in times of peace does not enlist much sympathetic interest. The only uniforms to be affectionately accepted are those of Postmen, Railwaymen, and Firemen. These represent to our selfish minds Convenience, Comfort, and Security. Only when war holds the stage do the troops become 'our dear lads'.

See LA W/F RECOLLECTIONS, Guthrie, Walter Edward.
13 IWM 92/36/1, Memoirs of 2nd Lt J.S. Handley, b. 1891. Handley worked in the building industry.
14 For an analysis of increase in striking, see James E. Cronin, 'Strikes, 1870–1914', in *A History of British Industrial Relations 1875–1914*, ed. Chris Wrigley (Boston: University of Massachusetts Press, 1982), 74–98. For a discussion that emphasizes

the Syndicalist interests of the new union members, see Henry Pelling, 'The Labour Unrest, 1911–1914', in Henry Pelling *Popular Politics and Society in Late Victorian Britain* (London: Macmillan, 1968), 147–164.
15 For example, see the chart of union growth in G.D.H. Cole, *Trade Unionism and Munitions* (Oxford: Clarendon Press, 1923), 24.
16 Quoted in Chris Wrigley, 'The Government and Industrial Relations', in *British Industrial Relations*, ed. Wrigley, 153.
17 Samuel Hynes, *A War Imagined* (New York: Collier Books (Macmillan), 1990), 7.
18 Martin Gilbert, *The First World War* (London: Weidenfeld & Nicolson, 1994), 22.
19 George N. Barnes, *From Workshop to War Cabinet* (London: Herbert Jenkins Ltd, 1923), 105–6.
20 Ibid., 105–6.
21 Quoted in Cameron Hazlehurst, *Politicians at War, July 1914 to May 1915: A Prologue to the Triumph of Lloyd George* (London: Jonathan Cape, 1971), 20.
22 A division which has been underemphasized. See Jo Vellacott, 'Feminist Consciousness and the First World War', *History Workshop* 23 (1987): 81–101; and Mary Sargant Florence, Catherine Marshall, and C.K. Ogden, *Militarism Versus Feminism* (London: Virago Press, 1987), esp. 1–36.
23 Barnes, *Workshop to War Cabinet*, 101. Two sources covering the suffragette campaign in detail are: Andrew Rosen, *Rise Up, Women! The Militant Campaign of the Women's Social and Political Union 1903–1914* (London: Routledge & Kegan Paul, 1974), and Leslie Parker Hume, *National Union of Women's Suffrage Societies, 1897–1914* (New York: Garland Publishing, 1982).
24 Hugh Armstrong Clegg, *History of British Trade Unions since 1889*, vol. 2 (Oxford: Clarendon Press, 1985), 24–25.
25 See PRO WO 33/688, A War Book for the War Office, 1914; WO 33/694, Home Defence – Central Force Scheme, August, 1914; Sydney Checkland, *British Public Policy 1776–1939: An Economic, Social, and Political Perspective* (Cambridge: Cambridge University Press, 1983), 222; IWM MISC29/ITEM522, Unidentified Diary, late July, 1914; for martial law, see PRO CAB 16/31–34, CID Documents Related to the War, Sub-Committee of the Committee of Imperial Defence: Emergency Powers in War, 30 June 1914.
26 Max Aitken, *Politicians and the War 1914–1916* (London: Oldbourne Book Co. Ltd, 1960), 12–13. See also Martin Pugh, *State and Society: British Political and Social History 1870–1992* (London: Edward Arnold, 1994), 137–146.
27 IWM 79/35/1, Starrett, D. (Papers), 1914–1918.
28 Charles B. Brown, Memoirs of a Private Soldier in the British Army in the First Great War, unpublished memoirs, IWM (uncatalogued). I have not been able to find a record of this in any of the secondary literature.
29 Jeremy Smith, 'Bluff, Bluster and Brinkmanship: Andrew Bonar Law and the Third Home Rule Bill', *Historical Journal* 36 (1993): 161–178. For 'managed extremism' see Geoffrey Searle, 'The "Revolt from the Right" in Edwardian Britain', in *Nationalist and Racialist Movements in Britain and Germany Before 1914*, ed. Paul Kennedy and Anthony Nicolls (London: Macmillan, 1978), 21–40.
30 John Gooch, *The Prospect of War: Studies in British Defence Policy* (London: Frank Cass, 1981), 116–123.
31 Quoted in the *Daily Mail*, 22 July 1914, 5. A cry echoed by Asquith, see Robin Wilson, 'Imperialism in Crisis: The "Irish Dimension"', in *Crises in the British State 1880–1930*, ed. Mary Langan and Bill Schwarz (London: Hutchinson, 1985), 163.
32 A useful and short analysis of this process can be found in Keith Wilson, ed., *Decisions for War, 1914* (New York: St Martin's Press, 1995).
33 Marvin Swartz, *Union of Democratic Control in British Politics During the First World War* (Oxford: Clarendon Press, 1971), 11–38.
34 For a useful analysis of socialist thinking about the war, both inside and outside the

Labour Party, see Jay Winter, *Socialism and the Challenge of War: Ideas and Politics in Britain 1912–1918* (London: Routledge & Kegan Paul, 1974).

35 Hazlehurst, *Politicians at War*, 20–122; Marvin Swartz, 'A Study in Futility: The British Radicals at the Outbreak of the First World War', in *Edwardian Radicalism, 1900–1914*, ed. A.J.A. Morris (London: Routledge & Kegan Paul, 1974), 246–261.
36 Quoted in Keith Robbins, *Abolition of War: The 'Peace Movement' in Britain, 1914–1919* (Cardiff: University of Wales Press, 1976), 34.
37 IWM 75/3/1, First World War Account of Major F. Mitchell, MC, nd.
38 Bertrand Russell, *Autobiography* (London: Unwin Paperbacks, 1967), 239.
39 IWM 74/61/1, First World War Recollections of H.D. Watson, nd. See also IWM 85/28/1, Papers of S.T. Kemp, nd; IWM 88/52/1, Memoirs of A.J. Jamieson, 1977–1980; IWM SR 4976/8, Catley, Eric (Interview), 1976.
40 For an account of this, see IWM 76/160/1, Papers of A.W. Bradbury, nd; IWM 90/37/1, Bate, Capt E.E.H. (Papers), 1914–1918.
41 Michael Macdonagh, *In London during the Great War* (London: Eyre & Spottiswoode, 1935), 95. See also: LA W/F RECOLLECTIONS, F.C. Formby, 4 August 1914; IWM 76/160/1, Papers of A.W. Bradbury, 1914–1918; LA TAPE 248, F.J. Bettis, b. 1899.
42 LA W/F RECOLLECTIONS, Sloan, James Alexander Cameron, 1979.
43 Russell, *Autobiography*, 240. For an analysis of his thought during the war, see Jo Vellacott, *Bertrand Russell and the Pacifists in the First World War* (Brighton: Harvester Press, 1980).
44 Martin Ceadal, *Pacifism in Britain 1914–1945: The Defining of a Faith* (Oxford: Clarendon Press, 1980), 32.
45 Swartz, 'A Study in Futility', 246–261.
46 Ibid.
47 For pro-strike, see the *Daily Herald*, London, 5 August 1914, 6. For pro-war see ibid., 17 August 1914, 6.
48 See his letter to *The Times* (London), 24 October 1914, 5.
49 Anti-war quote from Robbins, *Abolition*, 30; for PRC, see British Library (BL) AddMSS/54192A, Minutes of the Parliamentary Recruiting Committee, 27 August 1914.
50 Royden Harrison, 'The War Emergency Workers' National Committee, 1914–1920', in *Essays in Labour History 1886–1923*, ed. Asa Briggs and John Saville (London: Macmillan, 1971), 211–259; Clegg, *British Trade Unions*, 118–150. The reports published by the WEWNC can be seen in *War Emergency Workers' National Committee Publications* (London: War Emergency Workers' National Committee, 1914–1916); for strike cessation see Samuel Hurwitz, *State Intervention in Great Britain: A Study of Economic Control and Social Response 1914–1919* (London: Frank Cass, 1949), 241.
51 Figures are in A.R. Thatcher, ed., *British Labour Statistics: Historical Abstract 1886–1968* (London: HMSO, 1971), 396; Checkland, *British Public Policy*, 222; Clegg, *Trade Unions*, 25; Hurwitz, *State Intervention*, 241.
52 For a discussion of 'business as usual' see David French, *British Economic and Strategic Planning, 1905–1915* (London: Allen & Unwin, 1982), 22–38, 98–123; Gerald DeGroot, *Blighty: British Society in the Era of the Great War* (London: Longman, 1996), 54–78; David French, 'The Rise and Fall of "Business as Usual"', in *War and the State: The Transformation of British Government, 1914–1919*, ed. Kathleen Burk (London: George Allen & Unwin, 1982), 7–31. At a practical level, 'business as usual' meant that – although trading with the enemy was technically banned (see PRO CAB 1/10, Cabinet Documents regarding the War, #30 Report on the Opening of the War/1 Nov. 1914), James Sloan's company continued to receive the raw goods it needed from Germany, if by a more roundabout route: 'The slogan was "business as usual", taken so literally that, although it was at once made an

offence to trade with the enemy, Ohlenschlager Brothers continued, throughout the war, to receive German leather via Holland which remained neutral and made a fortune.' LA W/F RECOLLECTIONS, Sloan, James Alexander Cameron, 1979. For politicians and publishers believing that the war would end by Christmas, see LA SEVERAL FRONTS RECOLLECTIONS, Baker, W.E., Military Medal, 1977. For the popular belief that the war would end quickly, see Chapter 4.

53 For a detailed account, if one that relies perhaps a bit too much on Lloyd George's memoirs, see Peter Simkins, 'Kitchener and the Expansion of the Army', in *Politicians and Defence*, ed. Gooch and Beckett, 87–109. For a sense of how dominant Kitchener was within the War Office, an examination of the Army Council is instructive. In the pre-war era, the Council – consisting of the Secretary of State for War, the Parliamentary Under Secretary, the Financial Secretary, the Chief of the Imperial General Staff, the Adjutant General, the Quartermaster General, the Master General of the Ordnance, and the Secretary of the War Office – met twice monthly to set Army policy. During Kitchener's time as Secretary of State for War (August 1914– June 1916), the Army Council met a total of two times. In 1916, after Kitchener's death, the council met two to three times a month. In 1917, the council met anywhere from two to eleven times a month; in 1918, two to seven times a month. See PRO WO 163/19, Index of the Decisions of, and Précis Prepared for the Army Council (1914–1921).

54 IWM 81/14/1, Memoirs of H. Bartlett, 1914–1918.

55 R.J.Q. Adams and Philip Poirer, *Conscription Controversy in Great Britain, 1900–1918* (London: Macmillan, 1987), 59.

56 PRO WO 73/97, 156–161, Central Monthly Return of the Army, May–Aug. 1914. For doubling of the shortage, see PRO WO 163/20, Minutes of the Proceedings and Précis Prepared for the Army Council, 22 May 1914 meeting of the War Council, Précis no. 815.

57 PRO WO 159/3, 22. That shortage had grown worse since 1 January 1914, when it was 9,000. See WO 73/96, Central Monthly Return of the Army, January–April 1914.

58 PRO CAB 17/106, Committee for Imperial Defence (CID) Documents Relating to the War, Letter from Lord Esher to Hankey (11 August 1914). Kitchener's last experience of a volunteer military organization had been witnessing the ineffectual French units in the Franco-Prussian War of 1870–1871.

59 LA SEVERAL FRONTS RECOLLECTIONS, Turner, Frank, interviewed 1980.

60 IWM 80/32/1, Papers of Colonel Sir Geoffrey Christie-Miller, 1914–1918, and WO 162/26, Letter on Recruits, 10 October 1914. LA W/F RECOLLECTIONS, H. Bagenal, nd; PRO WO 159/18, The Creedy (K) Papers – Kitchener Letters, War Office Recruiting Memorandum (21 August 1914); PRO CAB 17/111A, CID Documents Relating to the War, Esher Memorandum (9 October 1914).

61 See PRO T 1/11626/9439, Press Censorship, 1912–1914.

62 Charles H. Carrington, *Soldier from the War Returning* (London: Hutchinson, 1965), 49.

63 Summary and quotes are from *The Times* (London), 30 August 1914, 1.

64 IWM P/472, Tower, Miss W.L.B. (Papers), nd.

65 *The Times* (London), 1 September 1914, 2, 9. See also the account in *The History of The Times, 1912–1948* (New York: Macmillan, 1952), 222–227; John Terraine, *The Impacts of War 1914–1918* (London: Hutchinson, 1970), 59–64.

66 IWM 77/156/1, West, Miss G.M. (Papers). See also IWM P/472, Tower, Miss W.L.B. (Papers), 29 August 1914. Even some officers and newspaper publishers believed the stories. IWM CON/SHELF Aston, Lt Colonel C.C. CBE (Papers); H.A. Gwynne, Letter to Countess Bathurst, 3 September 1914 in *The Rasp of War: The Letters of H.A. Gwynne to the Countess Bathurst*, ed. Keith Wilson (London: Sidgwick & Jackson, 1988), no page number. Even the Germans joined in, claiming

in a 12 September dispatch that any Russian force transported in such a way could have no effect on the outcome of the war. See: IWM P/401, 402, Robinson, F.A., 1914–1918.
67 PRO CAB 63/5, Hankey Papers, 1915, Note by the Secretary of State for War on 'The War' August 1914 to 31 May 1915.
68 Daily recruiting figures from PRO NATS 1/398.
69 Ibid.
70 LA GALLIPOLI RECOLLECTIONS, Battersby, F., 1972.
71 PRO WO 162/26, Letters on Recruits, 1914, Telegram of 1 September 1914 to commanders of the recruiting centres.
72 For capacity of the depots, see PRO WO 33/612, Report of the Committe on War Establishments (Home), 1912. PRO WO 159/18, War Office Memorandum, 4 September 1914; 'buried alive' at PRO T 1/11662/17287/14, Memoranda – War Proposals Committee, August–October 1914.
73 PRO WO 293/1, War Office Instructions, 8 September 1914. For a recollection of seeing hundreds of enlistees in their own clothes at the training depot, see LA GENERAL SECTION, Jaeger, W., Interviewed 1969, b. 1890.
74 For 'Kitchener's Blue', see LA SALONIKA RECOLLECTIONS, Dunning, Cabb, nd, and LA SALONIKA RECOLLECTIONS, Ransley, A.G., nd. Also LA MIDDLEBROOKE: SOMME, Wilkinson, G., 1974; LA GENERAL SECTION, Barley, W., nd, but post-war; LA W/F RECOLLECTIONS, Price, L.S., nd.
75 IWM 94/11/1, Papers of R.E. Foulkes, b. 1894. He was a plumber's apprentice when he enlisted. For 'motley' see Macdonagh, *In London during the Great War*, 35. 'Cossacks', R.J. Bailey thought his unit's mixed clothing made them look like. IWM 92/36/1, Bailey, R.J. (Papers), 16 Sept. 1914, letter.
76 For uniforms see IWM P/428, Papers of 2nd Lt C. Carter, 1914–1918. For other shortages, see PRO PRO 30/57/80, Miscellaneous Correspondence to Kitchener, 1914–1916, Letter of 12 Feb. 1915 from Archibald Hunter.
77 For Japanese rifles, see IWM 80/43/1, The Wartime Experiences of an Ordinary 'Tommy' by T.A. Bickerton, 1964. For sticks, see LA W/F RECOLLECTIONS, Henderson, Stanley, nd (probably 1974); LA GALLIPOLI RECOLLECTIONS, Attwood, J.C., 1972.
78 LA GENERAL SECTION, Barley, W., nd, but post-war.
79 IWM 81/44/1, Bless 'em All: The Long and the Short and the Tall, Memoirs of F. Palmer Cook, 1914–1918/1939–1945. See also LA GENERAL SECTION, Driver, P.T. 1982.
80 LA GENERAL SECTION, Smith, G.J., 1914 Diary. Although a great number of men complained about the food, many working-class enlistees found it delicious. F. Moakler, a middle-class man, could not stomach the rations but found his compatriot more than willing: ' ... breakfast ... [was] two slices of bread and some paloney [sic] sausage. No good I just could not face it. I sat and looked at it and the chap next to me said "Can't manage it?" and promptly stuck his fork in it and it was gone. I fed alright later on.' LA W/F RECOLLECTIONS, Moakler, F., b. 1899.
81 LA W/F RECOLLECTIONS, Hodge, D.A., nd.
82 For marching on the War Office, see LA TAPE 8, Lawson, G., nd; for complaints, see LA GENERAL SUBJECT, Wilson, R.N.P., Letters and Papers, 1914–1916.
83 For date, see WO 162/24, New Armies – Recruiting Officers and Other Ranks – Statistical Returns, 1914–1915, 4 September 1914: War Office Telegram. For enlistees who experienced it, see LA GALLIPOLI RECOLLECTIONS, Smith, E., 1980; LA GENERAL SECTION, Hooker, W.J., interviewed 1989; IWM 73/124/1, Memoirs of J.C.J. Bailey, 1914–1918; IWM 85/39/1, Field, F.J. (Papers), 1914–1918; IWM P/262, Diary of H.T. Bolton (7 September 1914).
84 PRO WO 159/18, Telegram from War Office to Officers Commanding Districts, 11 September 1914.

85 Returns are at PRO WO 159/3, 22; for drafting of NCOs, see PRO WO 159/18, Letter from Kitchener to Recruiting Officers, 21 August 1914. For police sergeants, see PRO WO 293/1, War Office Instructions, 4 September 1914.
86 PRO WO 159/19, Matters Concerning Recruiting, 1915, 'Description of Recruiting Since Mobilization'.
87 Parliamentary Recruiting Committee, *Leaflets of the Parliamentary Recruiting Committee* (London: HMSO, 1914–1916), 28 October 1914.
88 The height requirement was moved back to 5ft 4ins in October 1914, and then back to 5ft 3ins on 6 November 1914. See *The Times* (London), 6 November 1914, 5. The story of the Bantams is usefully told in Sidney Allinson, *The Bantams: The Untold Story of World War I* (London: Howard Baker, 1981); for first-person accounts, see IWM 94/46/1, Papers of K. Fraser, (1914–1918); IWM 79/17/1, Jennings, Thomas Alfred, 'Hark! I Hear the Bugles Calling', nd.
89 Ibid.
90 For shunning of military service, see John Gooch, 'The Armed Services', in *First World War*, ed. Constantine, Kirby, and Rose, 189; Gilbert, *First World War*, 224; P.E. Dewey, 'Military Recruiting and the British Labour Force during the First World War', *Historical Journal* 27 (1984): 199–223. For badly organized recruiting, see Keith Grieves, *Politics of Manpower, 1914–1918* (Manchester: Manchester University Press, 1988), 7; Peter Simkins, *Kitchener's Army: The Raising of the New Armies, 1914–1916* (Manchester: Manchester University Press, 1981), xv.
91 PRO WO 33/612, Report of the Committee on War Establishments (Home), 1912.
92 Even excluding the boom months of August and September 1914, when casualties were relatively low, the 15-month enlistment average was 113,659 as opposed to a wastage rate of 25,449. All figures taken from PRO WO 161/82, 83–84.
93 PRO CAB 27/2. Report from the CID on War Policy (6 September 1915); PRO CAB 63/11, Hankey Papers, Remarks on the Reports of the Cabinet War Policy Committee (14 September 1915).
94 PRO WO 159/3, 22 and PRO WO 161/82, 83. Precise figures for the Territorials were not kept until after October 1914.
95 PRO WO 159/3, The Creedy (K) Papers – Lord Kitchener's Strategical, Political, and Miscellaneous Papers, The War: Note by the Secretary of State for War (31 May 1915). See also PRO WO 162/18, Miscellaneous Correspondence on Mobilization, Letter from Beveridge to the War Office (31 July 1914). For some examples, see William Turner, *Accrington Pals: 11th (Service) Battalion (Accrington) East Lancashire Regiment* (Lancashire: Lancashire County Books, 1992); Michael Stedman, *Salford Pals: A History of the 15th, 16th, 19th and 20th Battalions Lancashire Fusiliers 1914–1919* (London: Leo Cooper, 1993); John M. Garwood, *Chorley Pals: 'Y' Company, 11th (Service) Battalion, East Lancashire Regiment* (Manchester: Neil Richardson, 1989); IWM P/115, Papers of Major C.H. Emerson, 1914–1918. Emerson helped organize the Grimsby Pals Battalion in September 1914.
96 PRO WO 293/1, War Office Instructions (7 August 1914, 4 September 1914).
97 PRO PRO 30/57/59. Kitchener Correspondence with Lord Esher and items from the Fitzgerald Papers (21 July 1915).
98 For party organizations, see Roy Douglas, 'Voluntary Enlistment in the First World War and the Work of the Parliamentary Recruiting Committee', *Journal of Modern History* 42 (1970): 564–585; BL AddMSS/54192A, Minutes of the Parliamentary Recruiting Committee, 1914–1916; for trade union efforts, see *War Emergency Workers' National Committee Publications*. For women's groups, see Sandra Stanley Holton, *Feminism and Democracy: Women's Suffrage and Reform Politics in Britain 1900–1918* (Cambridge: Cambridge University Press, 1986), 132; personal memories of wartime women's organizations are in Annie Kenney, *Memories of a Militant* (London: Edward Arnold, 1924). For labour registries, see PRO MUN

5/50/300/33/5, Circulars to Divisional Officers (Board of Trade, Labour Exchanges, and Unemployment Insurance), 1 January–31 March 1915. For the Church, see LA W/F RECOLLECTIONS, Price, L.S., 3 September 1914, who was recruited into a unit organized by the Vicar of Slaugham.

99   A.J.P. Taylor, *English History, 1914–1945* (Oxford: Oxford University Press, 1965), 58; Lloyd George quote from Randolph S. Churchill, *Lord Derby: King of Lancashire* (London: Heinemann, 1959), 187.
100 Grieves, *Politics of Manpower*, 7; Graham Maddocks, *Liverpool Pals: A History of the 17th, 18th, 19th, and 20th (Service) Battalions the King's (Liverpool Regiment) 1914–1919* (London: Leo Cooper, 1991), 27; For 'Lord Derby's Whirlwind Recruiting Campaigns', see PRO WO 161/112, Statements of Work Since August 1914 by Certain County Territorial Force Associations, Memorandum by West Lancashire Territorial Force (October 1915); LA GENERAL SECTION, Cowles, E., b. 30 September 1897.
101 PRO WO 293/2, War Office Instructions (8 February 1915). See also PRO MUN 5/50/300/33/5, Circulars to Divisional Officers (Board of Trade, Labour Exchanges, and Unemployment Insurance), Memorandum of 26 February 1915.
102 PRO WO 159/3, The Creedy (K) Papers – Lord Kitchener's Strategical, Political, and Miscellaneous Papers, The War: Note by the Secretary of State for War (31 May 1915).
103 *Daily Mail*, 5 November 1914, 4. For a list of advertising totals spent by the War Office, see PRO WO 113/5, War Notes (December 1915).
104 IWM PP/MCR/116, Rice, C.J. (Papers), nd; PRO WO 293/2, War Office Instructions (29 April 1915).
105 PRO WO 161/112, Statements of Work since August 1914 by Certain County Territorial Force Associations, 22 September 1917; IWM 88/57/1, Rhodes, Vernon (Papers), nd.
106 NAM 8307/56, Recruiting Posters, 1914–1918.
107 PRO WO 161/112, Statements of Work since August 1914 by Certain County Territorial Force Associations, 22 September 1917; IWM 82/3/1, Papers of N.J. Fowler, 1914–1918.
108 PRO MUN 5/9/180/3, Memorandum on the Shortage of Labour by Sir George Askwith (28 January 1915).
109 PRO MUN 5/9/180/2, Limits of Enlistment (Balfour) and Comments (Beveridge and Llewellyn-Smith) (1 January 1915). For military agreement, see PRO WO 159/22, Memorandum on the War by General Callwell (24 June 1915).
110 PRO WO 159/3.
111 PRO RG 28/9, National Register (July 1915).
112 9 June 1915, 5. See also Sir R.A.S. Redmayne, *The British Coal-Mining Industry during the War* (Oxford: Clarendon Press, 1923), 15.
113 IWM 91/3/1, Papers of W. Watkins, b. 1897.
114 IWM 77/84/1, 'All for a Shilling a Day', Autobiography of William F. Pressey, 1914–1918.
115 Minnie [no last name] writing to her brother Eddy on 11 November 1914, IWM MISC 340/BOX 15.
116 PRO PRO 30/57/76, Correspondence between Kitchener and Asquith.
117 6 September 1914, 8.
118 IWM MISC 94/ITEM 1441 23 November 1914.
119 In the *Pall Mall* (London). Noted by IWM P/401, 402. Robinson, F.A. (papers), 23 November 1914. For a discussion of recruiting efforts through the governing body, the Football Association, see Cate Haste, *Keep the Home Fires Burning: Propaganda in the First World War* (London: Allen Lane, 1977), 59.
120 27 November 1914, 9. The pressure on football grew so strong that the Football Association decided, in April 1915, to cancel all matches for the remainder of the war. See *Daily Mail* (London), 20 April 1915, 3.

Notes 145

121 See, for example, the *Daily Mail*, 7, 8 October 1914, 6 July 1915, 20 October 1915, 5 January 1916, all p. 4. Similar articles appeared in *The Times* (London), 19 November 1914, 5; 14 July 1915, 9; 26 August 1915, 7; 3 November 1915, 11; 29 December 1915, 9. See also the *Weekly Dispatch* (London), 10 January 1915, 1; 23 May 1915, 5. 'Unmarried loafers' from a letter from Edmund Talbot to Fitzgerald, IWM PP/MCR/118, Fitzgerald, Lt Col. B. (Papers) 2 March 1915.

122 21 May 1914, 4.

123 Memorandum of 6 October 1915 in PRO RG 28/11, National Registration Committee Minutes and Miscellaneous Papers, 1915–1916; for the government analysis of the figures, see PRO CAB 27/2, Report from the CID on War Policy, 6 September 1915.

124 See an unsigned memorandum that pointed out exactly this problem at PRO RG 28/1, National Registration, 1915–1919, volume 1.

125 PRO CAB 27/2, Report from the CID on War Policy, 6 September 1915; PRO WO 159/18, The Creedy (K) Papers – Kitchener Letters, 1914–1915.

126 See Chapter 3.

127 See the memorandum of 6 October 1915 in PRO RG 28/1, National Registration, 1915–1919, vol. 1.

128 IWM 76/41/1, Papers of P.E. Williamson, nd; William Hall, *The Lone Terrier* (Shropshire: Cadre of the King's Shropshire Highland Light Infantry, 1969), no page numbers; IWM 77/186/1, A.R. Reid, Letter (9 December 1914); IWM 79/49/1, Papers of A. Russell, October 1914; IWM 81/35/1, Papers of S. Bradbury, October 1915.

129 PRO PRO 30/57/73, Manpower and Recruiting/Correspondence; PRO RG 28/12, National Registration Committee – Interim Report and Sir H. Monro's Papers (Secretary of the Local Government Board).

130 PRO PRO 30/57/82, WX11, Munitions, 1914–1916; P.E. Dewey, 'Military Recruiting and the British Labour Force During the First World War', *Historical Journal* 27 (1984): 199.

131 A.J.P. Taylor, ed., *My Darling Pussy: The Letters of Lloyd George and Frances Stevenson, 1913–1941* (London: Weidenfeld & Nicolson, 1975), 7; Martin Pugh, *Lloyd George* (London: Longman, 1988), 78–81.

132 *The Times* (London), 14 May 1915, 8; LA SEVERAL FRONTS RECOLLECTIONS, Baker, W.E., Military Medal, 1977.

133 When the *Daily Mail* (London) attacked Kitchener's handling of the munitions situation, angry crowds burned copies of it in the street. See DeGroot, *Blighty*, 78. For the King's opinion of Kitchener, see PRO PRO 30/57/104, Royal Correspondence, Letter from Stamfordham (on behalf of George V), 22 May 1915; George Cassar, *Kitchener: Architect of Victory* (London: William Kimber, 1977), 190. For Kitchener's position in the Cabinet and nation during the Shells Crisis, see Hew Strachan, *The Politics of the British Army* (Oxford: Clarendon Press, 1997), 128–131. For the manoeuvring that went on to circumvent Kitchener after this, on both the military and political side, see David R. Woodward, *Field Marshal Sir William Robertson: Chief of the Imperial General Staff in the Great War* (London: Praeger, 1998), 14–32.

134 PRO MUN 5/10/180/17, Mobilization of War Industries – Conference between the Government and the Representatives of Trade Unions and Federations, 17–19 March 1915.

135 PRO WO 159/22, Memorandum on the War by General Callwell, 24 June 1915.

136 PRO MUN 5/19/221.1/1–4, Munitions of War Bill, 16–21 June 1915.

137 PRO MUN 5/49/300/15, Report of the Labour Department, 2 December 1915.

138 Walter Long, President of the Local Government Board, at the Second Reading of the National Registration Bill, 15 June 1915. PRO RG 28/12, National Registration Committee – Interim Report and Sir H. Monro's Papers (Secretary of the Local Government Board), 15 June–15 October 1915.

139 War Office Memorandum, 9 July 1915 in PRO WO 159/19, Matters Concerning Recruiting, 1915.
140 IWM P97, Blumenfeld.
141 A.J. Balfour warned of 'a great body of hostile opinion' opposing conscription, while Walter Long believed that conscription would create massive working-class unrest and lead to a 'great strike'. For Balfour, see PRO CAB 1/13, Cabinet Documents regarding the war, 1914–1915, #10: Note by A.J. Balfour on Efficiency in War and Compulsion September 1915. For Long, see 10 August 1915 Memorandum in PRO RG 28/12, National Registration Committee – Interim Report and Sir H. Monro's Papers (Secretary of the Local Government Board), 15 June–15 October 1915.
142 Memorandum by Arthur Henderson in PRO CAB 27/2, Report from the Committee for Imperial Defence (CID) on War Policy, 30 October 1915.
143 Kitchener remained opposed for two reasons. First, he had undertaken to the trade union leaders that he would use conscription only as a last resort in return for their allowing labour dilution. Second, Asquith appealed to him personally not to come out in favour of conscription because such a statement would seriously undermine the Prime Minister's position in the government. See Cassar, *Kitchener*, 444–456.
144 PRO CAB 37/135/15. Kitchener Memo on Recruiting (8 October 1915); PRO WO 159/4, The Creedy (K) Papers – Lord Kitchener's Strategical, Political and Miscellaneous Papers, June–December 1915.
145 PRO WO 293/3, War Office Instructions, July–December 1915, 23 October 1915.
146 Note by Asquith, 15 October 1915, in PRO PRO 30/57/73, Manpower and Recruiting/Correspondence, 1914–1916.
147 Letter of October 1915 in PRO PRO 30/57/73, Manpower and Recruiting/Correspondence, 1914–1916.
148 6 October 1915, 8.
149 Exactly how the Army calculated the figure of 240,000 is unclear. The permanent wastage (killed and those too badly wounded to return to the front) suffered by the BEF in those two months was 51,325 men (of whom 16,007 were killed). See PRO WO 161/82, 83. Allowing the number wounded as 48,000 (about three times the number killed), the average rate for the entire war, see PRO WO 161/82, 237 gives total casualties as about 99,000 men, less than half of those recruited. For Derby quote, see Memorandum on Recruiting by Lord Derby, 12 December 1915, in PRO WO 159/4, The Creedy (K) Papers – Lord Kitchener's Strategical, Political and Miscellaneous Papers, June–December 1915.
150 E. Golledge, for example, was working as a fitter and a turner and his firm forbade him to enlist, LA TAPE 155, E. Golledge, b. 1897.
151 PRO WO 293/3, War Office Instructions (4 December 1915).
152 See for example Asquith's speeches, reported in *The Times* (London), 3, 12 November 1915, 11, 9.
153 Adams and Poirer, *Conscription*, 125.
154 See PRO HO 45/10782/278537, Publications Regarding the War (Home Office – Cont), 1916 for a series of warnings about the public consequences of introducing conscription.
155 For public opinion, see Poirer and Adams, *Conscription*, 133–143; For MPs' votes, see J.M. Bourne, *Britain and the Great War, 1914–1918* (London: Edward Arnold, 1989), 123. The NCF, for example, claimed, as its highest membership, 15,000 people (in the summer of 1916) and even this was almost certainly an exaggeration. See Ceadel, *Pacifism*, 33.
156 Dewey, 'Military Recruiting', 199–223, discusses the control of British workers after the introduction of conscription.
157 The Labour Department laid out its plans in PRO MUN 5/49/300/15, Report of the Labour Department, 2 December 1915. For British factories equipping American armies, see Paul Y. Hammond, *Organizing for Defense: The American Military*

Establishment in the Twentieth Century (Princeton, NJ: Princeton University Press, 1961), 49.
158 PRO WO 161/82, 83.
159 PRO CAB 27/3, Cabinet Committee on the Size of the Army, 18 April 1916.
160 Roy Douglas, 'Voluntary Enlistment in the First World War and the Work of the Parliamentary Recruiting Committee', *Journal of Modern History* 42 (1970): 585.
161 PRO CAB 17/156. CID Documents Relating to the War, Manpower Distribution Board – Memoranda by the Adjutant General, 16 August 1916.
162 James Hinton, *Labour and Socialism: A History of the British Labour Movement 1867–1974* (London: Wheatsheaf Books, 1983), 30.
163 PRO RG 28/1, National Registration, 1915–1919, vol. 1.
164 PRO WO 162/28, Memos on Recruiting, Recruiting memo by the Adjutant General on Recruiting (31 May 1917).
165 Quoted in Bourne, *Britain*, 90.

3 Currents within the flood: who were the volunteers?

1 PRO WO 394/20, Monthly Recruiting Figures, 1914–1918.
2 PRO CAB 27/2, Estimate of the Condition of the Industrial Population of the United Kingdom, August 1915.
3 Ibid.
4 John Morton Osborne, *Voluntary Recruiting Movement in Britain, 1914–1916* (New York: Garland Publishing, 1982), 8.
5 'Backward' from PRO WO 159/19, Matters Concerning Recruiting, 1915; PRO CAB 1/10, Cabinet Documents regarding the War, 1914, #35, Recruiting in Proportion to Population, November 1914. For rural inhabitants who journeyed to a town to enlist, see IWM SR 12269/4, Barker, Albert (Interview), b. 21 August 1892 and LA GENERAL SECTION, Waring, F.E., interviewed 1980.
6 PRO WO 159/3, 23.
7 Census figures are in PRO CAB 27/2, Appendix XVIII; Agricultural enlistment figures are apparently not available. However, the Derby Scheme registration found the number of agricultural men of military age remaining in England in August 1915 to be 374,263 which shows an enlistment of 175,000, or 32 per cent.
8 PRO CAB 27/2, Appendix XVIII.
9 LA SEVERAL FRONTS RECOLLECTIONS, Fraser Harris, A.A., nd.
10 For restraints on agricultural professions, see PRO RG 28/1, Derby's Report on Recruiting, 12 December 1915; for urban, see PRO CAB 27/2, Appendix XIII.
11 Quoted in Alun Howkins, *Poor Labouring Men: Rural Radicalism in Norfolk, 1870–1923* (London: Routledge, 1985), 116. For other examples, see IWM SR 9118/8, Crow, Jim (Interview), b. 5 November 1893, IWM 85/28/1, Papers of S.T. Kemp, 1914–1918. Assistance: PRO MUN 5/50/300/33/7, Circulars to Divisional Officers (Board of Trade, Labour Exchanges, and Unemployment Insurance), 1 July–30 September 1915.
12 P.E. Dewey, 'Government Provision of Farm Labour in England and Wales, 1914–1918', *Agricultural History Review* 27 (1979): 110–121. The use of soldiers caused some hard feelings among the rural labourers as the soldiers were paid more than they were. In one case, a labourer gave notice rather than work alongside a soldier. See Howkins, *Labouring Men*, 118.
13 PRO WO 159/3, 23.
14 PRO WO 161/82.
15 Quoted in Edward Spiers, 'The Scottish Soldier at War', in *Facing Armageddon: The First World War Experienced*, ed. Peter Liddle and Hugh Cecil (London: Leo Cooper, 1996), 315.

16. T. Chalmers, *An Epic of Glasgow: History of the 15th Battalion the Highland Light Infantry (City of Glasgow Regiment)* (Glasgow: John McCallum, 1934), x.
17. Cyril Parry, 'Gwynedd and the Great War, 1914–1918', *Welsh History Review* 4 (June 1988): 78–117.
18. Anthony Mór O'Brien, 'Patriotism on Trial: The Strike of the South Wales Miners, July 1915', *Welsh History Review* 12 (June 1984): 86.
19. For 1914, see *The Times* (London), 24 August 1914, 2. For 1917, see PRO NATS 1/6, Recruitment of Miners, Post-War and Pre-War, September 1917. For a Kitchener's battalion that consisted of 50 per cent Welsh miners, see Richard Hilton, *Nine Lives: The Autobiography of an Old Soldier* (London: Hollis & Carter, 1955).
20. Keith Jeffrey, 'The Irish Military Tradition and the British Empire', in *'An Irish Empire?' Aspects of Ireland and the British Empire*, ed. Keith Jeffrey (Manchester: Manchester University Press, 1996), 94–123.
21. IWM Uncatalogued., 'Memoirs of a Private Soldier in the British Army in the First Great War', Charles B. Brown, 1914–1918.
22. Two of whose members remembered joining up: LA GENERAL SECTION, Nicholls, P., nd, LA DOMESTIC FRONT (IRELAND), Grange, R., Letters and Papers, 1914–1916. See also Pauline Codd, 'Recruiting and Responses to the War in Wexford', in *Ireland and the First World War*, ed. David Fitzpatrick (Dublin: Trinity History Workshop, 1986), 15–26.
23. David Howie and Josephine Howie, 'Irish Recruiting and the Home Rule Crisis of August–September 1914', in *Strategy and Intelligence: British Policy During the First World War*, ed. Michael Dockrill and David French (London: The Hambledon Press, 1996), 20.
24. Quoted in the *Irish Independent* excerpted in PRO PRO 30/57/60, Irish Affairs (Kitchener Papers), 1914–1916.
25. Frank M. Laird, *Personal Experiences of the Great War* (Dublin: Eason & Son, 1925), 2–3. See also IWM 75/16/1, Memoirs of A.W. Fenn, 1914–1918 who, as a soldier, was given a bag of fruit by Irish women when leaving Curragh for France in 1914 with a pamphlet inside asking 'Why should Ireland fight England's battles?'.
26. IWM P/262, Brennan, A.R. (Papers), 1914–1918. Brennan's unit was cheered by crowds through Dublin as it marched to the ships on 27 May 1915.
27. Quotes are from Myles Dungan, *They Shall Not Grow Old: Irish Soldiers and the Great War* (Dublin: Four Courts Press, 1997), 197, 24, 18–19.
28. Thomas Dooley, *Irishmen or English Soldiers: The Times and World of a Southern Catholic Irishman Enlisting in the British Army During the First World War* (Liverpool: Liverpool University Press, 1995).
29. PRO WO 159/3, The Creedy (K) Papers – Lord Kitchener's Strategical, Political, and Miscellaneous Papers, January–May 1915.
30. PRO CAB 27/2, Estimate of the Condition of the Industrial Population of the United Kingdom, August 1915.
31. See PRO RG 28/1, National Register, Appendix (C), Occupational Groups and Age, August 1915; PRO CAB 27/2, Estimate of the Condition of the Industrial Population of the United Kingdom, Appendix XVIII, August 1915.
32. PRO RG 28/1, National Register, Appendix (B), Estimates of the 46 Occupation Groups, August 1915.
33. PRO WO 394/20, Monthly Recruiting Figures, 1914–1918 and PRO CAB 27/2, Estimate of the Condition of the Industrial Population of the United Kingdom, August 1915.
34. PRO CAB 27/2, Estimate of the Condition of the Industrial Population of the United Kingdom, Appendix XVIII, August 1915. Total number from 1911 Census.
35. J.M. Winter, *The Great War and the British People* (Cambridge, MA: Harvard University Press, 1986), 25. See also W.J. Reader, *At Duty's Call: A Study in Obsolete Patriotism* (Manchester: Manchester University Press, 1988), 15–18.

36 23 July 1915, 5.
37 J.M. Winter, 'Britain's "Lost Generation" of the First World War', *Population Studies* 31 (1978): 449–466.
38 Alan Ramsay Skelley, *The Victorian Army at Home: The Recruitment and Terms and Conditions of the British Regular, 1859–1899* (London: Croom Helm, 1977), 238.
39 PRO CAB 17/17, Universal Military Training, The Financial Effect of the Introduction of Universal Military Service in the United Kingdom, 1905.
40 S.T. Beggs, *Selection of the Recruit* (London: Bailliere, Tindall & Cox, 1915), 27–29.
41 Ibid.
42 PRO CAB 17/17.
43 Beggs, *Recruit*, 13.
44 LA TAPE 218, 220, Tom Easton, nd; IWM P/370, The First and Second World War Memoirs of E.C. Palmer, 1914–1918.
45 IWM CON/SHELF, Dible, Captain J.H. (Papers), 1914–1918.
46 IWM SR 8849/8, Edmed, Thomas (Interview), 1914–1918; IWM 94/46/1, McPake, R. (Papers of), 1914–1918.
47 LA W/F RECOLLECTIONS, Robertson, Robert S., My Memories of the First World War, 1967; LA GENERAL SECTION, Price, D.J., nd; see LA GALLIPOLI RECOLLECTIONS, Hepworth, C.R., nd; LA TAPE 417, William Bradley, b. 1898; IWM 75/77/1, My Experiences in the Great War by Frederick William Dean, 1914–1919; LA GENERAL SUBJECT, A. Bartlett and C. Bartlett, letters to, 1914–1918, Letter from Bartlett, 14 August 1916.
48 IWM 76/80/1, Palmer, Lt K. (Papers), 1914–1918; IWM DS/MISC/54, Diary of H.V. Drinkwater, 1914–1920.
49 PRO WO 159/18, The Creedy (K) Papers – Kitchener Letters, 1914–1915.
50 LA W/F RECOLLECTIONS, E.A. Bond. Medical failures also occurred with men already enlisted. F.M. Packman seems to have developed epilepsy at some point during his military service. He suffered from fainting and thrashing spells. Nonetheless, the medical officer (who knew about his problems) let him go abroad. IWM P/316, Packman, F.M. (Papers), 1914–1918.
51 IWM SR 6656/3, Carroll, Syd (Interview), 1914–1918; LA GALLIPOLI RECOLLECTIONS, Whyte, A.G., 1971; IWM 67/71/1, Wright, H.E. (Papers), 1914–1918; see also IWM SR 8667/8, Boughton, Harold (Interview), b. 1895, and LA W/F RECOLLECTIONS, Iley, Robert William – news article in the *Sunderland Times*, 6 November 1986.
52 A requirement which, pre-war, had also proved difficult for many working-class men to pass. See LA MIDDLEBROOKE: SOMME, Sim, Robert, 1974. Sim, a miner, failed to get into the army in 1912 because he lacked enough teeth; W.G. Cadenhead's solution – having all his teeth pulled when he was a teenager and replaced by complete dentures – seems excessive. IWM 85/51/1, Papers of W.G. Cadenhead, b. 1896.
53 Robert Roberts, *The Classic Slum: Salford Life in the First Quarter of the Century* (London: Pelican, 1973), 187.
54 PRO WO 293/2, War Office Instructions, January–June 1915, letter of 20 February 1915.
55 IWM 71/64/1, Extracts from Personal Diary of Sgt J.T. Baldwin, 1914–1918.
56 PRO 30/57/0074, Manpower and Recruiting – Memos and Reports, 11 October 1915.
57 Laurie Milner, *Leeds Pals: A History of the 15th (Service) Battalion (1st Leeds) the Prince of Wales' Own (West Yorkshire Regiment) 1914–1918* (London: Leo Cooper, 1991), 27.
58 Ralph Gibson and Paul Oldfield, *The Sheffield City Battalion, the 12th (Service) Battalion York and Lancaster Regiment: A History of the Battalion Raised by Sheffield in World War One* (Barnsley, Yorkshire: Wharncliffe Publishing, 1988), 8.
59 *Weekly Dispatch* (London), 15 December 1915, 6.

60 See, for example, Table I in PRO CAB 27/2, Report from the CID on War Policy, 30 October 1915.
61 LA ENLISTMENT/RECRUITMENT/TRAINING ITEM 36, Lewis, S., Papers relating to, 1916.
62 David Coleman, 'Population', in *British Social Trends since 1900*, ed. A.H. Halsey (London: Macmillan, 1972), 105–108.
63 Figures from PRO RG 28/11, Table 1.
64 Ibid.
65 Examples can be found in: IWM 67/20/1, Chenery, B.W. (Papers), 1914–1918; IWM 67/20/1, Collis, F.E. (Papers), 1914–1918; IWM 78/36/1, Papers of J.W. Stephenson, 1914–1918; IWM 79/35/1, Starrett, D. (Papers), 1914–1918; IWM 81/41/1, Conn, A.V. (Papers), 1914–1918; IWM P/315, Tait, J.C. (Papers), 1914–1918; IWM SR 10061/6, Forrester, Harry (Interview), 1914–1918; IWM SR 12269/4, Barker, Albert (Interview), 1914–1918; IWM SR 737/16, Dixon, Fred (Interview), 1914–1918; IWM SR 9346/5, Baxter, Arthur William (Interview), 1914–1918; IWM SR 9992/2, Evans, Albert (Interview), 1914–1918; LA TAPE 120, Mr Maud, b. 1898; LA TAPE 248, F.J. Bettis, b. 1899; LA TAPE 251, V. F. King, b. 12 Feb. 1900; LA W/F RECOLLECTIONS, Walter Burton, nd; LA W/F RECOLLECTIONS, Matthews, G.W., nd; LA GENERAL SECTION, Horner, J.W., 1980; LA GENERAL SECTION, Nevell, George Thomas, b. 31 July 1897; LA W/F RECOLLECTIONS, Jackson, James Henry, b. 10 Jan. 1897; LA W/F RECOLLECTIONS, Powell, A.J., nd; LA W/F RECOLLECTIONS, Simpson, A.V., b. June 1897; LA SEVERAL FRONTS RECOLLECTIONS, Curdie, J., b. 1897, interviewed 1973; LA MIDDLEBROOKE: SOMME, Slater, W., b. October 1897, interviewed 1974; LA GENERAL SECTION, Newman, I.H., 1995; LA GENERAL SUBJECT, Ogley, Percy L., b. 1898; LA ROYAL NAVY/MERCHANT NAVY RECOLLECTIONS, White, Herbert J., b. 28 March 1897; LA ROYAL NAVY/MERCHANT NAVY RECOLLECTIONS, Chatwin, A.G., b. 12 April 1900, interviewed 1978; LA GALLIPOLI RECOLLECTIONS, Crighton, John David, b. 1897; IWM 67/20/1, Collis, F.E. (Papers), 1914–1918; IWM 85/43/1, Brittain, H.C. (Papers), 1914–1918.
66 IWM 85/28/1, Papers of S.T. Kemp, 1914–1918.
67 Quotes from: IWM 85/28/1, Papers of S.T. Kemp, 1914–1918; LA W/F RECOLLECTIONS, Hopkins, S.H., nd.
68 See, for example: LA TAPE 3, Lowry, James, b. 1897; LA SEVERAL FRONTS RECOLLECTIONS, Munro, Archibald M., b. 13 August 1897; IWM 86/77/1, Abbott, A. (Papers), 1914–1918; IWM SR 4121/B/A, Groves, Walter (Interview), 1914–1918.
69 Quotes from: IWM 83/23/1, Turner, F. (Papers), 1914–1918. Many others received similar help. See LA ROYAL NAVY/MERCHANT NAVY RECOLLECTIONS, Struidiron, Mr, 1971; IWM 86/77/1, Abbott, A. (Papers), 1914–1918; and IWM SR 4121/B/A, Groves, Walter (Interview), 1914–1918); LA GALLIPOLI RECOLLECTIONS, Bennett, Walter Albert, 1975; in one case, tobacco. See IWM SR 10/4, Collins, F. Adam (Interview), 1914–1918.
70 IWM 85/22/1, Papers of T.H. Edmed, 1914–1918.
71 For age 16, see: IWM SR 6838/2, Benwell, Howard (Interview), 1914–1918; IWM SR 9352/19, Cook, Walter (Interview), 1914–1918; LA W/F RECOLLECTIONS, W. F. Billingham, b. c1900; LA TAPE 120, Mr Maud, b. 1898; LA TAPE 251, King, V.F., b. 12 Feb. 1900; LA W/F RECOLLECTIONS, W.F. Billingham, b. c1900; LA MIDDLEBROOKE: SOMME, Conrad, H.H., 1974; LA MIDDLEBROOKE: SOMME, Logue, R.G., 1974; LA W/F RECOLLECTIONS, Wright, W.E., nd; LA W/F RECOLLECTIONS, Taylor, H.S., b. 1897, interviewed 1977; IWM 67/246/1, Hensher, A. (Papers), 1914–1918; IWM 87/33/1, Henwood, F. (Papers), 1914–1918; IWM 91/3/1, Papers of W. Watkins, b. 1897; IWM PP/MCR/137, The First World War Memoirs of E. Scullin, b. 1898; IWM SR 4087/D/C, Dunsford, C.B. (Interview),

b. 1896; IWM SR 9431/6, Grunwell, George (Interview), b. 30 October 1897; for age 15, see IWM SR 8849/8, Edmed, Thomas (Interview), 1914–1918; LA W/F RECOLLECTIONS, Harvey, Albert, nd; LA W/F RECOLLECTIONS, Moakler, F., b. 1899; LA W/F RECOLLECTIONS, Potts, W., nd; LA GALLIPOLI RECOLLECTIONS, Kibel, Joseph, b. 16 January 1900, interviewed 1977; LA ROYAL NAVY/MERCHANT NAVY RECOLLECTIONS, Stockton, Tom, b. 13 December 1899; Billy Cotton, *I Did It My Way: The Life Story of Billy Cotton* (London: George G. Harrap, 1970), 25; IWM MISC54/ITEM828, Discharge Certificate for an Underage Soldier, 1915; IWM P/315, Tait, J.C. (Papers), b. September 1899; IWM SR 9346/5, Baxter, Arthur William (Interview), 1914–1918; IWM SR 11387/2, Brady, James (Interview), b. 1898; for age 14, see: IWM PP/MCR/192, Memoirs of G.W. Albin, 1914–1918; Sidney Allinson, *The Bantams: The Untold Story of World War One* (London: Howard Baker, 1981), 30.
72 IWM 91/3/1, Papers of W. Watkins, 1914–1918.
73 IWM CON/SHELF, Papers of C. Jones, 1914–1918.
74 IWM 81/44/1, Bless 'em All: The Long and the Short and the Tall, 1914–1918/ 1939–1945, Memoirs of F. Palmer Cook.
75 Winter, 'Britain's "Lost Generation"', 449–456.

4 'A sense of the round world': the workers, Britain, Europe and the empire

1 IWM 67/297/1, Burns, F.L.B. (Papers), 1914–1918.
2 Ibid.
3 Anthony D. Smith, *Nationalism and Modernism* (London: Routledge, 1998), 140; Shula Marks, 'History, the Nation, and Empire: Sniping from the Periphery', *History Workshop* 29 (1990): 114–119.
4 For 1893, see David Vincent, *Literacy and Popular Culture: England 1750–1914* (Cambridge: Cambridge University Press, 1989), 97 and B. Stephens, *Education, Literacy, and Society, 1830–1870* (Manchester: Manchester University Press, 1987), 322–323; for earlier, Raymond Williams, 'The Press and Popular Culture: An Historical Perspective', in *Newspaper History from the Seventeenth Century to the Present Day*, ed. George Boyce, James Curran, and Pauline Wingate (London: Constable, 1978), 41–50.
5 R.K. Webb, *The British Working-Class Reader, 1790–1848: Literacy and Social Tension* (London: George Allen & Unwin, 1955), 23.
6 Historians have been slow to recognize this transformation. James Curran has argued that the radical press of the Napoleonic era 'afforded a national channel of communication' for a 'militant working-class sub-culture'. But the only effect he saw from the broader and more national press of the pre-First World War era was that it reinforced the 'lack of developed consciousness that rendered the working class vulnerable to ideological incorporation'. The national press did help the working class develop a consciousness. It was, however, not a consciousness of which Curran seems to have approved. See James Curran, 'The Press as an Agency of Social Control', in *Newspaper History*, ed. Boyce, Curran, and Wingate, 51–75.
7 Anna Davin, 'Imperialism and Motherhood', in *Patriotism: The Making and Unmaking of British National Identity*, vol. I, ed. Raphael Samuel (London: Routledge, 1989), 206.
8 José Harris, *Unemployment and Politics: A Study in English Social Policy, 1886–1914* (Oxford: Clarendon Press, 1972), 5.
9 Sydney Checkland, *British Public Policy 1776–1939: An Economic, Social, and Political Perspective* (Cambridge: Cambridge University Press, 1983), 204.
10 H. John Field, *Toward a Programme of Imperial Life: The British Empire at the Turn of the Century* (Westport, CT: Greenwood Press, 1982), 83–111.

152 Notes

11 PRO WO 163/20, Minutes of the Proceedings and Précis Prepared for the Army Council, 22 May 1914.
12 The Crimean war was reported in Britain, but in newspapers aimed at middle- and upper-class readers whose circulations numbered only in the tens of thousands. See Edward Spiers, *Army and Society 1815–1914* (London: Longman, 1980), 97.
13 LA TAPE 140, Brown, A.E., b. 1897. Another without shoes was LA SEVERAL FRONTS RECOLLECTIONS, Carr, no first name given, 1971, b. 1897.
14 For leaving school, see LA GALLIPOLI RECOLLECTIONS, Bradford, F., b. 14 August 1896; LA GENERAL SECTION, Ames, John, b. 12 April 1896; LA GENERAL SECTION, MacDonald, L., b. 22 October 1893; LA TAPE 115, Charters, J., b. 26 May 1892; LA TAPE 171, Bartlett, H.S., b. 1892; LA SALONIKA RECOLLECTIONS, Ransley, A.G., nd; LA SEVERAL FRONTS RECOLLECTIONS, Carr, no first name given, 1971, b. 1897; LA W/F RECOLLECTIONS, Hall, Percy Raymond, 1985, William Holt, *I Haven't Unpacked* (London: George G. Harrap, 1939), 33; IWM 67/43/1, Rolph, E. (Papers), b. 1892; IWM 88/57/1, Rhodes, Vernon (Papers), b. 1898; IWM SR 9419/14, Bracey, Tom (Interview), 1914–1918; IWM SR 11268/8, Clements, Joseph (Interview), 1914–1918; IWM SR 11039/3, Astin, Horace (Interview), 1914–1918. For the 86 per cent figures, see Geoffrey Sherington, *English Education, Social Change, and War 1911–1920* (Manchester: Manchester University Press, 1981), 4–5.
15 Gretchen R. Galbraith, *Reading Lives: Reconstructing Childhood, Books, and Schools in Britain 1870–1920* (New York: St Martin's Press, 1997), 25–41.
16 LA ROYAL NAVY/MERCHANT NAVY RECOLLECTIONS, Stockton, Tom, nd.
17 IWM 87/31/1, Papers of Lt P. Creek, b. c1899.
18 IWM 67/38/1, Hird, J.H. (Papers), b. 1898. Walter Ong pointed out that this suspicion of writing is characteristic of a society undergoing a transition from orality to literacy. Walter Ong, *Orality and Literacy: The Technologizing of the Word* (London: Methuen, 1982), 96–97.
19 For a discussion of the way the two mind-sets differed, see Ong, *Orality and Literacy*.
20 Though the town crier remained active in some smaller towns such as Western Super-Mare. See LA W/F RECOLLECTIONS, Pfaff, Karl, b. 1889. An interesting example of this occurred in R.J. Carrier's hometown. Before 1900, the band members had learned music by imitation and repetition. The introduction of written scoring put them all out of work: 'At that period none of the bandsmen had music, and when music was introduced it seems that many of the bandsmen who could not read it had to resign. To most of them this was a very bitter tragedy.' It was not that they could not play the music, it was that they could not read it. See LA GENERAL SECTION, Carrier, R.J., Memoirs, 1978, b. 29 September 1893.
21 IWM 67/31/1, Wallace, R.T., b. 14 December 1889. The choice of Whitsuntide and Martinmas (both connected to holy rituals) suggests a culture slowly making the transition to literacy. Oral groups (like the working class) would rely on literate groups (like Church ministers) to define their calendar for them. The religious calendar would thus underpin the secular calendar. See Ong, *Orality and Literacy*, 97–98, 105.
22 IWM 67/31/1, Wallace, R.T. (Papers), b. 14 December 1889.
23 Even for such low-level jobs as errand boy. E. Patterson 'saw in the "Sunderland Echo", "errand boy wanted" and I applied for the job.' See LA W/F RECOLLECTIONS, Patterson, E., 1971.
24 The ads in *The Times* (London) on the 5 and 7 August 1914 placed by the War Office, for example, were small ones in the centre of the classified pages, 3, 5. The same was true of the ads placed on 5, 6, and 13 August in the *Daily Mail*, 3, 3, 4.
25 LA GENERAL SECTION, Carrier, R.J., Memoirs, 1978, b. 29 September 1893.
26 IWM 87/8/1, Papers of Luther, R.M., 1914–1918.
27 IWM 87/31/1, Papers of Lt P. Creek, b. c1899.

Notes 153

28 Ibid.
29 LA GENERAL SECTION, Carrier, R.J., Memoirs, 1978, b. 29 September 1893.
30 IWM 87/31/1, Papers of Lt P. Creek, b. c1899.
31 Alun Howkins, 'The Discovery of Rural England', in *Englishness: Politics and Culture 1880–1920*, ed. Robert Colls and Philip Dodd (London: Croom Helm, 1986), 62–88.
32 Benedict Anderson, *Imagined Communities: Reflections on the Origin and Spread of Nationalism* (London: Verso, 1983).
33 Stephen Heathorn, '"Let Us Remember that We, Too, are English": Constructions of Citizenship and National Identity in English Elementary School Reading Books, 1880–1914', *Victorian Studies* 38 (Spring 1995): 395–428.
34 IWM 77/113/1, Buffey, E., 1914–1918.
35 LA GENERAL SECTION, Wootton, Herbert John, interviewed 1960.
36 IWM P/457, To Pashendale [sic] and Back by James Murray, 1895–1919.
37 For multi-ethnic, see John S. Ellis, 'Reconciling the Celt: British National Identity, Empire, and the 1911 Investiture of the Prince of Wales', *Journal of British Studies* 37 (October 1998): 391–418; for English, see Philip Dodd, 'Englishness and the National Culture', in *Englishness: Politics and Culture, 1880–1920*, ed. Dodd and Colls, 1–28.
38 LA GENERAL SECTION, MacDonald, L., b. 22 October 1893. For dialect/accent, see P.J. Waller, 'Democracy and Dialect, Speech and Class', in *Politics and Social Change in Modern Britain*, ed. P.J. Waller (New York: St Martin's Press, 1987), 1–33.
39 See Dave Marson, *Children's Strikes in 1911* (London: Routledge & Kegan Paul, 1973).
40 IWM 67/38/1, Hird, J.H., b. 1898.
41 LA GENERAL SECTION, Carrier, R.J., Memoirs, 1978.
42 LA GENERAL SECTION, Cockell, R.A., b. January 1887.
43 Patricia Anderson, *The Printed Image and the Transformation of Popular Culture 1790–1860* (Oxford: Clarendon Press, 1991), 157–191; Stephen Koss, *Rise and Fall of the Political Press in Britain*, 2 vols (London: Hamish Hamilton, 1984).
44 Alan J. Lee, *Origins of the Popular Press in England 1855–1914* (London: Croom Helm, 1976); Sally J. Taylor, *The Great Outsiders: Northcliffe, Rothermere and the Daily Mail* (London: Weidenfeld & Nicolson, 1996); Paul Ferris, *The House of Northcliffe: A Biography of an Empire* (New York: World Publications, 1972); Geoffrey Cranfield, *The Press and Society: From Caxton to Northcliffe* (London: Longman, 1978); an eyewitness view of life with Northcliffe can be found in Tom Clarke, *My Northcliffe Diary* (London: Victor Gollancz, 1931).
45 For the *Daily Mail*, see *Circulation Figures: The Daily Mail, Evening News, Weekly Dispatch* (London: Associated Newspapers Ltd, 1912), no page numbers; *The Times'* circulation in 1914 showed a large increase over 1913, resulting from Northcliffe's decision to cut the price of the paper to one penny in a partial emulation of the success of the *Daily Mail*. *The History of the Times, 1912–1948*, pt 1 (New York: Macmillan, 1952), 154. A steadfastly upper- or middle-class paper such as the *Morning Post* sold 85,000 papers daily in 1914. Keith Wilson, ed., *The Rasp of War: The Letters of H.A. Gwynne to the Countess Bathurst 1914–1918* (London: Sidgwick & Jackson, 1988), 1–10.
46 IWM P/268, Hunt, H.E. (Papers), 1914–1918. H.S. Bartlett, the son of a carpenter, 'rushed home to read [the newspaper]. I was very interested in the Boer War and collected cigarette cards with famous generals.' See LA TAPE 171, Bartlett, H.S., b. 1892. Also IWM SR 9955/19, Calvert, Horace (Interview), b. 3 September 1899.
47 IWM 67/38/1, Hird, J.H. (Papers), b. 1898.
48 For farm labourers, see LA TAPE 140, Brown, A.E., b. 1897; LA GENERAL SECTION, Ames, John, b. 12 April 1896.

49 LA SALONIKA RECOLLECTIONS, Ransley, A.G., nd.
50 IWM 67/43/1, Rolph, E. (Papers), b. 1892.
51 IWM 67/38/1, Hird, J.H. (Papers), b. 1898.
52 See *Penny Dreadfuls and Comics* (London: Victoria & Albert Museum, 1983); Joseph McAleer, *Popular Reading and Publishing in Britain, 1914–1950* (Oxford: Clarendon Press, 1992), 12–41; C.C. Eldridge, *The Imperial Experience: From Carlyle to Forster* (London: Macmillan, 1996), 55–102; 50,000 periodicals are listed in McAleer, *Popular Reading*, 25; 3,000 works of fiction are in Penny Dreadfuls.
53 Holt, *I Haven't Unpacked*, 32. Blake first appeared as a character in the *Halfpenny Marvel* in 1893. See *Penny Dreadfuls*, 58.
54 Pamphlet found in IWM P/406, Duke, W., 1909.
55 LA GENERAL SECTION, Carrier, R.J., Memoirs, 1978. See also IWM P/457, To Pashendale [sic] and Back by James Murray, 1895–1919.
56 IWM 87/31/1, Papers of Creek, Lt P., b. c1899.
57 LA W/F RECOLLECTIONS, Ward, Arthur, b. 1895; see also IWM SR 9419/14, Bracey, Tom (Interview), 1914–1918.
58 LA GALLIPOLI RECOLLECTIONS, Chapman, Herbert Stanley, nd.
59 See Hugh Cunningham, 'The Language of Patriotism', in *Patriotism*, vol. 1, ed. Samuel, 79; Richard Price, *An Imperial War and the British Working Class: Working-Class Attitudes and Reactions to the Boer War 1899–1902* (London: Routledge & Kegan Paul, 1972), 176; Richard Price, 'Society, Status, and Jingoism: The Social Roots of Lower Middle-Class Patriotism', in *The Lower Middle Class in Britain 1870–1914*, ed. Geoffrey Crossick (London: Croom Helm, 1977), 95. Both Price and Cunningham attempt to absolve the working class of any real imperialist interest in the Boer War by defining 'jingoism' as consisting only of actual attempts to break up peace rallies rather than any of the 'processions' mentioned in the text. For a useful corrective to this view, see Penny Summerfield, 'Patriotism and Empire: Music-Hall Entertainment 1870–1914', in *Imperialism and Popular Culture*, ed. John M. Mackenzie (Manchester: Manchester University Press, 1990), 17–48.
60 IWM SR 10061/6, Forrester, Harry (Interview), b. c1898.
61 C.H. Rolph, *London Particulars* (Oxford: Oxford University Press, 1980), 88.
62 Cecil Eby, *Road to Armageddon* (Durham, NC: Duke University Press, 1987), 11.
63 IWM P/268, Hunt, H.E. (Papers), 1914–1918. The paranoia about Germany extended to non-fictional outlets as well. Albert Williams remembered the illustrated magazines he found in the public library in Bolton growing up:

> I would often go into the Reading Room to look at magazines like the 'Illustrated London News', the 'Graphic' and the 'Strand' magazine. There was one monthly called the 'Review of Reviews' and this was crammed full of cartoons which openly accused Germany of making plans of aggression against Britain

See Albert Williams, *Thirty-Six Stewart Street, Bolton: An Exercise in Nostalgia 1901–1914* (Manchester: Neil Richardson, 1983), 28. Nor were the large publishers the only ones making their living off the demand for the written word, as C.H. Baker, the son of a carpenter, remembered:

> A colporteur used to visit outlying homes; he had a light box and a baize bag that rode on his back. He was a hawker of books, well read and entertaining. He would open his bag. You could just look or make a choice which he recorded in his shiny black book. A few days later he would deliver the order and collect payment. These were my first books. I remember his comment on people who turned down corners: 'A man who maltreats a book would kick a woman.'

See IWM 87/25/1, Baker, C.H. (Papers), b. 1911.

Notes 155

64 James Barnes, *The Unpardonable War* (New York: Macmillan, 1904), 64.
65 I.F. Clarke, 'The Battle of Dorking, 1871–1914', *Victorian Studies* 4 (1965): 309–328, and I.F. Clarke, *Tale of the Future* (London: Library Association, 1972).
66 Entry of 8 October 1911 in IWM P/351, Leftwich.
67 J.S. Bratton, 'Of England, Home, and Duty: The Image of England in Victorian and Edwardian Juvenile Fiction', in *Imperialism*, ed. Mackenzie, 73–93.
68 Raphael Samuel, 'Continuous National History', in *Patriotism*, vol. I, ed. Samuel, 8.
69 The phrase is Rudyard Kipling's, of course, well analysed in Harry Ricketts, *The Unforgiving Minute: A Life of Rudyard Kipling* (London: Chatto & Windus, 1999), 233–235.
70 A vision and its reception usefully analysed in Price, *An Imperial War*.
71 LA GENERAL SUBJECT, Stanbridge, S.T., My Life During the First World War, written 1972, b. 1899.
72 LA MIDDLEBROOKE: SOMME, Archer, G.W., b. 20 December 1896.
73 IWM P/351, Leftwich, Joseph, The 1911 Diary, Entry of 11 August 1911.
74 Aled Jones, *Powers of the Press* (Aldershot: Scolar Press, 1996), discusses this scepticism, although not on an explicitly class basis, and usefully points out the way in which the letters to the editor section of newspapers, which grew immensely in the second half of the nineteenth century, reflected such wariness. See 180–203.
75 LA GENERAL SECTION, Carrier, R.J., Memoirs, 1978, b. 29 September 1893.
76 IWM 67/7/1, Tritton, A.E. (Papers), b. c1896. Interesting to note the use of the passive voice here, though. Eric Catley, a grocer's assistant, also mentioned the special editions published in the first days of the war. IWM SR 4976/8, Catley, Eric (Interview), 1914–1918. Others mentioning reading newspapers after the war started: IWM 79/23/1, Whitehead, J.A. (Papers), 1914–1918; IWM 79/29/1, Meacham, A.G., b. 28 November 1893.
77 IWM 79/29/1, Meacham, A.G., b. 28 November 1893.
78 LA GENERAL SUBJECT, Stanbridge, S.T., 'My Life during the First World War', 1972.
79 William J. Tucker, *Autobiography of an Astrologer* (Sidcup: Pythagorean Publications, 1960), 42.
80 LA GENERAL SUBJECT, Cave, Arthur Charles, letter of 23 October 1915.
81 NAM 9001/32, Kay, Wilfred (Memoirs), 1914–1918; IWM P/375, Papers of W. Daly, 1914–1918. For others, see Letter from Private R. McCoubrie, 16 Jan. 1916 in LA GENERAL SUBJECT, Smythe, Y.M., 1914–1918; IWM 87/33/1, Thwaites, Private H.J., letter of 30 May 1915; NAM 9001/32, Kay, Wilfred.
82 IWM 76/153/1&2, McGregor, P. (Papers), 1914–1918.
83 G.R. Searle, *Quest for National Efficiency: A Study in British Politics and Political Thought, 1899–1914* (Oxford: Basil Blackwell, 1971), 65.
84 Bentley R. Gilbert, *The Evolution of National Insurance in Great Britain* (London: Michael Joseph, 1966), 234.
85 Mary Langan, 'Reorganizing the Labor Market: Unemployment, the State, and the Labour Movement', in *Englishness*, ed. Colls and Dodd, 104–125.
86 For OAPs, see Martin Pugh, *State and Society: British Political and Social History 1870–1992* (London: Edward Arnold, 1994), 111; for unemployment, see Sir Frank Tillyard, *Unemployment Insurance in Great Britain 1911–1948* (Leigh-on-Sea, Essex: Thames Bank Publishing Company Ltd, 1949), 12.
87 IWM 78/4/1, Papers of Patston, R.S., 1914–1918.
88 Memo of 26 February 1915 in PRO MUN 5/50/300/33/5, Circulars to Divisional Officers (Board of Trade, Labour Exchanges, and Unemployment Insurance), 1 January–31 March 1915; PRO MUN 5/50/300/33/3, Circulars to Divisional Officers (Board of Trade, Labour Exchanges, and Unemployment Insurance), 1 July–30 September 1914.

89 Baden-Powell quote from John Springhall, *Youth, Empire and Society: British Youth Movements, 1883–1940* (London: Croom Helm, 1977), 57; 'Conformity' quote from ibid., 16; see Robert H. MacDonald, *Sons of the Empire: The Frontier and the Boy Scout Movement, 1890–1918* (Toronto: University of Toronto Press, 1993), esp. pp. 176–202, for a countering view.
90 For a brief discussion of this, see Bill Schwarz, 'Politics and Rhetoric in the Age of Mass Culture', *History Workshop Journal* 46 (1998): 129–159
91 IWM SR 8721/8, Baker, Thomas (Interview), b. 23 January 1896.
92 LA SEVERAL FRONTS RECOLLECTIONS, Turner, Frank, 1980.
93 LA TAPE 979, Jack Armstrong, b. Jan. 1896.
94 IWM SR 9883/5, Groves, Arthur (Interview), 1914–1918; 'Army Cadets', see IWM SR 9184/5, Dann, William T. (Interview), b. 1898; Dixon, see IWM SR 737/16, Dixon, Fred (Interview), b. 1896.
95 For Territorials, see IWM PP/MCR/192, Albin, G.W., b. 1900; IWM 80/19/1, 'In the Face of Adversity, Smile' by F.H. Kibblewhite, b. 25 August 1898; for usefulness in military service, see IWM 87/51/1, Pearson, R., 1914–1918. The NCOs at the training depots, in fact, specifically asked for anyone with experience in the Boys' Brigades or the Territorials and appointed them acting corporals. See IWM 87/8/1, Papers of Luther, R.M., 1914–1918.
96 IWM 80/19/1, 'In the Face of Adversity, Smile' by F.H. Kibblewhite, 1914–1918.
97 Eric Hobsbawm and Terence Ranger, *The Invention of Tradition* (Cambridge: Cambridge University Press, 1983), 1.
98 Ibid.
99 IWM 73/206/1, Taylor, H.G., b. 27 September 1896. See Springhall, *Youth, Empire and Society*, for a discussion.
100 IWM CON/SHELF, Hobby, R.A., 1914–1918. For a discussion, see Sam Pryke, 'The Popularity of Nationalism in the Early British Boy Scout Movement', *Social History* 23 (October 1998): 309–324.
101 LA SALONIKA RECOLLECTIONS, Allcock, C.R., 1972.
102 LA TAPE 979, Armstrong, Jack, b. Jan. 1896.
103 George N. Barnes, *From Workshop to War Cabinet* (London: Herbert Jenkins Ltd, 1923), 39; James Hinton, *The First Shop Stewards' Movement* (London: George Allen & Unwin, 1973), 13.
104 See PRO WO 159/18, The Creedy (K) Papers – Kitchener Letters, 1914–1915, General Letter from War Office, 1 December 1914; Roy Douglas, 'Voluntary Enlistment in the First World War and the Work of the Parliamentary Recruiting Committee', *Journal of Modern History* 42 (1970): 564–585; *War Emergency Workers' National Committee Publications* (London: War Emergency Workers' National Committee, 1916).
105 LA TAPE 171, Bartlett, H.S., b. 1892. Others, like A.G. Ransley, treated crises like street theatre, attending the Siege of Sidney Street in east London in 1911 to watch Winston Churchill. See LA SALONIKA RECOLLECTIONS, Ransley, A.G., nd.
106 IWM P/351, Leftwich, Joseph, The 1911 Diary of, 1914–1918.
107 IWM 67/43/1, Rolph, E., b. 1892.
108 LA W/F RECOLLECTIONS, Ward, Arthur, b. 1895.
109 Quoted in Bernard Waites, 'The Government of the Home Front and the "Moral Economy" of the Working Class', in *Home Fires and Foreign Fields: British Social and Military Experience in the First World War*, ed. Peter Liddle (London: Brassey's, 1985), 178.
110 IWM P/351, Leftwich, Joseph, The 1911 Diary, 20 July 1911.
111 He was a woodcarver. IWM P/457, To Pashendale [sic] and Back by James Murray, 1895–1919.
112 IWM CON/SHELF, Macmillan, T., 1914–1918.
113 Ibid.

114 Eby, *Armageddon*, 27.
115 For 'cannon fodder', see Anna Davin, 'Imperialism', in *Patriotism*, vol. I, ed. Samuel, 226; for 'infected,' see Paul Thompson, *Edwardians: The Remaking of British Society* (London: Routledge, 1975), 185; for 'virus', see Hugh Cunningham, 'The Language of Patriotism', in *Patriotism*, vol. I, ed. Samuel, 81.
116 Patrick Brantlinger, *The Reading Lesson: The Threat of Mass Literacy in Nineteenth-Century British Fiction* (Bloomington, IN: Indiana University Press, 1998), 93–121.
117 IWM SR 11039/3, Astin, Horace (Interview), b. 27 September 1895.
118 IWM P/316, Diary of P. Tweed, 1914–1918. One of the ways of doing this was, as we have seen in Chapter 5, to personalize it through two familiar individuals. 'The bitterness was through the Kaiser and our King, because as far as we knew or as far as I was told the Kaiser thought that he had the right of the throne of England.' See LA TAPE 119, Lumsden, [no first name], b. 1895.
119 IWM 94/7/1, Rickus, E.E. (Papers), 1914–1918.
120 Quote from IWM 77/113/1, Buffey, E., 1914–1918.
121 LA GENERAL SECTION, Jaeger, W., Interviewed 1969, b. 1890.
122 LA GENERAL SUBJECT, Ogley, Percy L., b. 1898.
123 IWM 67/38/1, Hird, J.H., 1914–1918.
124 IWM 88/52/1, Papers of Wing Commander W.J. Shewry.
125 IWM 82/22/1, Wilkinson, J.A. (Papers), 1914–1918. Wilkinson was not alone in these kind of familial reassurances, which perhaps reveals more about the writer's state of mind than that of the receivers. Fred Odhams wrote to his mother on 7 April 1915, immediately before his ship left for the Dardanelles:

> We expect to land at Gallipoli I have no idea where it is only that it's somewhere in Turkey we expect to have a rough time there because the Turks are not going to let us land without giving us a good shelling and trying to stop us but don't you worry we shall get over that all right, there is 40,000 of them waiting for us at Gallipoli and you can bet that they are not going to let us have it all our own way, I think myself that this will be our hardest job.... P.S. remember me to all at home and tell them we are not downhearted yet, I hope to be with you all in about six months time.

Odhams's voice rings uncertainly in this quote; his obsession with the Turkish resistance reveals – unsurprisingly – his worry about the attack, and his postscript revealing that no one is 'downhearted yet' shows someone acknowledging the possibility of dislocation and death, a possibility caused by his enlistment. See IWM 93/25/1, Odhams, F.W. (Papers), 1914–1918.
126 IWM SR 11387/2, Brady, James (Interview), b. 1898.
127 H.G. Wells, *What the Worker Wants* (London: Hodder & Stoughton, 1912), 9.
128 John N. Horne, *Labour at War* (Oxford: Clarendon Press, 1991), 43.
129 IWM 75/111/1, Farrow, R.W. (Papers), 1914–1918.

5 'The monotony of the trivial round': enlistment and the escape from domesticity

1 This constriction of time and place has been called a 'second Industrial Revolution' by some historians. See Joe White, '1910–1914 Reconsidered', in *Social Conflict and the Political Order in Modern Britain*, ed. James E. Cronin and Jonathan Schneer (New Brunswick, NJ: Rutgers University Press, 1982), 73–95.
2 John R. Gillis, *For Better, for Worse: British Marriages, 1600 to the Present* (Oxford: Oxford University Press, 1985), 242.
3 Anna Davin, *Growing Up Poor: Home, School, and Street in London 1870–1914* (London: Rivers Oram Press, 1996), 29–51.

4 Female confinement was probably worse than male. Housewives were largely confined to their houses, only rarely escaping. Even women who worked probably did so in domestic service which was also highly confining. The situation grew worse for women as the century turned and more women moved from outside work to housewifery. See Joanna Bourke, *Husbandry to Housewifery: Women, Economic Change and Housework in Ireland, 1890–1914* (Oxford: Clarendon Press, 1993).
5 Delmar Bicker-Caarten writing in the *Southampton Times*, quoted in Martin Doughty, ed., *Dilapidated Housing and Housing Policy in Southampton, 1890–1914*, (Southampton: Southampton University Press, 1986), xii.
6 Mark Swenarton, *Homes Fit for Heroes* (London: Heinemann, 1981), 11.
7 Ibid., 11–18.
8 For average inhabitants, see Elizabeth Roberts, *A Woman's Place: An Oral History of Working-Class Women 1890–1940* (Oxford: Basil Blackwell, 1984), 227, 129–131; for Stockton, see LA ROYAL NAVY/MERCHANT NAVY RECOLLECTIONS, Stockton, Tom, nd.
9 Roberts, *A Woman's Place*, 125–201.
10 Mick Burke, *Ancoats Lad: The Recollections of Mick Burke* (Manchester: Neil Richardson, 1985).
11 LA SALONIKA RECOLLECTIONS, Phippen, G., nd.
12 Entry of 17 February 1911 in IWM P/351, Leftwich, Joseph, the 1911 Diary of, 1914–1918.
13 Albert Williams, *Thirty-six Stewart Street, Bolton: An Exercise in Nostalgia 1901–1914* (Manchester: Neil Richardson, 1983), 6.
14 IWM 67/31/1, Fensom, B.L. (Papers), 1914–1918, no page numbers.
15 William Holt, *I Haven't Unpacked* (London: George G. Harrap, 1939), 27.
16 IWM 78/31/1, Papers of Major W.J. Nicholson, 1914–1918.
17 LA GALLIPOLI RECOLLECTIONS, Chapman, Herbert Stanley, b. 13 February 1892.
18 Food consumption averages in Roberts, *A Woman's Place*, 153; for discussions of working-class diets, see Anna Davin, 'Loaves and Fishes: Food in Poor Households in Late 19th Century London', *History Workshop Journal* 41 (Spring 1996); Ellen Ross, *Love and Toil: Motherhood in Outcast London, 1870–1918* (Oxford: Oxford University Press, 1993), 30–36.
19 'Gristly' in LA GENERAL SUBJECT, Stone, H.R., 1914–1918; 'Splendid' in LA GENERAL SUBJECT, Jones, H.V., Letters, 1914–1918.
20 LA SALONIKA RECOLLECTIONS, Allcock, C.R., 1972.
21 IWM 85/39/1, Memoirs of B. Rudge, 1914–1918. See also John Burnett, ed., *Destiny Obscure: Autobiographies of Childhood, Education, and Family from the 1820s to the 1920s* (London: Routledge, 1994/1982), 79.
22 George K. Behlmer, *Child Abuse and Moral Reform in England, 1870–1908* (Stanford, CA: Stanford University Press, 1982), 11.
23 Ibid., 237–240. Part of this may have been the reluctance of women to report abuse of themselves and their children to an unreceptive legal system. See Shani D'Cruze, *Crimes of Outrage: Sex, Violence, and Victorian Working Women* (DeKalb, IL: Northern Illinois University Press, 1998), 2. The legal system not only avoided prosecuting cases of abuse, but also defined rape in a relatively narrow way. It was impossible, for example, for a husband to rape a wife under British law. See Mary Lyndon Shanley, *Feminism, Marriage, and the Law in Victorian England* (Princeton, NJ: Princeton University Press, 1989), 156–188. Other crimes – like domestic assault – were somewhat better dealt with, although the tendency was still to ignore all but the worst cases. See José Harris, *Private Lives, Public Spirit: Britain 1870–1914* (London: Penguin, 1993), 93–94.
24 IWM SR 9875/22, Ashurst, George (Interview), 1914–1918.
25 Quoted in Davin, *Growing Up Poor*, 88. Though Davin does have reservations about

that term, arguing that it is 'middle-class' in its assumption that the little mother was anticipating her future rather than simply doing her job.
26 LA SEVERAL FRONTS RECOLLECTIONS, Turner, Frank, 1980; IWM SR 9955/19, Calvert, Horace (Interview), 1914–1918. So, too, did J.H. Coombes, W. Smart, and Norman Smith. See LA TAPE 170, J.H. Coombes, nd; LA W/F RECOLLECTIONS, Smart, W., 1971; LA W/F RECOLLECTIONS, Smith, Norman, nd.
27 LA MIDDLEBROOKE: SOMME, Sim, Robert, 1974.
28 LA GENERAL SECTION, Horner, J.W., 1980.
29 LA SEVERAL FRONTS RECOLLECTIONS, Hancox, A.W., 1979. See also LA ROYAL NAVY/MERCHANT NAVY RECOLLECTIONS, Chadwick, R.C., 1990.
30 Geoffrey Sherington, *English Education, Social Change, and War 1911–1920* (Manchester: Manchester University Press, 1981), 5. For working-class children leaving at 14 or earlier, see Harry Forrest, who left at age 12. IWM SR 10061/6, Forrester, Harry (Interview), 1914–1918. G. Lawson left at age 13½. LA TAPE 17, Lawson, G., b. 1893. For Price's scholarship, see LA GENERAL SECTION, Price, D.J.
31 LA W/F RECOLLECTIONS, Kemp, W.J., 26 October 1972.
32 IWM 91/3/1, Papers of W. Watkins, 1914–1918.
33 Ross, *Love and Toil*, 37; see also John Tosh, 'What Should Historians Do With Masculinity? Reflections on 19th-Century Britain', *History Workshop Journal* 38 (Autumn 1994): 179–202.
34 Norman Angell, *War and the Workers* (London: National Labour Press Ltd, 1912/1914), 52.
35 IWM 85/28/1, Boydell, P., 'We Spend Our Years as a Tale that Is Told', 1914–1918.
36 LA TAPE 163, A. Sharpe, b. 1894.
37 IWM 88/52/1, And Truly Serve – Memoirs of Frederick Hunt, Sheriff of Lincoln 1959–1960, High Constable 1960–1961, 1914–1918.
38 Jeffrey Richards and John MacKenzie, *The Railway Stations: A Social History* (Oxford: Oxford University Press, 1986), 7.
39 IWM 79/29/1, Papers of A.G. Meacham, 1914–1918. See also LA GENERAL SECTION, Carrier, R.J., Memoirs, 1978, b. 29 September 1893.
40 For a recent examination of the motives that played a part in creating working-class emigration, see Paul Hudson and Dennis Mills, 'English Emigration, Kinship, and the Recruitment Process: Migration from Melbourn in Cambridgeshire to Melbourne in Victoria in the Mid-Nineteenth Century', *Rural History* 10 (1999): 55–74.
41 IWM SR 12269/4, Barker, Albert (Interview), 1914–1918; LA W/F RECOLLECTIONS, Allen, H.E., b. 28 February 1889.
42 LA W/F RECOLLECTIONS, Hodge, D.A., nd.
43 LA SEVERAL FRONTS RECOLLECTIONS, Biggle, H.A., 1971.
44 IWM 67/11/1, Hancox, A.W. (Papers), 1914–1918.
45 The words are J.D. Brew's, a working-class boy. See LA MIDDLEBROOKE: SOMME, Brew, J.D., 1975. For the distinction between the Regulars and the Territorials, see Michael Stedman, *Salford Pals: A History of the 15th, 16th, 19th and 20th Battalions Lancashire Fusiliers 1914–1919* (London: Leo Cooper, 1993), 15.
46 LA GENERAL SECTION, Moulds, H., nd.
47 LA TAPE 137, S.P. Shepherd, b. c1896. For others mentioning the summer camp as their reason for joining, see LA TAPE 197, T. Jordan, b. 1892; LA W/F RECOLLECTIONS, S.V. Edge, nd; LA W/F RECOLLECTIONS, Roebuck, Harold, nd; LA GALLIPOLI RECOLLECTIONS, Chapman, Herbert Stanley, nd; LA TAPE 135, Smith, B., b. 1894.
48 LA GENERAL SECTION, Smith, A.E., 1934.
49 LA TAPE 217, Mr Hannah, b. 1894. Such ease of mind may have come from restrictions on the use of the Territorial regiments, limiting them to home defence.

William Begbie's mother felt similarly worried when he joined up underage in April 1914, but his father told her that 'this will do him no harm – Territorials don't go to war.' LA GENERAL SUBJECT, Begbie, William, 1914–1919.
50. 'Adventure', see IWM SR 13672/C/A, Bell, A.A. (Interview), 1914–1918; Rolph quote in C.H. Rolph, *London Particulars* (Oxford: Oxford University Press, 1980), 130; 'Relief' from IWM SR 8866/4, Cowley, William (Interview), 1914–1918; 'Blow this!' from Charlie Byrne, *I Survived, Didn't I? The Great War Reminiscences of Private 'Ginger' Byrne*, ed. Joy B. Cave (London: Leo Cooper, 1993), 16.
51. Simpson's quote in IWM 84/1/1, Memoirs of T.J. Simpson, 1914–1918; Martin's quote in LA TAPE 147, M. Martin, b. 1895; Whiteley's in LA TAPE 139, A. Whiteley, b. 1897; Hird's in IWM 67/38/1, Hird, J.H., 1914–1918. Others expressing similar sentiments can be found in IWM SR 9419/14, Bracey, Tom (Interview), 1914–1918 and IWM SR 12269/4, Barker, Albert (Interview), 1914–1918.
52. For Bickerton, see IWM 80/43/1, The Wartime Experiences of an Ordinary 'Tommy' by T.A. Bickerton, 1964; for Bird, see IWM SR 10656/9, Bird, Robert (Interviews), 1914–1918.
53. For Jackson, see LA TAPE 142, J. Jackson, b. 1899; LA TAPE 158, J. Murray, b. 1896; Burgess quote is in Jon Cooksey, *13th and 14th York and Lancaster Regiment* (Barnsley: Graphics and Features Department, Barnsley Chronicle, 1986), 69.
54. IWM P/273, Hartsilver, J. (Papers), 1914–1918.
55. William J. Tucker, *Autobiography of an Astrologer* (Sidcup: Pythagorean Publications, 1960), 42.
56. Some spoke in simpler terms. Joseph Kibel enlisted in the Royal Naval Division because 'I always had a hankering after the sea.' Walter Burdon joined because 'I wanted to do something military. I liked that sort of thing, marching.' See LA GALLIPOLI RECOLLECTIONS, Kibel, Joseph, 1977 and IWM SR 11041/3, Burdon, Walter (Interview), 1914–1918.
57. IWM 67/31/1, Fensom, B.L. (Papers).
58. LA W/F RECOLLECTIONS, Macdonald, James Dixon, 1977. When A.G. Meacham, a domestic servant, enlisted in late 1914, he felt both patriotism and a desire for adventure. He was inspired by 'the murders in Sarajevo', a desire to defend Britain, and the chance for 'adventure and change, the opportunity to see life and new places'. IWM 79/29/1, Papers of A.G. Meacham, 1914–1918. The date of Meacham's enlistment is confused. He said November [1914] in this excerpt, but later claimed 7 September 1914 as the date on which he signed up. James Murray, an apprentice wood-carver, 'felt sufficiently patriotic' to enlist, but 'over and above that, I felt this would be a great adventure'. See IWM P/457, To Pashendale [sic] and Back by James Murray, 1895–1919.
59. LA SEVERAL FRONTS RECOLLECTIONS, Clark, H.F.M.
60. IWM SR 9118/8, Crow, Jim (Interview), 1914–1918.
61. IWM 81/14/1, Memoirs of H. Bartlett, 1914–1918.
62. IWM and LA sources. The problem here again is not the bias of the sources themselves, but of their collection. The Liddle Archive sources are biased towards men who were younger during the war and thus survived to be interviewed in the 1960s and 1970s. The same holds true, to a lesser extent, for the Imperial War Museum sources. This may exaggerate the number of men who joined in 1915, because they were simply too young to join in 1914.
63. LA TAPE 251, J.G. Barron, b. 1895.
64. LA TAPE 3, Lowry, James, b. 1897.
65. For Malcolm, see LA W/F RECOLLECTIONS, Malcolm, J.A., nd; for Slater, see LA MIDDLEBROOKE: SOMME, Slater, W., 1974.
66. IWM SR 9955/19, Calvert, Horace (Interview), 1914–1918.
67. These were all Imperial War Museum sources. All the Liddle Archive sources were

eliminated because they were interviews conducted in the late 1960s, 1970s, and 1980s.
68 NAM 9204/147, Keogh, B.A. (Papers), 1914–1918.

6 'Money was the attraction': enlistment and economic motives

1. William Cunningham writing in 1904. Quoted in B.W.E. Alford, *Britain in the World Economy since 1880* (London: Longman, 1996), 98.
2. Sidney Pollard, *Britain's Prime and Britain's Decline: The British Economy 1870–1914* (London: Edward Arnold, 1989), 260–271; Paul Kennedy, *The Rise and Fall of the Great Powers* (New York: Doubleday, 1987), 202; Lance E. Davis and Robert A. Huttenback, *Mammon and the Pursuit of Empire: The Political Economy of British Imperialism, 1860–1912* (Cambridge: Cambridge University Press, 1986), 1–30, 301–318; E.J. Hobsbawm, *Industry and Empire* (London: Weidenfeld & Nicolson, 1968); Roderick Floud and Donald McCloskey, eds, *The Economic History of Britain since 1700*, vol. 2 (Cambridge: Cambridge University Press, 1981).
3. Paul Kennedy, *The Rise of the Anglo-German Antagonism, 1860–1914* (New York: George Allen & Unwin, 1980), 251–440; Robert Massie, *Dreadnought: Britain, Germany, and the Coming of the Great War* (New York: Random House, 1991), 160–188, 373–546, 609–625.
4. M. Edelstein, 'Foreign Investment and Empire 1860–1914', in *The Economic History of Britain since 1700*, vol. 2, ed. Floud and McCloskey, 70–99.
5. Pollard, *Britain's Prime*, 18–57.
6. For wages, see John Benson, *The Working Class in Britain, 1850–1939* (London: Longman, 1989), 39–71. For unemployment, see José Harris, *Unemployment and Politics: A Study in English Social Policy* (Oxford: Clarendon Press, 1972), 374.
7. LA SEVERAL FRONTS RECOLLECTIONS, Carr, [no first name], 1971. See also IWM 67/37/1, Price, L.S. (Papers), 1914–1918. For a discussion of the minimum weekly wage needed to keep families fed and housed, see Ellen Ross, *Love and Toil: Motherhood in Outcast London, 1870–1918* (Oxford: Oxford University Press, 1993), 27–53.
8. LA SEVERAL FRONTS RECOLLECTIONS, Lane, J.M., 1971, b. May 1892; LA TAPE 119, W.W. Finlay, b. 1898.
9. LA SEVERAL FRONTS RECOLLECTIONS, Turner, Frank, 1980.
10. B. Seebohm Rowntree, *Poverty, a Study of Town Life* (London: Macmillan, 1906); Charles Booth, *Life and Labour of the People in London* (London: Macmillan, 1902).
11. Colin G. Pooley and Jean Turnbull, *Migration and Mobility in Britain since the Eighteenth Century* (London: UCL Press, 1998), 279.
12. LA TAPE 121, J.M. Lane, b. May 1892; IWM 67/43/1, Rolph, E. (Papers), 1914–1918.
13. LA GENERAL SECTION, Smith, A.E., 1934.
14. LA W/F RECOLLECTIONS, Patterson, E., 1971.
15. John Benson, *The Penny Capitalists* (New Brunswick, NJ: Rutgers University Press, 1983), 130.
16. IWM 77/113/1, Buffey, E. (Papers), 1914–1918.
17. LA MIDDLEBROOKE: SOMME, Slater, W., 1974.
18. Ibid.
19. Lynn H. Lees, *The Solidarities of Strangers: The English Poor Laws and the People, 1700–1948* (Cambridge and New York: Cambridge University Press, c1998).
20. Mick Burke, *Ancoats Lad: The Recollections of Mick Burke* (Manchester: Neil Richardson, 1985), 7.
21. LA SEVERAL FRONTS RECOLLECTIONS, Turner, Frank, 1980.
22. For an outline of unemployment insurance history, see Frank Tillyard, *Unemployment*

Insurance in Great Britain 1911–1948 (Leigh-on-Sea, Essex: Thames Bank Publishing, 1949). For a modern interpretation, see Harris, *Unemployment*.
23 LA W/F RECOLLECTIONS, Ward, Arthur. Ward was the son of goods driver.
24 IWM 78/4/1, Papers of R.S. Patston, 1914–1918.
25 PRO CAB 37/119/42, 50, Cabinet Papers, March, April 1914.
26 IWM SR 8866/4, Cowley, William (Interview), 1914–1918.
27 LA TAPE 129, G. Davis, b. c1896.
28 For unemployment, see G.D.H. Cole, *Trade Unionism and Munitions* (Oxford: Clarendon Press, 1923), 52; for inflation, see Arthur L. Bowley, *Prices and Wages in the United Kingdom, 1914–1920* (Oxford: Clarendon Press, 1921), 7, 106.
29 For the coal industry, see R.A.S. Redmayne, *The British Coal-Mining Industry During the War* (Oxford: Clarendon Press, 1923), 9–11; for the shipping and storage industries, see Mary B. Rose, 'Britain and the International Economy', in *The First World War in British History*, ed. Stephen Constantine, Maurice W. Kirby and Mary B. Rose (London: Edward Arnold, 1995), 231–251; for the northern textile industries, see Sidney Allinson, *The Bantams: The Untold Story Of World War One* (London: Howard Baker, 1981), 30.
30 Rosenberg quote from: *The Collected Works of Isaac Rosenberg*, ed. Gordon Bottomley and Denys Harding (London: Chatto & Windus, 1937), no page numbers; Battersby quote from LA GALLIPOLI RECOLLECTIONS, Battersby, F., 1972; Albin quote from IWM PP/MCR/192, Memoirs of G.W. Albin, 1914–1918.
31 P. Simkins, *Kitchener's Army: The Raising of the New Armies, 1914–1916* (Manchester: Manchester University Press, 1988), 107.
32 Newsted quote from LA SEVERAL FRONTS RECOLLECTIONS, Newsted, J., 1975; Ramshaw quote from LA TAPE 233, G.E. Ramshaw, b. 3 June 1890; William Muckle's father also lost his job in the mines as a result of the slowdown and thus enlisted. See William Muckle, *No Regrets* (Newcastle upon Tyne: People's Publications, 1981), 20.
33 IWM SR 8226/5, Bonney, Arthur (Interview), 1914–1918.
34 LA W/F RECOLLECTIONS, Pollard, George, 1982.
35 Russell Grenfell, *Service Pay* (London: Eyre & Spottiswoode, 1944), 17, 104.
36 Bowley, *Prices and Wages*, 171, 103, 113, 154.
37 Grenfell, *Service Pay*, 20.
38 P.E. Dewey, 'Military Recruiting and the British Labour Force during the First World War', *Historical Journal* 27 (1984): 199–223; Simkins, *Kitchener's Army*, 173.
39 LA TAPE 24, Carroll, b. c1897.
40 Grenfell, *Service Pay*, 17.
41 Foulkes in IWM 94/11/1, Papers of R.E. Foulkes, b. 5 May 1894; Ransley in LA SALONIKA RECOLLECTIONS, Ransley, A.G., nd.
42 Quoted in Allinson, *Bantams*, 30. P. Carroll also felt that enlisting was the 'best idea' because it would reduce the number of mouths to feed. See LA TAPE 24, Carroll, b. c1897.
43 IWM 80/40/1, Roworth, John William, 'A War Story, 1914–1918', b. 1897.
44 Quoted in Allinson, *Bantams*, 30.
45 LA SEVERAL FRONTS RECOLLECTIONS, Turner, Frank, 1980.
46 For Kingston, see IWM 88/27/1, Memoirs of A.J. Kingston, 1914–1918; for Orton, see LA GALLIPOLI RECOLLECTIONS, Orton, F.J., nd.
47 IWM 67/37/1, Price, L.S. (Papers), 1914–1918. G. Bird, already in the military, aimed for a similar post: 'I am thinking of volunteering to be an officer's groom, the commanding officer asked last week. . . . I am out to better myself if I can.' See LA GENERAL SECTION, Bird, G, Letters, 1914–1915.
48 IWM SR 6/7, Burne, Charles (Interview), 1914–1918.
49 IWM P/273, Memoirs of Guy Buckeridge, 1914–1918; see also IWM 86/30/1, Papers of John M. Cordy, 1914–1918.

50 Robert Roberts, *The Classic Slum: Salford Life in the First Quarter of the Century* (London: Pelican, 1973), 189. F. Perry joined up and found that 'I enjoyed my training ... we had plenty of food and a good variety and I was fit as could be.' See LA MIDDLEBROOKE: SOMME, Perry, F., 1974. Often the status of a man as working or middle class proved difficult to figure from sketchy memoirs, letters, or diaries. Many times, the surest sign that a man was working class proved to be his enjoyment of Army food. Conversely, an enlistee's revulsion at Army rations usually revealed a middle- or upper-class upbringing.
51 LA GENERAL SECTION, Bird, G., Letters, 1914–1915.
52 Clegg quote from IWM 88/18/1, Diary of H. Clegg, 1914–1918; Webster quote from IWM 78/74/1, Papers of Major F.W. Webster, b. 1895.
53 Roberts, *Classic Slum*, 189.
54 LA ENLISTMENT/RECRUITMENT/TRAINING ITEM 7, Recruiting Pamphlet – Army Form B. 218F, August 1914.
55 PRO MUN 5/50/300/33/3, Circulars to Divisional Officers (Board of Trade, Labour Exchanges, and Unemployment Insurance), 1 July–30 September 1914, Memo of 11 August 1914.
56 PRO HO 45/10741, Publications Regarding the War (Home Office), 1914. The Home Office reaction to the pamphlet was less than worried: 'I do not see much harm in the pamphlet – some parts are excellent. I do not think it will do much damage to recruiting.'
57 Ibid.
58 For overall wages, see A.R. Thatcher, *British Labour Statistics: Historical Abstract 1886–1968* (London: HMSO, 1971), 52; for war industry wage rises, see PRO MUN 5/49/300/15, Report of the Labour Department, 2 December 1915. For unemployment, see Frances Hirst, *The Consequences of the War to Great Britain* (London: Oxford University Press, 1934), 282. 'Irreducible minimum' from PRO RG 28/11, National Registration Committee Minutes and Miscellaneous Papers, 1915–1916. Report on the Course of Employment in the United Kingdom from July 1914–July 1915.
59 *Daily Mail* (London), 1 February 1915, 4.
60 Roberts, *Classic Slum*, 203.
61 LA GENERAL SECTION, Horner, J.W., 1980.
62 LA SEVERAL FRONTS RECOLLECTIONS, Baker, W.E., Military Medal, 1977.
63 IWM PP/MCR/110, The First World War Memories of Joe Woollin, 1914–1918.
64 PRO CAB 27/2, Report from the CID on War Policy, 30 October 1915.
65 All had an employment growth rate of between 5.4 per cent and 10.2 per cent. The growth rate range was chosen because that provided the most 'C' and 'A' industries. The industries also all had more than 10,000 workers. This minimum allows the elimination of small industries, which tended to be more volatile. The six industries used are the only ones that fit these criteria.
66 Bowley, *Prices and Wages*, 106.
67 Figures and quote from S.T. Beggs, *Selection of the Recruit* (London: Bailliere, Tindall & Cox, 1915), 27–29.
68 Ibid., 83.
69 Ibid.

7 'We were being patriotic. Or young and silly': enlistment and allegiance

1 IWM 78/4/1, Caseby, A. (Papers), 1914–1918. Caseby was the son of a boot maker.
2 IWM 77/186/1, Papers of A.R. Reid, Letter of 28 August 1914.
3 LA W/F RECOLLECTIONS, Samuel, Henry, nd.
4 LA GALLIPOLI RECOLLECTIONS, Page, James, interviewed 1980.

5   Alan Ramsay Skelley, *The Victorian Army at Home: The Recruitment and Terms and Conditions of the British Regular, 1859–1899* (London: Croom Helm, 1977).
6   Quoted in Brian Bond, *Victorian Army and the Staff College, 1854–1914* (London: Eyre Methuen, 1972), 327.
7   IWM SR 9955/19, Calvert, Horace (Interview), b. 3 September 1899.
8   IWM 67/43/1, Rolph, E. (Papers), b. 1892.
9   Edward Spiers, *Army and Society (1815–1914)* (London: Longman, 1980), 42–52.
10 IWM 77/47/1, Chaney, Bert (Papers), 1914–1918.
11 IWM 67/43/1, Rolph, E. (Papers), b. 1892.
12 W.A. Tucker, *The Lousier War* (London: New English Library (Times Mirror), 1974), 11.
13 Neal Blewett, 'The Franchise in the United Kingdom, 1885–1918', *Past & Present* 32 (1974): 27–56; Robert Colls, 'Englishness and the Political Culture', in *Englishness: Politics and Culture 1880–1920*, ed. Robert Colls and Philip Dodd (London: Croom Helm, 1986), 29–61.
14 Michael Blanch, 'Imperialism, Nationalism and Organized Youth', in *Working Class Culture: Studies in History and Theory*, ed. John Clarke, Charles Crichter, and Richard Johnson (London: Hutchinson, 1979), 103–120.
15 IWM 91/5/1, Batty, T. (Papers), 16 November 1914.
16 For Evans, see IWM SR 9992/2, Evans, Albert (Interview), b. 1897. There is, of course, the problem with a town being known as 'Little Moscow' before the Russian Revolution and the move of the Soviet capital from St Petersburg to Moscow. Moscow was known as a city of radicals before the First World War (most notably after the failed 1905 revolution) but not so much that it is likely that it would be taken as a byword for socialism. The other interpretation is that Evans is taking a post-1917 label and applying it, either for convenience or because of failing memory, to the pre-war town. It seems unlikely, however, that he is making up the town's radicalism, either pre- or post-war, wholesale; for Salford, see Michael Stedman, *Salford Pals: A History of the 15th, 16th, 19th and 20th Battalions Lancashire Fusiliers 1914–1919* (London: Leo Cooper, 1993), 13–14.
17 LA W/F RECOLLECTIONS, Hunter, R., Recollection of August 1914, nd.
18 LA GENERAL SECTION, Bird, G., Letters, 1914–1915.
19 LA GALLIPOLI RECOLLECTIONS, Page, James, Interviewed 1980.
20 IWM 87/8/1, Papers of R.M. Luther, 1914–1918.
21 LA W/F RECOLLECTIONS, Macdonald, James Dixon, 1977. Others protested about the food differently:

> Near where I was sitting, chap replied. 'Yes, I have a complaint.' Whereupon a Colour Sergeant with bristling moustache and 100 per cent military bearing, marched to complainant. 'What's your complaint?' he asked in a thunderous voice, 'Look at this tea', the complaining chap replied, adding 'It's covered with grease.' 'There's nothing wrong with that,' replied the sergeant, stirring the offending tea with two fingers. This act caused an explosion. Another chap [Ivor Rees] sitting alongside – whom we learned later was a pal of the complainant – without hesitation picked up the basin of tea and hurled it into the face of the sergeant. Hell was let loose for a minute or so before the two buddies were carried off to the Guard Room.

Such behaviour did not necessarily mark the man as a bad soldier; Rees, after serving his punishment for tea-throwing, won the Victoria Cross in France in 1917. See IWM 80/43/1, Perriman, A.E. (Papers of), 1914–1918. The same basins were used to hold both the main course and then the post-dinner tea. No washing equipment was provided between the two and thus grease and floating chunks of beef in the tea were not uncommon.

22 PRO CAB 27/2, Report from the CID on War Policy, 30 October 1915.
23 Quoted in Sidney Allinson, *The Bantams: The Untold Story of World War One* (London: Howard Baker, 1981), 24.
24 LA TAPE 855, G. Ives, b. 17 November 1881.
25 For Anthony quote, see Francis Anthony, *A Man's a Man* (London: Duckworth, 1932), 10; for Bromley quote, see IWM SR 9544/7, Bromley, Tom (Interview), b. 3 February 1897; for Gosling, see IWM 81/14/1, Gosling, A.J. (Papers), 1914–1918; IWM SR 9544/7.
26 LA W/F RECOLLECTIONS, Heptonstall, Mr and Mrs, January 1971.
27 LA ENLISTMENT/RECRUITMENT/TRAINING, ITEM 4, 19 Recruiting Posters, no. 110.
28 For Ward quote, see LA W/F RECOLLECTIONS, Ward, Arthur, nd; for Gosling, see IWM 81/14/1, Gosling, A.J. (Papers), 1914–1918; IWM 67/43/1, Burns, R. (Papers), 1914–1918.
29 Preben Kaarsholm, 'Kipling and Masculinity', in *Patriotism: The Making and Unmaking of British National Identity*, vol. III, ed. Raphael Samuel (London: Routledge, 1989), 216–226.
30 I.F. Clarke, 'The Battle of Dorking, 1871–1914', *Victorian Studies* 8 (1965): 309–328.
31 IWM CON/SHELF, Dible, Captain J.H. (Papers), 1914–1918.
32 IWM 85/28/1, Papers of S.T. Kemp, 1914–1918.
33 IWM 72/25/1, Papers of D. Stephen, 1914–1918.
34 IWM 67/20/1, Chenery, B.W. (Papers), 1914–1918.
35 Patrick Wright, *On Living in an Old Country* (London: Verso, 1985), 2 (iconography), 119 (geography).
36 See G.R. Searle, *Liberal Party: Triumph and Disintegration, 1886–1929* (London: Macmillan, 1992), 91.
37 LA GENERAL SECTION, Carrier, R.J., Memoirs, written 1978. Nor did the feelings necessarily end as the war continued. When Kitchener drowned off Scotland in 1916, after his ship struck a mine, the public reaction split between hysteria and near-catatonia. For catatonia, see LA GENERAL SUBJECT, Stanbridge, S.T., My Life During the First World War, 1972. For hysteria and the belief of a large part of the public that Kitchener was not dead but in hiding, waiting to emerge and win the war, see George H. Cassar, *Kitchener: Architect of Victory* (London: William Kimber, 1977), 478–481.
38 LA MIDDLEBROOKE: SOMME, Askew, A.W., interviewed 1974; others who mentioned the poster were IWM CON/SHELF, Papers of R.A. Hobby, 1914–1918; IWM P/438, Preston, R. (Papers), 1914–1918; LA TAPE 119, Mr Lumsden, b. 1895; IWM 88/52/1, Memoirs of A.J. Jamieson, written 1977–80. The quote describing the poster is from IWM 88/27/1, Papers of Flight Lt S.D. Evans, 1914–1918. For the date of first issue, see Keith Grieves, *Politics of Manpower, 1914–1918* (Manchester: Manchester University Press, 1988), 7. Kitchener's finger was called 'menacing' by J.H. Hird. See IWM 67/38/1.
39 Cassar, *Kitchener*, 203; Philip Warner, *Kitchener: The Man Behind the Legend* (New York: Atheneum, 1986), 175; IWM 88/52/1, Memoirs of A.J. Jamieson, written 1977–1980.
40 IWM CON/SHELF, Dale, G.E. (Papers), 1914–1918.
41 IWM 89/7/1, Lynas, W.J. (Papers), 1914–1918.
42 D.G. Boyce, '"The Marginal Britons": The Irish', in *Englishness*, ed. Colls and Dodd, 230–253.
43 LA MIDDLEBROOKE: SOMME, Brownlea, E.J., 1975.
44 IWM 79/35/1, Starrett, D. (Papers), 1914–1918.
45 John P. Duggan, *A History of the Irish Army* (Dublin: Gill & Macmillan, 1991), 4, 5.

46 Quoted in Myles Dungan, *They Shall Not Grow Old: Irish Soldiers and the Great War* (Dublin: Four Courts Press, 1997), 28.
47 IWM 79/35/1, Starrett, D. (Papers), 1914–1918.
48 Joseph Murray, a miner, thought that such an organization was very effective, 'propaganda-wise'. Joseph Murray, *Call to Arms: From Gallipoli to the Western Front* (London: William Kimber, 1980), 91.
49 William J. Tucker, *Autobiography of an Astrologer* (Sidcup: Pythagorean Publications, 1960), 42.
50 LA MIDDLEBROOKE: SOMME, Askew, A.W., interviewed 1974.
51 IWM 67/319/1, Crumpton, E.V. (Papers), 1914–1918.
52 For Pollard, see LA W/F RECOLLECTIONS, Pollard, George, 1982. Others expressing the same feelings can be found at LA TAPE 74, E.N. Harvey, b. 1896; IWM SR 10656/9, Bird, Robert (Interview), b. 24 May 1894; LA TAPE 116, H. Furneval, b. 18 April 1895; For joining in a group, see for example: IWM SR 8867/3, Dawson, Claude (Interview), b. 30 May 1896; IWM SR 10656/9, Bird, Robert (Interviews), b. 24 May 1894; IWM SR 8849/8, Edmed, Thomas (Interview), 1914–1918; for Dale, see IWM CON/SHELF, Dale, G.E. (Papers), 1914–1918.
53 Murray, *Call to Arms*, 18. Others expressing the same emotions can be found at: IWM SR 10642/3, Beard, Charles Alfred Ernest, 1914–1918; IWM SR 9352/19, Cook, Walter (Interview), 1914–1918; IWM SR 10441/7, Grover, Walter (Interview), 1914–1918; IWM 79/17/1, Jennings, Thomas Alfred, 'Hark! I Hear the Bugles Calling', b. 3 April 1894 ; IWM P/267, The First World War Papers of A.L. Atkins, 1914–1919; Evan Rogers, *A Funny Old Quist* (London: Dennis Dobson, 1981), 48; IWM 67/20/1, Chenery, B.W. (Papers), 1914–1918.
54 IWM 77/113/1, Buffey, E. (Papers), 1914–1918.
55 LA W/F RECOLLECTIONS, John Christopher, b. 1891.
56 For Bird, see LA GENERAL SECTION, Bird, G., Letters, 1914–1915; for Mortimer, see IWM 75/21/1, Mortimer, J.G., 'A Tyke in Khaki', 31 December 1895.
57 LA W/F RECOLLECTIONS, Potts, W., nd.
58 For Gerrard, see LA W/F RECOLLECTIONS, Gerrard, James, b. 1890; for Attwood, see Albert E. Attwood, *In the Running* (Elms Court: Arthur H. Stockwell, 1977).
59 LA W/F RECOLLECTIONS, Hodge, D.A., nd; see also IWM SR 13842/2, Bennett, James (Interview), b. 6 June 1898; IWM SR 9955/19, Calvert, Horace (Interview), b. 3 September 1899.
60 LA SEVERAL FRONTS RECOLLECTIONS, Hart, J.R., nd.
61 LA TAPE 125, Mr Carr, b. 1897; see also IWM SR 1/4, Berry, William (Interview), 1914–1918; IWM SR 10061/6, Forrester, Harry (Interview), 1914–1918 for somewhat less violent parents forbidding their children to enlist.
62 For Groves, see IWM SR 9883/5, Groves, Arthur (Interview), 1914–1918; for Barker, see IWM SR 12269/4, Barker, Albert (Interview), 1914–1918; for Leithead, see LA TAPE 167, T. Leithead, nd. See also LA TAPE 19, Laidlaw, J., b. 7 March 1895.
63 LA W/F RECOLLECTIONS, W.J. Barker, b. 1897.
64 IWM 78/2, Papers of Morgan, P., 1914–1918.
65 IWM 81/23/1, Memoirs of Heraty, A.J., b. 1897.
66 LA GENERAL SUBJECT, Cave, Arthur Charles, nd.
67 IWM 79/41/1, Papers of Orchard, W., 1914–1918.
68 *Echoes of the Great War: The Diary of Reverend Andrew Clark 1914–1919*, ed. James Munson (Oxford: Oxford University Press, 1985), 12.
69 IWM 67/315/1, Jarrod, F.J., 'Memoirs of the Great War, 1914–1918', 1914–1918. E.V. Crumpton's employer also forbade him to enlist. See IWM 67/319/1, Crumpton, E.V. (Papers), 1914–1918.
70 IWM 81/35/1, Papers of Bradbury, S., 1914–1918. A.R. Reid's employer did the same thing. See IWM 77/186/1, Papers of Reid, A.R., 1914–1918.

71 IWM 81/35/1, Papers of Bradbury, S., 1914–1918.
72 LA W/F RECOLLECTIONS, Riley, A.W., nd.
73 LA TAPE 191, Hunter, E., nd.
74 The lyrics went:

> A man and a maiden met a month ago
> She said there's one thing I should like to know
> Why aren't you in khaki or navy blue
> And fighting for your country like other men do?
> The man looked up and slowly shook his head
> Dear Madam, do you know what you have said?
> For I gladly took my chance
> Now my right arm's out in France
> I'm one of England's Broken Dolls.

See IWM 78/51/1.
75 David Silbey, 'Pressure to Volunteer: The Male Experience of the White Feather in Britain, 1914–1916', Paper presented at the North American Conference on British Studies, 17 October 1996.
76 The historian Cate Haste, for example, wrote of 'squads' of young women giving the white feather to all the men they encountered in civilian attire. See Cate Haste, *Keep the Home Fires Burning: Propaganda in the First World War* (London: Allen Lane, 1977), 56.
77 PRO HO 45/10741, Publications Regarding the War (Home Office), 1914.
78 LA SALONIKA RECOLLECTIONS, Ashton, W.W., nd.
79 IWM 85/39/1, Field, F.J. (Papers), 1914–1918.
80 IWM 77/121/1, Papers of Thomas, W.R., 1914–1918.
81 Peter Simkins, *Kitchener's Army: The Raising of the New Armies, 1914–1916* (Manchester: Manchester University Press, 1988), 186. See also Cassar, *Kitchener*, 203–205.
82 Eric Field, *Advertising: The Forgotten Years* (London: Ernest Benn, 1959), 29.
83 Gerald DeGroot, *Blighty: British Society in the Era of the Great War* (London: Longman, 1996), 175; see also Gary S. Messinger, *British Propaganda and the State in the First World War* (Manchester: Manchester University Press, 1992), 33. David Sweet, 'The Domestic Scene: Parliament and People', in *Home Fires and Foreign Fields: British Social and Military Experience in the First World War*, ed. Peter Liddle (London: Brassey's, 1985), 9–20; Haste, *Home Fires*, 50.
84 LA W/F RECOLLECTIONS, Hall, Percy Raymond, 1985. See also IWM PP/MCR/110, The First World War Memories of Joe Woollin, 1914–1918; see also LA TAPE 115, Charters, J., b. 26 May 1892.
85 Both quotes from LA W/F RECOLLECTIONS, Knabbit, R., A Royal Field Artillery Man Looks Back at 'The War to End Wars', 1976.
86 Abe Moffat, *My Life with the Miners* (London: Lawrence & Wishart, 1965), 26.
87 IWM 87/8/1, Papers of R.M. Luther, 1914–1918.
88 Ibid.
89 For an interesting analysis of the way the British government used gendered language in its propaganda about the Belgian situation, see Nicolleta F. Gullace, 'Sexual Violence and Family Honor: British Propaganda and International Law during the First World War', *American Historical Review* 102 (June 1997): 714–747.
90 IWM 87/18/1, Nimmo, P., Letter of 16 October 1914.
91 Frederick Hunt grew up in Kirton, Lincolnshire, and remembered the delayed and unorthodox methods by which news spread. Most familiar was the arrival of the papers on the morning train which he, working for the local news agent, would collect and deliver. But the postal carriers also used to read people's mail and spread

168 *Notes*

interesting tidbits (which included deaths in action) to the populace. See IWM 88/52/1, And Truly Serve – Memoirs of Frederick Hunt, Sheriff of Lincoln 1959–60, High Constable 1960–1961.
92 LA TAPE 144, J.T. Jenkins, b. 1892.
93 IWM 91/5/1, Batty, T. (Papers), Letter of 16 November 1914. See also IWM 94/11/1, Foulkes, R.E., 1914–1918.
94 For Crumpton, see IWM 67/319/1, Crumpton, E.V., b. 13 January 1891, interviewed 10 November 1977; for Hodge, see LA W/F RECOLLECTIONS, Hodge, D.A., 30 August 1914.
95 PRO NATS 1/398, Daily Recruiting Returns, August–December 1914. Londoners made up 18.6 per cent of the recruits, as opposed to a previous average of around 15 per cent.
96 Ibid. London's proportion of the recruits dropped to 10–12 per cent.
97 *The Times* (London), 12 September 1914, 4.
98 PRO WO 159/3, Weekly Return of Recruits for Regular Army and Territorial Force, 4 August 1914–22 May 1915, 22.
99 Simkins, *Kitchener's Army*, 169.
100 For Wallace, see IWM 67/31/1, Wallace, R.T. (Papers), b. 14 December 1889; for Clark, see *Echoes of the Great War*, ed. Munson, 11.
101 LA W/F RECOLLECTIONS, Hunter, R., Recollection of August 1914, nd.
102 Figures are from PRO NATS 1/398, Daily Recruiting Returns, August–December 1914 and War Office, *Statistics of the Military Effort of the British Empire During the Great War 1914–1920* (London: HMSO, 1922), 364.
103 IWM 76/225/1, Memoirs of R.L. Venables; see also IWM 76/134/1, Memoirs of Capt. G.A. Brett; IWM 76/225/1, Memoirs of R.L. Venables; IWM 88/11/1, Harrison, R.F. (Papers).
104 *Statistics of the Military Effort of the British Empire During the Great War 1914–1920*, 364.
105 IWM 85/4/1, Papers of Thompson, R., 1914–1918.
106 Independent Labour Party Pamphlet of 21 August 1914 in PRO HO 45/10741, Publications Regarding the War (Home Office), 1914.
107 Independent Labour Party Pamphlet of 21 August 1914 in PRO HO 45/10741, Publications Regarding the War (Home Office), 1914. Although occasionally the Home Office's indifference was based on an artistic judgement rather than a political one. Responding to a book called *Red Dawn*, a book of anti-war poetry published in 1916, the Home Office reviewer said 'This book seem rather nonsense and more or less harmless. Some of the "poems" rhyme or scan, but a good deal of it is prose cut into lengths.' See PRO HO 45/10742, Publications Regarding the War (Home Office – Cont), Oct. 1915 onward.
108 IWM CON/SHELF, Dible, Captain J.H. (Papers), Diary entry of 25 August 1914.
109 IWM 75/111/1, Farrow, R.W. (Papers), 1914–1918.
110 Speech at a meeting in Leeds, 4 September 1914 by Ernest Pack. Quoted in HO 45/10741, Publications Regarding the War (Home Office), 1914.
111 IWM 82/22/1, Wilkinson, J.A. (Papers), 1914–1918.

8 Conclusion

1 Niall Ferguson, *The Pity of War* (New York: Basic Books, 1999), 203.
2 R.W. Johnson, 'The Greatest Error of Modern History', *London Review of Books* 19 (February 18, 1999): 7–8.
3 Martin Middlebrooke, *The First Day of the Somme* (London: Penguin Books, 1971), xviii.
4 Ibid.
5 Ibid. 330.

6 Joseph Murray, *Call to Arms: From Gallipoli to the Western Front* (London: William Kimber, 1980), 91.
7 Middlebrooke, *First Day*, 306.
8 Jay Winter, *Sites of Memory, Sites of Mourning: The Great War in European Cultural History* (Cambridge: Cambridge University Press, 1995), 1.
9 John Keegan, *The First World War* (New York: Alfred A. Knopf, 1999), 299.
10 Hew Strachan, 'The Battle of the Somme and British Strategy', *Journal of Strategic Studies* 1 (March 1998): 80.
11 Winter, *Sites*, 2. See also Jay Winter and Emmanuel Sivan, 'Setting the Framework', in *War and Remembrance in the Twentieth Century*, ed. Jay Winter and Emmanuel Sivan (Cambridge: Cambridge University Press, 1999), 6–39 and Jay Winter, 'Forms of Kinship and Remembrance in the Aftermath of the Great War', in ibid., 40–60.
12 See, for example, Alan Clark, *The Donkeys* (London: Hutchinson, 1961) and Denis Winter, *Haig's Command: A Reassessment* (New York: Viking, 1991).
13 W.J. Reader, *At Duty's Call: A Study in Obsolete Patriotism* (Manchester: Manchester University Press, 1988), vii. Barry Hunt and Adrian Preston give a slightly different twist to this:

> Even a perspective of six decades has done little to lessen the feeling that the Great War was a senseless catastrophe, an incomprehensible tragedy which once begun seemed to set loose forces which cynical statesmen and myopic generals could barely comprehend, much less control.

See Barry Hunt and Adrian Preston, *War Aims and Strategic Policy in the Great War 1914–1918* (London: Croom Helm, 1977), 9.
14 Ferguson, *Pity of War*, 202.
15 Jay Winter, 'Army and Society: The Demographic Context', in *Nation in Arms: A Social Study of the British Army in the First World War*, ed. Ian F. Beckett and Keith Simpson (Manchester: Manchester University Press, 1985), 193–209.
16 George Anastaplo, 'Did Anyone "In Charge" Know What He was Doing? Thoughts on the Thirty Years' War of the Twentieth Century', in *A Weekend with the Great War*, ed. Steven Weingartner (Wheaton, IL: Cantigny First Division Foundation, 1995), 3–18.

References

Published primary sources

Primary Sources Archives used included the Imperial War Museum Departments of Documents and Sound Recording, the Liddle Archive at the Brotherton Library, University of Leeds, the National Army Museum, Chelsea, London, and the Public Records Office, Kew Gardens, London. For specific citations, see chapter endnotes.

Amyand, A. *With Rank and File or Sidelights on Soldier Life*. London: Osgood, McIlvaine, 1895.
Angell, N. *War and the Workers*. London: National Labour Press, 1912–1914.
Anthony, F. *A Man's a Man*. London: Duckworth, 1932.
Armstrong, W. *Saltwater Tramp*. London: Jarrods Publishers, 1944.
Asquith, M. *Autobiography of Margot Asquith*. Bath: Cedric Chivers, 1962.
Attwood, A.E. *In the Running*. Elms Court: Arthur H. Stockwell, 1977.
Barnes, G.N. *From Workshop to War Cabinet*. London: Herbert Jenkins, 1923.
Barnes, J. *The Unpardonable War*. New York: Macmillan, 1904.
Beckett, I.F. and Simpson, K. *Nation in Arms: A Social Study of the British Army in the First World War*. Manchester: Manchester University Press, 1985.
Beggs, S.T. *Selection of the Recruit*. London: Bailliere, Tindall & Cox, 1915.
Blatchford, R. *Can We Win?* London: Hodder & Stoughton, 1918.
—— *The War that was Foretold: Germany and England*. London: The Daily Mail, 1914.
Braddock, J. and B. *The Braddocks*. London: Macdonald, 1963.
Bridges, H. *As I Remember*. Preston: Carnegie Publishing, 1992.
Brock, M. and Brock, E. eds. *H.H. Asquith: Letters to Venetia Stanley*. Oxford: Oxford University Press, 1982.
Bruckshaw, H. *The Diaries of Private Horace Bruckshaw 1915–1916*. Edited by Martin Middlebrook. London: Scolar Press, 1979.
Burke, M. *Ancoats Lad: The Recollections of Mick Burke*. Manchester: Neil Richardson, 1985.
Burnett, J., ed. *Destiny Obscure: Autobiographies of Childhood, Education, and Family from the 1820s to the 1920s*. London: Routledge, 1994/1982.
Burnett, J., Vincent, D., and Mayall, D., eds. *Autobiography of the Working Class: An Annotated, Critical Bibliography, 1790–1900*. Brighton: Harvester Press, 1984.
—— eds. *Autobiography of the Working Class: An Annotated, Critical Bibliography, 1900–1945*. Brighton: Harvester Press, 1987.
Byrne, C. *I Survived, Didn't I? The Great War Reminiscences of Private 'Ginger' Byrne*. Edited by Joy B. Cave. London: Leo Cooper, 1993.

Carrington, C. H. *Soldier from the War Returning*. London: Hutchinson, 1965. *The Causes of War*. Manchester: National Labour Press, 1914.

Census Office. *Census of England and Wales, 1911*. London: HMSO, 1912.

Chew, D.N., ed. *Ada Nield Chew: The Life and Writings of a Working Woman*. London: Virago, 1982.

Circulation Figures: The Daily Mail, Evening News, Weekly Dispatch. London: Associated Newspapers, 1912.

Clark, A. *Echoes of the Great War: The Diary of Reverend Andrew Clark, 1914–1919*. Edited by James Munson. Oxford: Oxford University Press, 1985.

Clarke, A. *The Effects of the Factory System*. London: G. Richards, 1899.

Clayton, C.P. *The Hungry One*. Llandysul: Gomer Press, 1978.

Conway, M. *The Crowd in Peace and War*. New York: Longmans, Green, 1915.

Cook, D., ed. *1914: Letters from a Volunteer*. London: Cranbourn Press, 1984.

Cook, E. *The Press in War-Time*. London: Macmillan, 1920.

Corrigan, E. *Ups and Downs and Roundabouts*. Driffield: Ridings Publishing, 1972.

Cotton, B. *I Did It My Way: The Life Story of Billy Cotton*. London: George G. Harrap, 1970.

Cousland, K.H. *The Great War: A Former Gunner of the First World War Looks Back*. Toronto: by the author, 1982.

The Daily Mail and the Liberal Press: A Reply to 'Scaremongerings' and an Open Letter to Lord Northcliffe. London: privately printed, 1914.

Dawson, A. *The Story of the 1st Chiswick Early Years, 1908–1939*. London: by the author, no date given.

Dilke, C. *Army Reform*. London: Service & Paton, 1898.

Edmonds, C. *A Subaltern's War*. London: Peter Davies, 1929.

Emmerson, H.C. *Masters and Servants: A Career in the Civil Service*. Berkhamsted, Herts: Harold Emmerson, 1978.

An Englishman's Call to Arms. London: Macmillan, 1914.

Field, E. *Advertising: The Forgotten Years*. London: Ernest Benn, 1959.

Flanagan, B. *My Crazy Life*. London: Frederick Muller, 1961.

Fletcher, H. *A Life on the Humber: Keeling to Shipbuilding*. London: Faber & Faber, 1975.

Florence, M.S., Marshall, C. and Ogden, C.K. *Militarism versus Feminism*. London: Virago Press, 1915.

Hall, W. *The Lone Terrier*. Shropshire: Cadre of the King's Shropshire Highland Light Infantry, 1969.

Hankey, M. *The Supreme Command, 1914–1918*. London: George Allen & Unwin, 1961.

Hawke, J. *From Private to Major*. London: Hutchinson, 1938.

Hilton, R. *Nine Lives: The Autobiography of an Old Soldier*. London: Hollis & Carter, 1955.

Holt, W. *I Haven't Unpacked*. London: George G. Harrap, 1939.

Hunter-Weston, A. *Manpower*. London: Hayman, Christie & Lilly, 1918.

Joseph, M., ed. *The Autobiography of a Journalist*. London: Hutchinson, 1928.

Kennedy, B. *Bill Kennedy, MM: Egypt, Gallipoli, France, and Flanders with the 42nd East Lancashire Division in the Great War, 1914–1919*. Manchester: Neil Richardson, 1989.

Kenney, A. *The Memories of a Militant*. London: Edward Arnold, 1924.

Kernahan, C. *The Experiences of a Recruiting Officer: True Pictures of Splendid Patriotism*. London: Hodder & Stoughton, 1915.

Laird, F. M. *Personal Experiences of the Great War*. Dublin: Eason & Son, 1925.

Lupton, A., ed. *Statements by Asquith and Kitchener on the Debate between Compulsory and Voluntary Service*. London: Vacher & Sons, 1915.
Mann, T. *Tom Mann's Memoirs*. London: Labour Publishing Company, 1923.
Maxwell, W.N. *A Psychological Retrospect of the Great War*. London: George Allen & Unwin, 1923.
Milligan, J. *Memoirs of John Milligan of Dreghorn*. Dreghorn: by the author, 1975.
Moffat, A. *My Life with the Miners*. London: Lawrence & Wishart, 1965.
Muckle, W. *No Regrets*. Newcastle Upon Tyne: People's Publications, 1981.
Murray, J. *Call to Arms: From Gallipoli to the Western Front*. London: William Kimber, 1980.
Murray, S.L. 'The Internal Condition of Great Britain During a Great War', *Journal of the Royal United Service Institute* 57 (1913): 1561–1615.
The Narrow Waters: the First Volume of the Life and Thoughts of a Common Man. London: William Hodge, 1935.
Newsholme, A.K. *Elements of Vital Statistics in their Bearing on Social and Public Health Problems*. London: George Allen & Unwin, 1923.
Norman, C.H. *Nationality and Patriotism*. Manchester: National Labour Press, 1915.
Parliamentary Recruiting Committee. *How the Great War Arose*. London: Parliamentary Recruiting Committee, 1914.
—— *Leaflets of the Parliamentary Recruiting Committee*. London: HMSO, 1914–1916.
Purdom, C.B. *Everyman at War: Sixty Personal Narratives of the War*. London: J.M. Dent, 1930.
Recruiting by Poster: A Remarkable Patriotic Campaign. London: The Windsor Magazine, 1915.
Roberts, R. *The Classic Slum: Salford Life in the First Quarter of the Century*. London: Pelican, 1973.
Robertson, W. *From Private to Field Marshal*. London: Constable, 1921.
Robinson, C. *These We Have Loved*. London: New Horizon, 1982.
Rogers, E. *A Funny Old Quist*. London: Dennis Dobson, 1981.
Rogers, S.A.B. *Four Acres and a Donkey*. London: Dennis Dobson, 1979.
Rolph, C.H. *London Particulars*. Oxford: Oxford University Press, 1980.
Rosenberg, I. *The Collected Works of Isaac Rosenberg*. Edited by Gordon Bottomley and Denys Harding. London: Chatto & Windus, 1937.
Russell, B. *Autobiography*. London: Unwin Paperbacks, 1967.
Simpkins, H.E. *Pro Patria: Record and Extracts from Correspondence of Our Employees Serving their King and Country in the Great European War*. London: Shaw & Sons, 1915.
Taylor, A.J.P., ed. *My Darling Pussy: The Letters of Lloyd George and Frances Stevenson, 1913–1941*. London: Weidenfeld & Nicolson, 1975.
Tressell, R. *The Ragged-Trousered Philanthropists*. London: Lawrence & Wishart, 1914.
Tucker, W.A. *The Lousier War*. London: Times Mirror, 1974.
Tucker, W.J. *The Autobiography of an Astrologer*. Sidcup: Pythagorean Publications, 1960.
Wade, A. *A Gunner on the Western Front*. London: B.T. Batsford, 1959/1936.
War Emergency Workers' National Committee. *War Emergency Workers' National Committee Publications*. London: War Emergency Workers' National Committee, 1916.
War Office. *Statistics of the Military Effort of the British Empire During the Great War 1914–1920*. London: HMSO.
Wells, H.G. *War and the Future: Italy, France and Britain at War*. London: Cassell, 1917.

Wells, H.G. and Angell, N. *What the Worker Wants*. London: Hodder & Stoughton, 1912.
Williams, A. *Thirty-Six Stewart Street, Bolton: An Exercise in Nostalgia, 1901–1914*. Manchester: Neil Richardson, 1983.
Wilson, K., ed. *The Rasp of War: The Letters of H.A. Gwynne to the Countess Bathurst, 1914–1918*. London: Sidgwick & Jackson, 1988.
Wynne, F.C. *Fourpence a Day and All Found*. London: New Horizon, 1981.

Secondary sources

Adams, M.C.C. *The Great Adventure: Male Desire and the Coming of World War I*. Bloomington, IN: Indiana University Press, 1990.
Adams, R.J.Q. and Poirer, P.P. *The Conscription Controversy in Great Britain, 1900–1918*. London: Macmillan, 1987.
Aitken, M. *Politicians and the War 1914–1916*. London: Oldbourne Book Co., 1960.
Alford, B.W.E. *Britain in the World Economy Since 1880*. London: Longman, 1996.
Allinson, S. *The Bantams: The Untold Story of World War One*. London: Howard Baker, 1981.
Altick, R. *The English Common Reader: A Social History of the Mass Reading Public, 1800–1900*. Chicago: University of Chicago Press, 1957.
Anderson, B. *Imagined Communities: Reflections on the Origin and Spread of Nationalism*. London: Verso, 1983.
Anderson, P. *The Printed Image and the Transformation of Popular Culture 1790–1860*. Oxford: Clarendon Press, 1991.
Arnstein, W., ed. *Recent Historians of Great Britain*. Ames, IA: Iowa State University Press, 1990.
Aron, R. *Peace and War: A Theory of International Relations*. London: Weidenfeld & Nicolson, 1966.
Aston, J. and Duggan, L.M. *The History of the 12th Bermondsey Battalion, East Surrey Regiment*. London: Union Press, 1936.
Barnes, R.M. *The British Army of 1914*. London: Seeley Service, 1968.
Barnett, C. *The Swordbearers: Studies in Supreme Command in the First World War*. London: Eyre & Spottiswoode, 1963.
—— *Britain and Her Army, 1509–1970*. London: Penguin, 1970.
—— *The Collapse of British Power*. London: Methuen, 1972.
—— *The Great War*. London: Park Lane Press, 1979.
Behlmer, G.K. *Child Abuse and Moral Reform in England, 1870–1908*. Stanford, CA: Stanford University Press, 1982.
Beiriger, E.E. *Churchill, Munitions, and Mechanical Warfare*. New York: Peter Lang, 1997.
Belchem, J. *Industrialization and the Working Class: The English Experience, 1750–1900*. Aldershot: Scolar Press, 1990.
Benson, J. *British Coalminers in the Nineteenth Century*. New York: Holmes & Meier Publishers, 1980.
—— *The Penny Capitalists*. New Brunswick, NJ: Rutgers University Press, 1983.
—— *The Working Class in Britain, 1850–1939*. London: Longman, 1989.
Berghahn, V.R. *Germany and the Approach of War in 1914*. New York: St Martin's Press, 1973.
Biagini, E. and Reid, A., eds. *Currents of Radicalism: Popular Radicalism, Organized Labour and Party Politics in Britain, 1859–1914*. Cambridge: Cambridge University Press, 1991.

Billington, J.H. *Fire in the Minds of Men*. New York: Basic Books, 1980.
Bond, B. *Victorian Army and the Staff College, 1854–1914*. London: Eyre Methuen, 1972.
—— *War and Society in Europe 1870–1970*. London: Fontana, 1984.
—— ed. *Fallen Stars: Eleven Studies of Twentieth Century Military Disasters*. London: Brassey's, 1991.
—— *The First World War and British Military History*. Oxford: Clarendon Press, 1991.
Bond, B. and Roy, I., eds. *War and Society: A Yearbook of Military History*, vols 1 and 2. London: Croom Helm, 1975–1977.
Booth, C. *The Life and Labour of the People in London*. London: Macmillan, 1902.
Bourke, J. *Husbandry to Housewifery: Women, Economic Change, and Housework in Ireland, 1890–1914*. Oxford: Clarendon Press, 1993.
Bowle, J. *Imperial Achievement: The Rise and Transformation of the British Empire*. Boston: Little, Brown, 1974.
Bowley, A.L. *Prices and Wages in the United Kingdom, 1914–1920*. Oxford: Clarendon Press, 1921.
Boyce, G., Curran, J., and Wingate, P., eds. *Newspaper History from the Seventeenth Century to the Present Day*. London: Constable, 1978.
Brantlinger, P. *The Rule of Darkness: British Literature and Imperialism, 1830–1914*. Ithaca, NY: Cornell University Press, 1988.
—— *The Reading Lesson: The Threat of Mass Literacy in Nineteenth Century British Fiction*. Bloomington, IN: Indiana University Press, 1998.
Braybon, G. *Women Workers in the First World War*. London: Croom Helm, 1981.
Bridge, F.R. and Bullen, R. *The Great Powers and the European States System 1815–1914*. London: Longman, 1980.
Briggs, A. and Saville, J., eds. *Essays in Labour History*. New York: St Martin's Press, 1967.
Brophy, J. and Partridge, E. *The Long Trail: What the British Soldier Sang and Said in the Great War of 1914–1918*. London: André Deutsch, 1965/1931.
Brown, M. *Tommy Goes to War*. London: J.M. Dent & Sons, 1978.
Buitenhuis, P. *The Great War of Words*. Vancouver: University of British Columbia Press, 1987.
Bullock, A. *The Life and Times of Ernest Bevin*, vols 1 and 2. London: Heinemann, 1960.
Burk, K. *War and the State*. London: George Allen & Unwin, 1982.
Cain, P.J. *The Economic Foundations of British Overseas Expansion 1815–1914*. London: Macmillan, 1980.
Cannadine, D. *The Decline and Fall of the British Aristocracy*. New Haven, CT and London: Yale University Press, 1990.
Carrington, C. *Rudyard Kipling: His Life and Work*. London: Penguin, 1970.
Carsten, F.L. *War Against War*. London: Batsford Academic & Educational, 1982.
Cassar, G. *Kitchener: Architect of Victory*. London: William Kimber, 1977.
Ceadel, M. *Pacifism in Britain 1914–1945: The Defining of a Faith*. Oxford: Clarendon Press, 1980.
Chalmers, T. *An Epic of Glasgow: History of the 15th Battalion the Highland Light Infantry (City of Glasgow Regiment)*. Glasgow: John McCallum, 1934.
Chamberlain, W.J. *Fighting for Peace: The Story of the War Resistance Movement*. London: No More War Movement, 1928.
Chambers, F.P. *War Behind the War 1914–1918*. London: Faber & Faber, 1939.
Chase, M. and Dyck, I., eds. *Living and Learning: Essays in Honour of J.F.C. Harrison*. Aldershot, England: Scolar, 1996.

Checkland, S. *British Public Policy 1776–1939: An Economic, Social, and Political Perspective*. Cambridge: Cambridge University Press, 1983.
Churchill, R.S. *Lord Derby: King of Lancashire*. London: Heinemann, 1959.
Churchill, W. *The World Crisis*, vol. 1. New York: Charles Scribner's Sons, 1923.
Clark, A. *The Donkeys*. London: Hutchinson, 1961.
Clarke, I. *Tale of the Future*. London: Library Association, 1972.
—— *Voices Prophesying War: Future Wars 1763–3749*. Oxford: Oxford University Press, 1992.
Clarke, J., Crichter, C., and Johnson, R. *Working-Class Culture: Studies in History and Theory*. London: Hutchinson, 1979.
Clarke, P. *Hope and Glory*. London: Allen Lane, 1996.
Clarke, T. *My Northcliffe Diary*. London: Victor Gollancz, 1931.
Clegg, H.A. *History of British Trade Unions Since 1889, Volume II: 1911–1933*. Oxford: Clarendon Press, 1985.
Cole, G.D.H. *Trade Unionism and Munitions*. Oxford: Clarendon Press, 1923.
Cole, G.D.H. and Postgate, R. *The British People, 1746–1946*. London: Methuen, 1961.
Colley, L. *Britons: Forging the Nation 1707–1837*. New Haven, CT: Yale University Press, 1992.
Constantine, S., Kirby, M.W., and Rose, M.B., eds. *The First World War in British History*. London: Edward Arnold, 1995.
Cooksey, J. *The 13th and 14th York and Lancaster Regiment*. Barnsley: Graphics and Features Department, Barnsley Chronicle, 1986.
Cookson, J.E. *The British Armed Nation*. Oxford: Clarendon Press, 1997.
Cooper, T., ed. *The Wheels Used to Talk to Us*. Sheffield: Sheaf Publishing, 1977.
Cranfield, G. *The Press and Society: From Caxton to Northcliffe*. London: Longman, 1978.
Critchley, T.A. *The Conquest of Violence: Order and Liberty in Britain*. London: Constable, 1970.
—— *The History of Police in England and Wales*. London: Constable, 1978/1967.
Cronin, J. *Politics of State Expansion: War, State and Society in Twentieth-Century Britain*. London: Routledge, 1991.
Cronin, J.E. and Schneer, J., eds. *Social Conflict and the Political Order in Modern Britain*. New Brunswick, NJ: Rutgers University Press, 1982.
Crook, P. *Darwinism, War and History: The Debate over the Biology of War from the 'Origin of Species' to the First World War*. Cambridge: Cambridge University Press, 1994.
Cross, C. *The Liberals in Power*. London: Barrie & Rockliffe, 1963.
Crossick G., ed. *The Lower Middle-Class in Britain, 1870–1914*. London: Croom Helm, 1977.
Crossick, G. and Haupt, H.G., eds. *Shopkeepers and Master Artisans in Nineteenth-Century Europe*. London: Methuen, 1984.
Cruttwell, C.R.M.F. *A History of the Great War, 1914–1918*. Oxford: Clarendon Press, 1934.
Cunningham, H. *The Children of the Poor: Representations of Childhood since the Seventeenth Century*. Oxford: Blackwell, 1991.
—— *Children and Childhood in Western Society Since 1500*. London: Longman, 1995.
D'Cruze, S. *Crimes of Outrage: Sex, Violence, and Victorian Working Women*. DeKalb, IL: Northern Illinois University Press, 1998.

Davin, A. *Growing Up Poor: Home, School, and Street in London 1870–1914*. London: Rivers Oram Press, 1996.
Davis, L.E. and Huttenback, R. *Mammon and the Pursuit of Empire*. Cambridge: Cambridge University Press, 1986.
DeGroot, G. *Blighty: British Society in the Era of the Great War*. London: Longman, 1996.
Dietz, P. *The Last of the Regiments: Their Rise and Fall*. London: Brassey's, 1990.
Dooley, T. *Irishmen or English Soldiers*. Liverpool: Liverpool University Press, 1995.
Doughty, M., ed. *Dilapidated Housing and Housing Policy in Southampton, 1890–1914*. Southampton: Southampton University Press, 1986.
Duggan, J.P. *A History of the Irish Army*. Dublin: Gill & Macmillan, 1991.
Dungan, M. *They Shall Not Grow Old: Irish Soldiers and the Great War*. Dublin: Four Courts Press, 1991.
—— *Irish Voice from the Great War*. Dublin: Irish Academic Press, 1995.
Dunlop, J.K. *Development of the British Army 1899–1914*. London: Methuen, 1938.
Eby, C. *Road to Armageddon*. Durham, NC: Duke University Press, 1987.
Eksteins, M. *Rites of Spring: The Great War and the Birth of the Modern Age*. New York: Houghton Mifflin, 1989.
Eldridge, C.C. *The Imperial Experience: From Carlyle to Forster*. London: Macmillan, 1996.
Engel, M. *Tickle the Public: 100 Years of the Popular Press*. London: Victor Gollancz, 1996.
Enloe, C. *Does Khaki Become You?* London: South End Press, 1983.
Falls, C. *The Great War*. New York: G.P. Putnam's Sons, 1959.
Ferris, P. *The House of Northcliffe: A Biography of an Empire*. New York: World Publications, 1972.
Field, H.J. *Toward a Programme of Imperial Life: The British Empire at the Turn of the Century*. Westport, CT: Greenwood Press, 1982.
Fitzpatrick, D., ed. *Ireland and the First World War*. Dublin: Trinity History Workshop, 1986.
Floud, R. and McCloskey, D., eds. *The Economic History of Britain since 1700*, 2 vols. Cambridge: Cambridge University Press, 1981.
Foot, M.R.D., ed. *War and Society: Historical Essays in Honour and Memory of J.R. Western, 1928–1971*. London: Paul Elek, 1973.
Fulbrook, M., ed. *National Histories and European History*. Boulder, CO: Westview Press, 1993.
Fuller, S. *The Poetry of War, 1914–1989*. London: Longmans, 1990.
Fussell, P. *The Great War and Modern Memory*. London: Oxford University Press, 1975.
Galbraith, G.R. *Reading Lives: Reconstructing Childhood, Books, and Schools in Britain 1870–1920*. New York: St Martin's Press, 1997.
Garwood, J.M. *The Chorley Pals: 'Y' Company, 11th (Service) Battalion, East Lancashire Regiment*. Manchester: Neil Richardson, 1989.
Gellner, E. *Nations and Nationalism*. Ithaca, NY: Cornell University Press, 1983.
Germains, V. *The Kitchener Armies: The Story of a National Achievement*. London: Peter Davies, 1930.
Gibson, R. and Oldfield, P. *The Sheffield City Battalion, The 12th (Service) Battalion York and Lancaster Regiment: A History of the Battalion Raised by Sheffield in World War One*. Barnsley, Yorkshire: Wharncliffe Publishing, 1988.

Gilbert, B.R. *The Evolution of National Insurance in Great Britain*. London: Michael Joseph, 1966.

Gilbert, M. *The First World War: A Complete History*. New York: H. Holt, 1994.

Gillis, J.R. *For Better, for Worse: British Marriages, 1600 to the Present*. Oxford: Oxford University Press, 1985.

Girouard, M. *The Return to Camelot: Chivalry and the English Gentleman*. New Haven, CT: Yale University Press, 1981.

Gooch, J. *Plans of War: The General Staff and British Military Strategy c. 1900–1916*. London: Routledge & Kegan Paul, 1974.

—— *The Prospect of War: Studies in British Defence Policy 1847–1942*. London: Frank Cass, 1981.

Gooch, J. and Beckett, I., eds. *Politicians and Defence: Studies in the Formulation of British Defence Policy 1845–1970*. Manchester: Manchester University Press, 1981.

Goodspeed, D.J. *The German Wars, 1914–1945*. Boston: Houghton Mifflin, 1977.

Grainger, J.H. *Patriotisms: Britain, 1900–1939*. London: Routledge & Kegan Paul, 1986.

Green, H. *The British Army in the First World War: The Regulars, the Territorials, and Kitchener's Army*. London: J. Trahern, 1968.

Grenfell, R. *Service Pay*. London: Eyre & Spottiswoode, 1944.

Grieves, K. *Politics of Manpower, 1914–1918*. Manchester: Manchester University Press, 1988.

Guinn, P. *British Strategy and Politics 1914–1918*. Oxford: Clarendon Press, 1965.

Halsey, A.H., ed. *British Social Trends since 1900*. London: Macmillan, 1972.

Hammond, P.Y. *Organizing for Defense: The American Military Establishment in the Twentieth Century*. Princeton, NJ: Princeton University Press, 1961.

Hardach, G. *The First World War*. London: Penguin, 1987.

Harris, J. *Unemployment and Politics: A Study in English Social Policy, 1886–1914*. Oxford: Clarendon Press, 1972.

—— *Private Lives, Public Spirit: Britain 1870–1914*. London: Penguin, 1993.

Harvey, A.D. *Collision of Empires: Britain in Three World Wars, 1793–1945*. London: The Hambledon Press, 1992.

Haste, C. *Keep the Home Fires Burning: Propaganda in the First World War*. London: Allen Lane, 1977.

Haupt, G. *Socialism and the Great War*. Oxford: Clarendon Press, 1972.

Hayes, D. *Conscription Conflict: The Conflict of Ideas in the Struggle for and against Military Conscription in Britain between 1901–1939*. London: Sheppard Press, 1949.

Hayes, P., ed. *Themes in Modern European History 1890–1945*. London: Routledge, 1992.

Hazlehurst, C. *The Politicians at War, July 1914 to May 1915: A Prologue to the Triumph of Lloyd George*. London: Jonathan Cape, 1971.

Higonnet, M. *et al.*, eds. *Behind the Lines: Gender and the Two World Wars*. New Haven, CT: Yale University Press, 1987.

Hinton, J. *The First Shop Stewards' Movement*. London: George Allen & Unwin, 1973.

—— *Labour and Socialism: A History of the British Labour Movement 1867–1974*. London: Wheatsheaf Books, 1983.

Hirst, F.W. *The Consequences of the War to Great Britain*. London: Humphrey Milford, 1934.

The History of The Times, 1912–1948, part I. New York: Macmillan, 1952.

Hobsbawm, E.J. *Labouring Men: Studies in the History of Labour*. London: Weidenfeld & Nicolson, 1964.

—— *Industry and Empire*. London: Weidenfeld & Nicolson, 1968.

—— *Worlds of Labour: Further Studies in the History of Labour*. London: Weidenfeld & Nicolson, 1984.
—— *The Age of Empire*. London: Weidenfeld & Nicolson, 1987.
Hobsbawm, E. and Ranger, T. *The Invention of Tradition*. Cambridge: Cambridge University Press, 1983.
Holton, S.S. *Feminism and Democracy: Women's Suffrage and Reform Politics in Britain 1900–1918*. Cambridge: Cambridge University Press, 1986.
Horn, P. *Children's Work and Welfare, 1780–1880s*. London: Macmillan, 1994.
Horne, J. *Labour at War*. Oxford: Clarendon Press, 1991.
—— ed. *State, Society, and Mobilization in Europe During the First World War*. Cambridge: Cambridge University Press, 1997.
Host, J. *Victorian Labour History*. London: Routledge, 1998.
Howard, M. *The Continental Commitment*. London: Penguin, 1974/1972.
—— *War in European History*. Oxford: Oxford University Press, 1976.
Howarth, P. *Play Up and Play the Game*. London: Eyre Methuen, 1973.
Howkins, A. *Poor Labouring Men: Rural Radicalism in Norfolk, 1870–1923*. London: Routledge, 1985.
Hume, L.P. *The National Union of Women's Suffrage Societies, 1897–1914*. New York: Garland Publishing, 1982.
Humphries, S. *Hooligans or Rebels? An Oral History of Working-Class Childhood and Youth 1889–1939*. Oxford: Basil Blackwell, 1981.
Humphries, S. and Gordon, P. *A Labour of Love: The Experience of Parenthood in Britain, 1900–1950*. London: Sidgwick & Jackson, 1993.
Hunt, B. and Preston, A. *War Aims and Strategic Policy in the Great War 1914–1918*. London: Croom Helm, 1977.
Hurwitz, S. *State Intervention in Great Britain: A Study of Economic Control and Social Response 1914–1919*. London: Frank Cass, 1949.
Hynes, S. *The Edwardian Turn of Mind*. Princeton, NJ: Princeton University Press, 1968.
—— *A War Imagined*. New York: Collier Books, Macmillan, 1990.
Inwood, S. *A History of London*. London: Macmillan, 1998.
James, D. and French, J., eds. *The Gendered Worlds of Latin American Women Workers*. Durham, NC: Duke University Press, 1997.
James, R.R. *The British Revolution: British Politics, 1880–1939, Volume 1: From Gladstone to Asquith, 1880–1914*. London: Hamish Hamilton, 1976.
Jeffrey, K., ed. *'An Irish Empire': Aspects of Ireland and the British Empire*. Manchester: Manchester University Press, 1996.
Johnson, F.A. *Defence by Committee: The British Committee of Imperial Defence 1885–1959*. Oxford and London: Oxford University Press, 1960.
Johnson, P. *Saving and Spending: The Working-Class Economy in Britain 1870–1939*. Oxford: Clarendon Press, 1985.
Joll, J. *Origins of the First World War*. London: Longman, 1992/1984.
Jones, A. *The Powers of the Press*. Aldershot: Scolar Press, 1996.
Jones, B. and Howell, B. *Popular Arts of the First World War*. London: Studio Vista, 1972.
Jones, D. *Bullets and Bandsmen*. Salisbury: Owl Press, 1992.
Jones, D. *The Selected Works of David Jones*. Edited by John Matthias. Cardiff: University of Wales Press, 1992.
Jones, G.S. *The Languages of Class: Studies in English Working Class History, 1832–1982*. Cambridge: Cambridge University Press, 1983.

—— *Outcast London: A Study in the Relationship Between Classes in Victorian Society.* New York: Pantheon, 1984/1971.
Joyce, P. *Work, Society, and Politics: The Culture of the Factory in Later Victorian England.* London: Methuen, 1982/1980.
—— ed. *The Historical Meanings of Work.* Cambridge: Cambridge University Press, 1987.
—— *Visions of the People: Industrial England and the Question of Class, 1848–1914.* Cambridge: Cambridge University Press, 1991.
—— *Democratic Subjects: The Self and the Social in Nineteenth-Century England.* Cambridge: Cambridge University Press, 1994.
Keegan, J. *The First World War.* New York: Alfred A. Knopf, 1999.
Kennedy, P. *The Rise of the Anglo-German Antagonism.* London: George Allen & Unwin, 1980.
—— ed. *War Plans of the Great Powers 1880–1914.* Boston: Allen & Unwin, 1985.
—— *The Rise and Fall of the Great Powers.* New York: Doubleday, 1987.
Kennedy, P. and Nicholls, A., eds. *Nationalist and Racialist Movements in Britain and Germany Before 1914.* Oxford and London: Macmillan, 1978.
Kent, S.K. *Sex and Suffrage in Britain, 1860–1914.* London: Routledge, 1990.
Kirk, N. *Labour and Society in Britain and the USA, Volume 2: 1850–1939.* London: Scolar Press, 1994.
Koss, S. *The Rise and Fall of the Political Press in Britain: The Twentieth Century.* London: Hamish Hamilton, 1984.
Langan, M. and Schwarz, B., eds. *Crises in the British State 1880–1930.* London: Hutchinson, 1985.
Lawrence, J. *Speaking for the People.* Cambridge: Cambridge University Press, 1998.
Lawton, R., ed. *The Census and Social Structure: An Interpretive Guide to Nineteenth Century Censuses for England and Wales.* London: Frank Cass, 1978.
Lee, A.J. *The Origins of the Popular Press in England 1855–1914.* London: Croom Helm, 1976.
Leed, E.J. *No Man's Land: Combat and Identity in World War One.* Cambridge: Cambridge University Press, 1981.
Lees, L.H. *The Solidarities of Strangers: The English Poor Laws and the People, 1700–1948.* Cambridge: Cambridge University Press, c1998.
Levine, K. *The Social Context of Literacy.* London: Routledge & Kegan Paul, 1986.
Liddell Hart, B. *The Real War, 1914–1918.* Boston: Little, Brown, 1930.
Liddington, J. *Long Road to Greenham: Feminism and Anti-Militarism in Britain since 1820.* London: Virago, 1989.
Liddington, J. and Norris, J. *One Hand Tied Behind Us: The Rise of the Women's Suffrage Movement.* London: Virago, 1978.
Liddle, P. *The Testimony of War 1914–1918.* London: Michael Russell, 1979.
—— ed. *Home Fires and Foreign Fields: British Social and Military Experience in the First World War.* London: Brassey's, 1985.
—— *The Soldier's War.* London: Blandford Press, 1988.
—— *The Voices of War.* London: Leo Cooper, 1988.
Liddle, P. and Cecil, H., eds. *Facing Armageddon: The First World War Experienced.* London: Leo Cooper, 1996.
Liesner, T. *Economic Statistics, 1900–1983, UK, USA, France, Germany, Italy, Japan.* London: Economist Publications, 1985.
Lloyd, T.O. *Empire, Welfare State, Europe: English History 1906–1992.* Oxford: Oxford University Press, 1993.

Lummis, T. *The Labour Aristocracy: 1851–1914*. Aldershot, UK: Scolar Press, 1994.
Macdonagh, M. *In London during the Great War*. London: Eyre & Spottiswoode, 1935.
Macdonald, L. *1914*. London: Michael Joseph, 1987.
—— *1915: The Death of Innocence*. London: Headline, 1993.
MacDonald, R.H. *The Sons of the Empire: The Frontier and the Boy Scout Movement, 1890–1918*. Toronto: University of Toronto Press, 1993.
—— *The Language of Empire: Myths and Metaphors of Popular Imperialism, 1880–1918*. Manchester: Manchester University Press, 1994.
Mackenzie, J., ed. *Imperialism and Popular Culture*. Manchester: Manchester University Press, 1990.
—— ed. *Popular Imperialism and the Military 1850–1950*. Manchester: Manchester University Press, 1992.
Maddocks, G. *The Liverpool Pals: A History of the 17th, 18th, 19th, and 20th (Service) Battalions The King's Liverpool Regiment, 1914–1919*. London: Leo Cooper, 1991.
Magnus, P. *Kitchener: Portrait of an Imperialist*. London: John Murray, 1958.
Mann, M., ed. *The Rise and Decline of the Nation State*. Oxford: Blackwell, 1990.
Manning, F. *Her Privates We*. London: Hogarth Press, 1986.
Marson, D. *Children's Strikes in 1911*. London: Routledge & Kegan Paul, 1973.
Marwick, A. *The Deluge: British Society and the First World War*. London: Bodley Head, 1965.
—— *Britain in the Century of Total War: War, Peace, and Social Change*. Boston: Little, Brown, 1968.
—— *Britain in Our Century: Images and Controversies*. London: Thames & Hudson, 1984.
Marx, K. and Engels, F. *The Communist Manifesto: New Interpretations*, ed. Mark Cowling. New York: New York University Press, 1998.
Massie, R. *Dreadnought: Britain, Germany and the Coming of the Great War*. New York: Random House, 1991.
McAleer, J. *Popular Reading and Publishing in Britain, 1914–1950*. Oxford: Clarendon Press, 1992.
McGuffie, T.H., ed. *The Rank and File: The Common Soldier at Peace and War 1642–1914*. London: Hutchinson, 1964.
McKibbin, R. *The Evolution of the Labour Party 1910–1924*. Oxford: Clarendon Press, 1974.
—— *Ideologies of Class: Social Relations in Britain 1880–1950*. Oxford: Clarendon Press, 1990.
Meacham, S. *A Life Apart: The English Working Class 1890–1914*. London: Thames & Hudson, 1977.
Messinger, G.S. *British Propaganda and the State in the First World War*. Manchester: Manchester University Press, 1992.
Middlebrooke, M. *The First Day on the Somme*. London: Allen Lane, 1971.
Milner, L. *The Leeds Pals: A History of the 15th (Service) Battalion, 1st Leeds, The Prince of Wales' Own (West Yorkshire Regiment), 1914–1918*. London: Leo Cooper, 1991.
Mitchell, J. *Robert Tressell and the Ragged Trousered Philanthropists*. London: Lawrence & Wishart, 1969.
Moore, D.C. *The Politics of Deference*. New York: Harvester Press, 1976.
More, C. *Skill and the English Working-Class, 1870–1914*. New York: St Martin's Press, 1980.
Morgan, D. *Suffragists and Liberals: The Politics of Woman Suffrage in England*. Oxford: Basil Blackwell, 1975.

Morgan, K.O. *Wales in British Politics, 1868–1922*. Cardiff: University of Wales Press, 1991.
—— *Modern Wales: Politics, Places, and People*. Cardiff: University of Wales Press, 1995.
Morris, A.J.A. *Radicalism Against War, 1906–1914: The Advocacy of Peace and Retrenchment*. London: Longman, 1972.
—— ed. *Edwardian Radicalism, 1900–1914*. London: Routledge & Kegan Paul, 1974.
—— *The Scaremongers: The Advocacy of War and Rearmament 1896–1914*. London: Routledge & Kegan Paul, 1984.
Morris, H.F. *Bermondsey's 'Bit' in the Greatest War*. London: Clifton Publishing House, 1923.
Moynihan, M. *Greater Love: Letters Home, 1914–1918*. London: W.H. Allen, 1980.
Müller, D.K., Ringer, F., and Simon, B., eds. *The Rise of the Modern Educational System: Structural Change and Social Reproduction 1870–1920*. Cambridge: Cambridge University Press, 1987.
Murphy, P.T. *Toward a Working-Class Canon: Literary Criticism in British Working-Class Periodicals, 1816–1858*. Columbus, OH: Ohio State University Press, 1994.
News of Our Time: The Golden Jubilee Book of the Daily Mail. London: Associated Newspapers, 1946.
Newton, D.J. *British Labour, European Socialism, and the Struggle for Peace 1889–1914*. Oxford: Clarendon Press, 1985.
Newton, J.L., Ryan, M.P., and Walkowitz, J.R., eds. *Sex and Class in Women's History*. London: Routledge, 1983.
Offer, A. *Property and Politics 1870–1914*. Cambridge: Cambridge University Press, 1981.
—— *The First World War: An Agrarian Interpretation*. Oxford: Clarendon Press, 1989.
Ong, W. *Orality and Literacy: The Technologizing of the Word*. London: Methuen, 1982.
Osborne, J.M. *The Voluntary Recruiting Movement in Britain, 1914–1916*. New York: Garland Publishing, 1982.
Parker, A., Russo, M., Sommer, D. Yaeger, P. *Nationalism and Sexualities*. London: Routledge, 1992.
Parker, P. *The Old Lie: The Great War and the Public-School Ethos*. London: Constable, 1987.
Peacock, A. and Wiseman, J. *The Growth of Public Expenditure in the United Kingdom*. Princeton, NJ: Princeton University Press, 1961.
Pelling, H. *The Social Geography of British Elections, 1885–1910*. London: Macmillan, 1967.
—— *Popular Politics and Society in Late Victorian Britain*. London: Macmillan, 1968.
Penny Dreadfuls and Comics. London: Victoria & Albert Museum, 1983.
Pick, D. *The War Machine: The Rationalization of Slaughter*. New Haven, CT: Yale University Press, 1993.
Playne, C. *Pre-War Mind in Britain: An Historical Review*. London: George Allen & Unwin, 1928.
—— *Society at War, 1914–1916*. London: George Allen & Unwin, 1931.
Pollard, S. *Britain's Prime and Britain's Decline: The British Economy 1870–1914*. London: Edward Arnold, 1989.
Pooley, C.G. and Turnbull, J. *Migration and Mobility in Britain since the Eighteenth Century*. London: UCL Press, 1989.
Poovey, M. *Making a Social Body*. Chicago: University of Chicago Press, 1995.
Porter, B. *Britain, Europe and the World 1850–1982: Delusions of Grandeur*. London: Allen & Unwin, 1987.

—— *Origins of the Vigilant State*. London: Boydell Press, 1987.
—— *Lion's Share: Short History of British Imperialism 1850–1970*. London: Longman, 1996.
Porter, B. *War and the Rise of the State*. New York: Free Press, 1994.
Pound, R. *The Lost Generation*. London: Constable, 1964.
Powell, D. *The Edwardian Crisis: Britain, 1901–1914*. London: Macmillan, 1996.
Price, R. *An Imperial War and the British Working Class: Working-Class Attitudes and Reactions to the Boer War 1899–1902*. London: Routledge & Kegan Paul, 1972.
Pugh, M. *Lloyd George*. London: Longman, 1988.
—— *State and Society: British Political and Social History 1870–1992*. London: Edward Arnold, 1994.
Purvis, J. *Hard Lessons: The Lives and Educations of Working-Class Women in Nineteenth-Century England*. Minneapolis: University of Minnesota Press, 1989.
Read, D., ed. *Edwardian England*. New Brunswick, NJ: Rutgers University Press, 1982.
Read, J.M. *Atrocity Propaganda*. New Haven, CT: Yale University Press, 1941.
Reader, W.J. *At Duty's Call: A Study in Obsolete Patriotism*. Manchester: Manchester University Press, 1988.
Redmayne, R.A.S. *The British Coal-Mining Industry during the War*. Oxford: Clarendon Press, 1923.
Reeves, N. *Official British Film Propaganda during the First World War*. London: Croom Helm, 1986.
Richards, J. and MacKenzie, J. *The Railway Stations: A Social History*. Oxford: Oxford University Press, 1986.
Ricketts, H. *The Unforgiving Minute: A Life of Rudyard Kipling*. London: Chatto & Windus, 1999.
Robbins, K. *The Abolition of War: The 'Peace Movement' in Britain, 1914–1919*. Cardiff: University of Wales Press, 1976.
—— *The First World War*. Oxford: Oxford University Press, 1984.
—— *Politicians, Diplomacy, and War in Modern British History*. London: The Hambledon Press, 1994.
Roberts, E. *A Woman's Place: An Oral History of Working-Class Women 1890–1940*. Oxford: Basil Blackwell, 1984.
Rolph, C.H. *London Particulars*. Oxford: Oxford University Press, 1980.
Rosen, A. *Rise Up, Women! The Militant Campaign of the Women's Social and Political Union 1903–1914*. London: Routledge & Kegan Paul, 1974.
Rosenthal, M. *The Character Factory: Baden-Powell and the Origins of the Boy Scout Movement*. New York: Pantheon Books, 1984.
Roskill, S. *Hankey: Man of Secrets*. London: Collins, 1970.
Ross, E. *Love and Toil: Motherhood in Outcast London, 1870–1918*. Oxford: Oxford University Press, 1993.
Rowntree, B. Seebohm. *Poverty, A Study of Town Life*. London: Macmillan, 1906.
Royle, T. *The Kitchener Enigma*. London: Michael Joseph, 1985.
Rubinstein, S. *German Atrocity or British Propaganda: The Seventieth Anniversary of a Scandal: German Corpse Utilization Establishments in the First World War*. Jerusalem: Acadamon, 1987.
Russell, D. *Popular Music in England, 1840–1914: A Social History*. Manchester: Manchester University Press, 1987.
Ryan, J.R. *Picturing Empire: Photography and the Visualization of the British Empire*. Chicago: University of Chicago Press, 1997.

Samuel, R. *Village Life and Labour*. London: Routledge, 1975.
—— ed. *People's History and Socialist Theory*. London: Routledge, 1981.
—— *Patriotism: The Making and Unmaking of British National Identity*, vols 1–3. London: Routledge, 1989.
Samuel, R. and Stedman Jones, G., eds. *Culture, Ideology, and Politics: Essays for Eric Hobsbawm*. London: Routledge & Kegan Paul, 1982.
Sanders, M.L. and Taylor, P. *British Propaganda during the First World War, 1914–1918*. London: Macmillan, 1982.
Savage, M. and Miles, A. *The Remaking of the British Working-Class*. London: Routledge, 1994.
Schmitt, B.E. and Vedeler, H.C.L.B. *The World in the Crucible*. New York: Harper & Row, 1984.
Searle, G.R. *Quest for National Efficiency: A Study in British Politics and Political Thought, 1899–1914*. Oxford: Basil Blackwell, 1971.
—— *Liberal Party: Triumph and Disintegration, 1886–1929*. London: Macmillan, 1992.
Shanley, M.L. *Feminism, Marriage, and the Law in Victorian England*. Princeton, NJ: Princeton University Press, 1989.
Sheffield, G. *Forgotten Victory, the First World War: Myths and Realities*. London: Headline Books, 2001.
Sherington, G. *English Education, Social Change, and War 1911–1920*. Manchester: Manchester University Press, 1981.
Simkins, P. *Kitchener's Army: The Raising of the New Armies, 1914–1916*. Manchester: Manchester University Press, 1980.
Skelley, A.R. *The Victorian Army at Home: The Recruitment and Terms and Conditions of the British Regular, 1859–1899*. London: Croom Helm, 1977.
Smith, A.D. *Nationalism and Modernism*. London: Routledge, 1998.
Smithers, A.J. *Fighting Nation: Lord Kitchener and His Armies*. London: Leo Cooper, 1994.
Soloway, R.A. *Birth Control and the Population Question in England, 1877–1930*. Chapel Hill, NC: University of North Carolina Press, 1982.
Spiers, E. *The Army and Society, 1815–1914*. London: Longman, 1980.
Springhall, J. *Youth, Empire and Society: British Youth Movements, 1883–1940*. London: Croom Helm, 1977.
—— *Coming of Age: Adolescence in Britain 1860–1960*. Dublin: Gill & Macmillan, 1986.
—— *Youth, Popular Culture, and Moral Panics: Penny Gaffs to Gangsta-Rap, 1830–1996*. New York: St Martin's Press, 1998.
Stedman, M. *The Salford Pals: A History of the 15th, 16th, 19th and 20th Battalions Lancashire Fusiliers 1914–1919*. London: Leo Cooper, 1993.
Steedman, C., ed. *The Radical Soldier's Tale*. London: Routledge, 1988.
Steedman, C., Urwin, C., and Walkerdine, V. *Language, Gender, and Childhood*. London: Routledge, 1985.
Stephens, B. *Education, Literacy and Society, 1830–1870*. Manchester: Manchester University Press, 1978.
Steppler, G.A. *Britons, To Arms! The Story of the British Volunteer Soldiers*. London: Alan Sutton, 1992.
Stone, J. and Schmidl, E.A. *The Boer War and Military Reforms*. New York: University Press of America, 1988.

Stone, L., ed. *Imperial State at War: Britain from 1689 to 1815*. London: Routledge, 1994.
Strachan, H. *European Armies and the Conduct of War*. London: Routledge, 1983.
—— *The Politics of the British Army*. Oxford: Clarendon Press, 1997.
—— ed. *The Oxford Illustrated History of the First World War*. Oxford: Oxford University Press, 1998.
Streets, H. '"The Right Stamp of Men": Military Imperatives and Popular Imperialism in Late Victorian Britain.' PhD diss., Duke University, 1998.
Swartz, M. *The Union of Democratic Control in British Politics during the First World War*. Oxford: Clarendon Press, 1971.
Swenarton, M. *Homes Fit for Heroes*. London: Heinemann, 1981.
Tanner, D. *Political Change and the Labour Party 1900–1918*. Cambridge: Cambridge University Press, 1990.
Taylor, A.J.P. *English History, 1914–1945*. Oxford: Oxford University Press, 1965.
—— *Politicians, Socialism, and Historians*. London: Hamish Hamilton, 1980.
—— *Great Outsiders: Northcliffe, Rothermere and the 'Daily Mail'*. London: Weidenfeld & Nicolson, 1996.
Taylor, S.J. *Shock! Horror! The Tabloids in Action*. London: Corgi, 1991.
Terraine, J. *The First World War 1914–1918*. London: Macmillan, 1965.
—— *Impacts of War, 1914 and 1918*. London: Hutchinson, 1970.
—— *Smoke and the Fire: Myths and Anti-Myths of War 1861–1945*. London: Sidgwick & Jackson, 1980.
—— *The White Heat: The New Warfare 1914–1918*. London: Leo Cooper, 1982.
Thatcher, A.R., ed. *British Labour Statistics: Historical Abstract 1886–1968*. London: HMSO, 1971.
Thompson, E.P. *The Making of the English Working Class*. New York: Vintage, 1963.
Thompson, F.M.L., ed. *Cambridge Social History of Britain 1750–1950*. Cambridge: Cambridge University Press, 1990.
Thompson, L. *Robert Blatchford: Portrait of an Englishman*. London: Victor Gollancz, 1951.
—— *The Enthusiasts: A Biography of John and Katharine Bruce Glasier*. London: Victor Gollancz, 1971.
Thompson, P. *The Edwardians: The Remaking of British Society*. London: Routledge, 1992/1975.
Tilly, C., ed. *Citizenship, Identity, and Social History*. Cambridge: University of Cambridge Press, 1995.
Tillyard, F. *Unemployment Insurance in Great Britain 1911–1948*. Leigh-on-Sea, Essex: Thames Bank Publishing, 1949.
Travers, T. *The Killing Ground: The British Army, the Western Front, and the Emergence of Modern Warfare, 1900–1918*. London: Allen & Unwin, 1987.
Trollope, J. *Britannia's Daughters: Women of the British Empire*. London: Hutchinson, 1983.
Turner, J. *British Politics and the Great War: Coalition and Conflict 1915–1918*. New Haven, CT: Yale University Press, 1992.
Turner, W. *The Accrington Pals: 11th (Service) Battalion, Accrington, East Lancashire Regiment*. Lancashire: Lancashire County Books, 1992.
Vellacott, J. *Bertrand Russell and the Pacifists in the First World War*. Brighton: Harvester Press, 1980.
—— *From Liberal to Labor with Women's Suffrage: The Story of Catherine Marshall*. Montreal: McGill-Queen's University Press, 1993.

Vincent, D. *Literacy and Popular Culture: England 1750–1914*. Cambridge: Cambridge University Press, 1989.
Waites, B. *A Class Society at War: England, 1914–1918*. Leamington Spa: Berg Publishers, 1987.
Wall, R. and Winter, J., eds. *The Upheaval of War: Family, Work and Welfare in Europe, 1914–1918*. Cambridge: Cambridge University Press, 1988.
Wallace, S. *War and the Image of Germany: British Academics 1914–1918*. Edinburgh: John Donald Publishers, 1988.
Waller, P.J., ed. *Politics and Social Change in Modern Britain*. New York: St Martin's Press, 1987.
Warner, P. *Kitchener: The Man Behind the Legend*. London: Atheneum, 1985.
Webb, R.K. *The British Working-Class Reader, 1790–1848: Literacy and Social Tension*. London: George Allen & Unwin, 1955.
Whelan, P. *The Accrington Pals*. London: Methuen, 1982.
White, J.A. *Transition to Global Rivalry: Alliance Diplomacy and the Quadruple Entente, 1895–1907*. Cambridge: Cambridge University Press.
Williams, B. *Raising and Training the New Armies*. London: Constable, 1918.
Williams, J. *The Home Fronts: Britain, France, and Germany*. London: Constable, 1972.
Williamson, S.R., Jr. *Politics of Grand Strategy: Britain and France Prepare for War, 1904–1914*. Cambridge, MA: Harvard University Press, 1969.
Willis, I.C. *England's Holy War: A Study of English Liberal Idealism during the Great War*. New York: Alfred Knopf, 1928.
Wilson, K., ed. *Decisions for War, 1914*. New York: St Martin's Press, 1995.
Wilson, T. *Downfall of the Liberal Party 1914–1935*. London: Collins, 1966.
—— *The Myriad Faces of War: Britain and the Great War, 1914–1918*. New York: Basil Blackwall, 1986.
Wiltsher, A. *A Most Dangerous Women*. London: Pandora, 1985.
Winter, D. *Death's Men: Soldiers of the Great War*. London: Penguin, 1979.
Winter, J.M. *Socialism and the Challenge of War: Ideas and Politics in Britain 1912–1918*. London: Routledge & Kegan Paul, 1974.
—— ed. *Working Class in Modern British History*. Cambridge: Cambridge University Press, 1983.
—— *The Great War and the British People*. Cambridge, MA: Harvard University Press, 1986.
—— *Experience of World War I*. London: Papermac, 1989.
Winter, J.M. and Sivan, E. eds. *War and Economic Development*. Cambridge: Cambridge University Press, 1975.
—— *War and Remembrance in the Twentieth Century*. Cambridge: Cambridge University Press, 1999.
Wohl, R. *The Generation of 1914*. Cambridge, MA: Harvard University Press, 1979.
Woodward, D.R. *Lloyd George and the Generals*. London: Associated University Presses, 1983.
—— *Field Marshal Sir William Robertson: Chief of the Imperial General Staff in the Great War*. London: Praeger, 1998.
Woodward, E.L. *Great Britain and the German Navy*. London: Frank Cass, 1935.
—— *Great Britain and the War of 1914–1918*. London: Methuen, 1967.
Wright, P. *On Living in an Old Country*. London: Verso, 1985.
Wrigley, C. *History of British Industrial Relations, 1875–1914*. Amherst, MA: University of Massachusetts Press, 1982.

Index

adventure 69–70, 74–6, 91, 105, 130; and bank holidays 75; bleak ending of 81; effect of education on 74; and enlistment 75–81, 160(n58); longing for 73–4; and the railways 74–5; travel/emigration 75
allegiance 13, 104–5, 130; external pressures 116–20; family 114–15; generality of motives 120–3; genuiness of 123; geographic loyalties 108–12; internal motivations 123–4; personal loyalties 113–16; as specific type of patriotism 106–8, *see also* patriotism
American Expeditionary Force 37
Amery, Leo 17
Anderson, Benedict 53
Angell, Norman 73
anti-war groups 89–91
army *see* Regular Army; Territorial Army (TA)
Askwith, George 17, 64
Asquith, Herbert Henry 2, 18–19, 22, 33, 35, 108, 129

Baden-Powell, Robert 61, 67
Balfour, Arthur 29, 146(n141)
Barnes, George 17
Begbie, Harold 30
The Belgian Official Report (1914) 23
Boer War 15, 16, 43, 44, 53, 56–7, 67, 105, 154(n59)
Bonar-Law, Andrew 18
books 56, 57, 60, 154–5(n63), 168(n107)
Booth, Charles 3–4
Boy Scouts 16, 61, 62, 75
Boys' Brigades 156(n95)
British Empire 53–4, 57, 58, 59, 109, 110
British Expeditionary Force (BEF) 21, 22, 23–4, 33, 37, 79, 119, 128
Buller, Redvers 57, 67

Carson, Sir Edward 18, 41
Census (1911) 4, 42
children 53, 54, 72–3, 83–4, 91
Church Lads Brigade (CLB) 16, 61–2
Churchill, Winston 18, 35
Clarke, Allen 4
class 3, 134(n16); appeals to solidarity 89; attitudes to war 19–21; boundaries of 4–5; breakdown of enlistment 42–5; consciousness 63–5; distinctions 3–4; feminist view 4; physical structure 4; and rate of rejection 45; segregations 4, *see also* middle class; upper class; working class
conscription 15, 91, 106, 119, 129, 130, 138(n8), 146(n141); arrival of 34–7; idea of 29–33; industrial factors 29–30, 33–4; propaganda campaign 35–6, 146(n149); support for 35, *see also* enlistment; recruitment

Daily Chronicle 30
Daily Herald 20
Daily Mail 29, 31, 37, 55, 145(n133), 153–4(n45)
Davin, Anna 16
Derby, Lord 28, 35–6, 37, 119, 128, 129
domesticity, and children 72–3; economics of 83–4; and excitement of war 76–9; female domain 70–1; and food 72; gender relations 73; physical aspects 70; and recreation 71, 72; restrictive nature of 69–70, 158(n2); and violence 72, 158–9(n23); and visions of escape 73–6; work aspects 70
Dreadnoughts 15, 138(n7)

Eby, Cecil 57
economics, complex calculations 87–9; downturn in economy 85–7; of

enlistment 82, 87–103; expansion of economy 91–2; external stresses 82–3; general motivations for enlistment 92–9; government/anti-war groups 89–91; incomes/safety nets 83–5; pre-war situation 82; problems with statistical analysis of enlistment 99–103, *see also* industry
education 49; assumptions concerning 51–2; changes in 50–1; move from orality to literacy 51, 152(n20, n21); rural/urban link 53; value of 52–3; wariness concerning 60; and world view 53–4
Educational Reform Acts (1870, 1902) 50
Edward, VII, King 110
elites 8, 134(n16); changing view of 58, 60; enlistment of 42–5; working class view of 63
enlistment, adolescent exuberance for 79, 80–1; by profession 40; different from recruitment 27, 43; economic motives 82, 87–103; employer pressure 116–17; governmental pressure 118–20; industrial constraints 29–30; influence of media on 59, 110–11, 121; and local/national loyalties 108–12; as means of escape 75–81, 160(n58); medical exemption/acceptance 37, 44–5, 101; motivations 120–3; peer/gender pressure 117–18, 119–20, 167(n74, n76); physical benefits 88–9, 163(n50); political/geographical differences 40–2; and retaining of civilian skills 88, 163(n47); rural/urban divide 39–40, 147(n12); and servant/elite relationships 88, 163(n47); trade breakdown 92–9; training problems 21–3; as voluntary 27–9, *see also* conscription; recruitment
Entente Cordiale 15
Esher, Lord 28, 128

Ferguson, Niall 125, 127
Festubert (Aubers Ridge) 33
First World War 50; casualties 125–6; domestic reactions to Mons retreat 23–6; events leading up to 17–21; as industrialized mass war 2; myths/ambiguities of 11; outbreak of 76–9; press coverage of 23–4; roots of 15, 137(n1); as senseless catastrophe 169(n13)
Football Cancer 31

Franz Ferdinand, Archduke 17
French, Sir John 33

General Strike (1926) 3, 134(n15)
George V, King 18, 20
Germany, antipathy toward 109–10, 119, 127; external pressures 15; invasion of Belgium 19–20, 23, 108–9; paranoia concerning 57, 154–5(n63)
government 8; anti-German sentiment 15–16; business as usual attitude 21, 26, 127, 130, 140–1(n52); economic arguments for war 89–91; mandate for war 18–20; new bureaucracies 60–2, 84–5; propaganda 118–20; and push for conscription 34–7; social/domestic problems 16–17
Great Shells Scandal 33, 35
Grey, Edward 18–19, 35

Haggard, H. Rider 109
Haig, Douglas 37
Haldane, Reginald 16, 105
Hankey, Maurice 27
Henderson, Arthur 21, 34–5
Hobsbawm, Eric 62
Housing of the Working Classes Act (1890) 70
Howard, Michael 2
Howkins, Alun 53

income *see* economics
Independent Labour Party (ILP) 20, 90, 123
industry, and Army advertising 87–8; and conscription 29–30, 33–4; and employment 85–7, 91, 163(n65); enlistment figures 99–103, 129; occupations/trades 38–9, 92–9, *see also* economics
invasion literature 57, 109
Ireland 40, 41–2, 111–12, 129
Irish Home Rule 17–18, 111

Jones, Gareth Stedman 3
Joyce, Patrick 3

Keegan, John 126
kinematograph 29
Kipling, Rudyard 109
Kitchener, Herbert Horatio 13, 21–3, 26–8, 31, 33, 35, 41–2, 67, 77, 106, 110–11, 118, 119, 125, 128, 141(n53), 145(n133), 146(n143), 165(n37)

188 *Index*

Labour Exchanges 61, 84, 90
Lancashire Territorial Force Regiment 29
Liddle, Peter 6
'Little Moscow' 106, 164(n16)
Lloyd George, David 18, 28, 33–4, 35, 59, 61, 84, 129, 130
Long, Walter 32–3, 34

MacDonald, Ramsay 21
Maclean, John 19
middle class 1, 45, 47, 65
Miners' Federation of Great Britain 17
Mons 23–6, 121
Moore, Arthur 23
Munitions of War Act (1915) 34

National Register 31–2, 34, 35, 42
National Registration Act (1915) 31
National Transport Workers' Federation 17
National Union of Railwaymen 17
nationalism 10–11, 49, 63, 65, 68, 79, 108–9, 131
Navy 15, 49, 127
newspapers/magazines 50, 121–2, 151(n6), 153–5(n45, n46, n63), 168(n91); advertising in 51–2, 87–8, 110–11, 118; availability of 54–5; essential nature of 60; influence on world view 55–60, 127; and New Journalism 55; scepticism concerning 59, 155(n74); technological advances in 55, *see also* named papers eg. *The Times*
No-Conscription Fellowship (NCF) 36, 146–7(n155)
Norman, C.H. 8–9
Northcliffe, Lord 33

Old Age Pension Bill (1911) 60–1

Pack, Ernest 90–1
Pals Battalions 28–9, 45, 112–13, 125
Parliamentary Recruiting Committee (PRC) 21, 26
patriotism 64, 65, 91, 126; and adventure 78; autobiographical memories of 9–11; and avoidance of interrogation 8; catch phrases associated with 11–12; as cloak for true enlistment motives 77–8; as combination of motives 7–8; as conceptual minefield 104; construction of 8–9; external considerations 8; false 10–11; internal considerations 7–8; and jingoism 57, 154(n59); as justification for volunteering 7; language of 9–13; meanings of 7–14; misguided/ambiguous 11; particular kind of 106–8; problems with 7, 9; role of groups in 8–9, *see also* allegiance
peace movement 19, 20–1
Peace Society 20
Poor Law 84
propaganda campaigns 11, 35–6, 51–2, 79, 87–8, 90, 118–20, 146(n149)

Recruiting Offices 90
recruitment, advertising posters for 79; and breakdown of infrastructure 24–6; different from enlistment 27, 43; effect of *Times* article on 24, 121; food/clothing 25–6, 142(n80); and idea of slackers/shirkers 30–3, 37, 130; lack of experienced NCOs 22–3; local/national system 27–9; numbers needed 27; physical requirements 26, 43–5, 121–2, 143(n88), 149(n52n); shortages 29–30; urban/rural patterns 122–3, *see also* conscription; enlistment
Redmond, John 112
Regular Army 16, 22, 27–8, 29, 43, 75–6; advertising for trades in 87–8; change in attitude toward 105; food in 107, 164–5(n21); pre-war enlistment 83; propaganda used by 90; reform of 15–16, 105; specific reasons for joining 106–8; suspicions concerning 105; unreliability of 18; view of 138(n12); wages in 86–7, 91
Roberts, Lord 18, 44
Rosenberg, Isaac 85
Ross, Ellen 73
Royal Air Service (RAS) 88
Royal Army Medical Corps (RAMC) 44
Royal Sussex Regiment 29
rush to colours 2, 7, 67, 76, 77–8, 127–9
Russell, Bertrand 19, 20

Samuel, Raphael 8, 58
Scotland 40–1
Somme 1, 125–6
South Wales Miners' Federation (SWMF) 41
spies 15
Staunton, C.B. 41
strikes 1–2, 3, 17, 20, 21, 54, 59, 107, 134(n15)
suffrage movement 17, 28, 63

Index   189

Taylor, H.G. 62
Territorial Army (TA) 22, 27, 76, 83, 125, 156(n95), 160(n49)
Territorial Field Ambulance 114
Territorial Force 16
The Times 23–4, 30, 31, 36, 43, 55, 121–2, 153–4(n45)
trade unions 21, 28, 35, 36, 62–3, 146(n143)

Ulster Brigade 111
Ulster Volunteer Force (UVF) 18, 41, 111
unemployment insurance 61, 63, 84–5
Union for Democratic Control 20
The Union Jack 56
upper class 1, 4, 45, 50, 63, 65

volunteers 1, 91; acceptance/rejection of 31–2, 43–5; age breakdown 46; beliefs of 130–1; class differences 1–3, 42–5, 47–8; geographical location 39–42; imperial fantasies of 79; motivations of 1–3; occupations of 38–9; and perception of unfairness 30–1; rate of enlistment 22, 121, 128, 129; recruitment/enlistment dichotomy 27–9; regarded as 'not needed' 26; success of system 37, 130

Waites, Bernard 14
Wales 41, 106, 164(n16)
War Emergency Workers' National Committee 21
War Office 12, 18, 22, 26, 28, 29, 32, 37, 44–5, 61, 128–9
Weavers' Union 65
Webb, R.K. 49

Weekly Dispatch 30, 45
Wells, H.G. 67–8
Wilhelm II, Kaiser 110
Winter, J.M. 47
working class, boundaries 4–5; and children's strikes 54; and class consciousness 63–5; constraints on 73–4; definition 4; and dreams of adventure 74–6; education/literacy of 49, 50–4; enrolment of 42–5, 47; false consciousness amongst 3, 134–5(n19); generational differences 66–7, 157(n125); health of 16, 43, 47; and helpful bureaucracy 49–50, 60–2; historical awareness of 78; increased awareness/sophistication of beliefs 67–8; insecurity/poverty of 83–4; and the media 50, 54–60; mental reinvigoration of 16–17; and move from resistance to cooperation 65–8; movement within/beyond 4; political awareness of 63, 156(n105); rights/responsibilities 64, 65–6; sacrifices made by 14; scepticism of 64–5; as shirkers 30–1, 129; sources of information 5–7; support for war 14, 21, 65; supposed view on conscription 34–5; willingness/motivation to fight 1–3, 125, 126–7, 130–1; world view 49, 50, 62–8
world view 49, 50; contrast with home 69; and education 53–4; influence of newspapers/books on 55–60; and rush to colours 67–8; working class connections 62–8

youth movements 61–2

eBooks – at www.eBookstore.tandf.co.uk

A library at your fingertips!

eBooks are electronic versions of printed books. You can store them on your PC/laptop or browse them online.

They have advantages for anyone needing rapid access to a wide variety of published, copyright information. eBooks can help your research by enabling you to bookmark chapters, annotate text and use instant searches to find specific words or phrases. Several eBook files would fit on even a small laptop or PDA.

NEW: Save money by eSubscribing: cheap, online access to any eBook for as long as you need it.

Annual subscription packages

We now offer special low-cost bulk subscriptions to packages of eBooks in certain subject areas. These are available to libraries or to individuals.

For more information please contact webmaster.ebooks@tandf.co.uk

We're continually developing the eBook concept, so keep up to date by visiting the website.

www.eBookstore.tandf.co.uk